Drawn Fabric Work
Close-up of Fig. 137, embroidered by the late Mrs. G. Newall

Mary Thomas's
EMBROIDERY
BOOK

Including Appliqué, Patchwork, Quilting,
Initials and Monograms, Fringes and Tassels,
Smocking, Seams and Hems

DOVER PUBLICATIONS, INC.
NEW YORK

This Dover edition, first published in 1983, is an unabridged and unaltered republication of the edition published by Hodder and Stoughton Limited, London, in 1936, under the title *Mary Thomas's Embroidery Book.*

Manufactured in the United States of America
Dover Publications, Inc., 180 Varick Street, New York, N.Y. 10014

Library of Congress Cataloging in Publication Data

Thomas, Mary, 1889–
  Mary Thomas's Embroidery book.

  Reprint. Originally published: London : Hodder and Stoughton, 1936.
  Includes index.
  1. Embroidery. 2. Needlework. I. Title. II. Title: Embroidery book.
TT770.T52   1983   746.44   83-5183
ISBN 0-486-24530-6

DEDICATION

THIS BOOK IS DEDICATED WITH LOVE AND AFFECTION

TO MY MOTHER

AND TO ALL THOSE WOMEN,

WHO,

THROUGHOUT THE LONG PAST AGES,

HAVE CONTRIBUTED TO THE JOYS OF LIFE

THROUGH THEIR EMBROIDERIES

CONTENTS

CONTENTS

PREFACE

EMBROIDERY, like every other art—or sport, for that matter—needs to be understood to be enjoyed. Once the rules of the game are known, there not only comes the urge to create with needle and thread, but a knowledge which enables the better appreciation of the old masterpieces, as well as of those produced in our own day. We are enjoying a revival in all arts and crafts—it is fashionable to be dextrous—and since it is better to be out of the world than out of fashion—it is as well to know something of the art which will soon be the pastime of every woman in the million houses where the wireless is turned on nightly. Besides, there is always infinitely more joy and satisfaction derived from the simplest tray-mat evolved by one's own brain and fingers than from twenty ready-made articles of more elaborate conception. Embroidery has been woman's art through innumerable ages, how long can only be surmised. Each archæological expedition throws the beginning back still earlier and earlier; the excavations at Ur reveal how high the standard must have been centuries before the hanging gardens of Babylon became a seventh wonder of the earth. Since those days women of all countries and all centuries have quietly added their quota, and in the days of the Renaissance, such heights of beauty and technique were reached that the value of the work was often beyond its own weight in gold. Throughout the Elizabethan, the Jacobean and the Georgian eras, this glory continued practically undiminished; and it was only at the beginning of the 19th century, with the advent of the machine age, that it began to wane and, later, almost vanish, stifled beneath the avalanche of " art needlework " and Berlin wool-work so beloved of the Victorians.

Now comes this great Renaissance of the 20th century! full of life, virility and promise, and it is up to this age to see its struggling efforts mature.

My first book likened stitches to the " scales and exercises " of embroidery, and in this book the different works conveniently progress to the " counterpoint " of embroidery, as the stitches are grouped and arranged in different sequential melodies or works, each containing the principle upon which still grander and greater works can be founded. These various types of embroidery are not the invention of this age, nor of any one age in particular, but the collective efforts of countless ages, and mainly developed from a peasant origin.

Photographs and diagrams of a simple nature have been chosen throughout as illustrations, and each section or chapter shows the gradual progressive development of each work, so that all can take the particular amount of information needed to suit their own individual requirements. The enthusiast will go ahead and visit museums and exhibitions ; there to seek the further elaborate developments, and I hope, find a new appreciation of the ingenious intricacies of the old workers, and the sparkling, adventurous methods of our own age.

There may appear less time to-day than of yore, in which to produce works of elaborate nature; but there is always time to produce good small pieces. Besides, count the assets of modern civilisation. Material already woven, threads of fast dyes, inexpensive and perfect needles, transfers with designs ready prepared, shops with demonstrators, museums free of access where the best works of any age can be seen, and libraries where books can be read free of charge. Half the work is already done! There are those who decry the use of the printed transfers, but it is one of the necessary pillars in rebuilding this great art so long neglected and untaught.

Again, many are too nervous to attempt original design and would forever miss the joy of the work were it not for the transfer and the stencilled canvases. This prejudice is a hindrance rather than an aid to progress, as manufacturers are not encouraged to improve the standard of design. We need better transfer designs drawn by experts, who understand embroidery. At the moment we suffer from designs made by artists who perhaps understand drawing as applied to line and water-colours, but not the requirements of the needle.

The day will come to each student when she will discard all copy-book methods and aim to express herself in original design, and with this object suggestions are given throughout the book as to method and principle. Those embroideries worked on counted threads offer the best beginnings, and should a transfer ever be used for these, such as cross stitch, then it is better to use a fine or silk material, to give reason for the method.

As a hint to beginners, it is advisable to work a small article when first attempting a new form of work, in order to perfect the technique, and test out the appearance of the different stitches in different threads. Always experiment, as this will bring new ideas—your ideas—to the work.

A clever worker does not seek constant change of colours as a means of variety. She changes her stitch, or the direction of her stitch (but with reason), as this will produce the illusion of colour change by the play of light on the thread. The method of doing this distinguishes the artist from the amateur. It cannot be taught, it is just felt, known; the result of industry and observation. Teachers will find that a small specimen of each different type of embroidery, framed for class work, is an inspiring means of teaching embroidery in schools.

The pitfalls of each work are marked throughout the book thus △—the familiar danger signal. This may often stand at seemingly unimportant points, but heed and slow up, as it indicates the spot where most amateurs meet with difficulties.

The technical hints at the end of the book will, I hope, be useful, and the timely warning that embroidery is the art of enriching a fabric, and only the best fabrics are worth this trouble, be heeded. Good materials inspire good work, and if these are really " embroidered " and not just covered with thoughtless stitchery, the result is one of lasting joy and satisfaction.

Further, I would urge the habit of signing and dating embroidery, and thus avoid that great tragedy of the past when works of genius were created, and showered upon the world, leaving alas! so few names to record and venerate.

MARY THOMAS

NOTE: Throughout this book *Mary Thomas's Dictionary of Embroidery Stitches* is referred to in brief as *The Dictionary*, and any stitch marked with an asterisk, thus *, indicates that it will be found fully described and illustrated in this book.

$\triangle$ = *See* previous page.

ACKNOWLEDGMENTS

I N presenting this second book on the subject of embroidery, I would like to acknowledge with my sincere thanks and gratitude the ever-ready assistance of Miss H. Lyon Wood and Miss Dorothy Goslett. Miss Lyon Wood's technical knowledge of the subject has doubly ensured that the drawings and diagrams are rendered in a simple, direct and comprehensive manner, a laborious task in which she was notably assisted by two young technical experts, Miss Margot Stanley and Miss Joan Loewenthal.

My thanks are also due to Miss Mary Kirby who executed the drawings for the Jacobean section, and to Mr. Frank Ormrod who designed the jacket and Miss Jeffreys who worked the embroidery; and last but not least to Miss Dorothy Moss who typed the entire MS., often, I fear, rather illegibly written! The great kindness of various societies and people who have worked and loaned articles for illustration is acknowledged with thanks beneath the pictures respectively reproduced.

MARY THOMAS

WHENEVER YOU SEE THIS SIGN

STOP!

CAUTION!!

GO!!!

Fig. 12. Picture Appliqué " Punch and Judy " by Miss Barbara Lack

APPLIED WORK
OR APPLIQUÉ

PPLIED WORK, OR APPLIQUÉ, is the method of applying one material to another by means of decorative
stitchery. There are two forms, " onlay " and " inlay,"
and the work was probably invented by the Persians or
the Indians as an inexpensive imitation of richer embroideries. Applied work has a long and ancient history,
occurring and recurring in waves of great popularity through
the centuries. It was lavishly used by the Egyptians and
Greeks; appeared again during the Crusades as a decoration
on knights' surcoats, horse trappings, tents, etc., and later
still was revived by Botticelli, who used it for church banners.
After this last revival it reached a height of classic importance.
The designs took on a delicate and lacy character akin to
fretwork, embroidered upon rich luxurious fabrics suitable
only for ecclesiastical or heraldic embroideries.

Of late it has enjoyed yet another wave of popularity but
one in which all classic tradition has given way to modern
experiment, as beyond all other forms of needlecraft, Appliqué
affords the widest scope for individual expression; admitting
no limit to subject or material. Modern designs are moulded
and built on a heroic scale, in much the same way as a sculptor
uses his lumps of clay. Any kind of stuff—plain and printed
cotton, silks, braid, buttons, felt, leather, or American cloth—
is used, and in cases where embroidery is literally designed by
the mile, as for theatre curtains, Appliqué work produces the
maximum effect with the minimum labour of the needle.

This does not imply that the finer forms are neglected, and
indeed, those who wish to create on the heroic scale must first
feel their way through the " scales and exercises " of the
technique, for which purpose the simpler and more delicate

Fig. 1

types afford the best school. Light and dainty Appliqué on net offers just as much scope for skill and originality as some of the larger subjects, and may, in the end, prove more attractive; since all minds do not run along gargantuan lines!

DESIGNS

The beauty of this work lies in the design, which must be well planned, well executed and the colours pleasingly distributed, before the embroidery stitches are considered. Futile attempts are often made to disguise a bad design by the over-lavish use of stitchery, but this being contrary to the basic law of the work is never satisfactory. Start off with a good design, no matter how simple, and the work will be a success. Finishing touches of stitchery to express the smaller details are quite sufficient and should be worked on the applied motifs and the foundation material after the preliminary work is completed. Bold conventional shapes with simple outlines lend themselves more readily to the technique, and any attempt to reproduce naturalistic flowers should be avoided, except in the finer forms on net, as thin materials lend themselves quite easily to more intricate shapes.

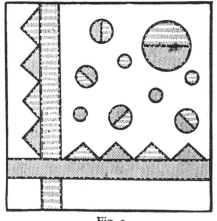

Fig. 2

An example of simple applied work is shown in *Fig.* 1 in different coloured linens on a neutral background. Very few stitches are suggested on the applied pieces, yet the design is compact and pleasing. A simple first effort in design where the forms and colours provide the effect, rather than the stitchery, is shown in *Fig.* 2. These small circles are cut from the outline of coins or simple geometrical shapes, and obviate the use of a transfer, a knowledge of drawing or any transferring method.

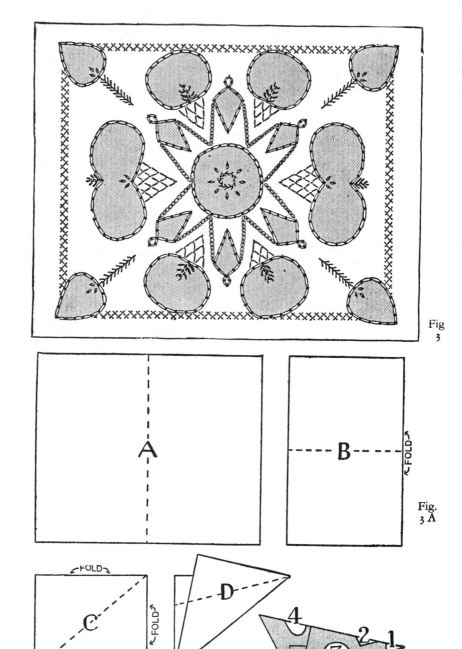

Fig
3

Fig.
3 A

Other simple designs can be evolved by the kindergarten method of paper cutting, *see Figs.* 3 and 4, the process being explained in *Figs.* 3 A and B. Cut a sheet of paper (A), fold this four times (B, C and D), then cut away four spaces as indicated by the figures 1 to 4. On opening out this will produce the design in *Fig.* 3 B, and by referring again to *Fig.* 3 it will be seen how the stitchery links up the separate pieces into an interesting whole. More elaborate patterns

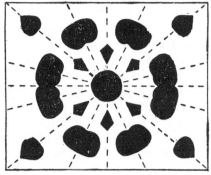

Fig. 3 B

may be obtained by varying the shape of the paper, the folds and the cuts, as exampled in *Fig.* 4.

COLOURS AND MATERIALS

Colour is mainly supplied to this work by the applied fabrics and secondly by embroidery threads, but the latter is subservient to the first, just as the stitches are subservient to the design. The applied motifs need not be of the same material as the background, and an impression of contrast can be given to a colour scheme by applying a different material of the same colour. Different shades of one colour are also pleasing. Small designs appear more harmonious in soft colours, leaving the more violent

Fig. 4

contrasts to larger works on which their brilliance becomes somewhat subdued by breadth and space. The background should be neutral in colour, and not detract from the interest of the design. The edges of the applied pieces are covered with a thread to match or blend with each patch, but a whole colour scheme can be toned down and unified by using only one thread to match the background. All kinds of embroidery threads, silks or wools can be used, but a fine cotton is necessary for overcasting the edges. Gold is generally used for church work. Non-fraying materials of firm weave are preferable, leaving any eccentric choice for Picture Appliqué. For household articles, linen should be applied to linen, but velvet, silks, satins and furnishing fabrics of all kinds may be used for cushions, curtains, screens, etc., while for lingerie, crêpe-de-chine, satin, georgette and net are all suitable.

Figures cut from chintz should be applied to a ground which matches the darkest shade in the design. This form of Appliqué is sometimes called Broderie Perse. All work of an elaborate nature should be carried out in a frame. △ Before beginning any Appliqué work, study the warp and weft of the material, and see that those of the ground and the applied pieces correspond. Any motif applied on the bias to the ground fabric, will "pull" in a contrary direction, causing the patch to wrinkle; a catastrophe which can only be corrected by cutting a new patch or motif.

LYON WOOD

Fig. 5   △ = *See* preface

WORKING METHODS

Transfer the whole design upon the ground material, then each applied portion on to its own particular colour and cut out carefully. Arrange each patch in its correct position and fasten down with a pin and then tack (*see Fig.* 5). The next step is to oversew all the cut

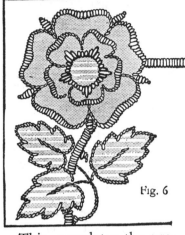

Fig. 6

edges, using a fine thread and neat stitches. The process of pinning, tacking and oversewing are all shown in *Fig.* 5.

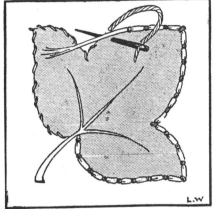

Fig. 7

This completes the preparation, and the decorative stitches are now added, a process which permits of great individual treatment. A large variety of stitches are available for the purpose, but buttonhole and blanket stitch are the most popular (*Fig.* 5). The many varieties of buttonhole*, chain stitch*, coral*, feather*, herring-bone*, etc., are all successful. Satin stitch looks effective graded in width and padded as in *Fig.* 6. Couching (*Fig.* 7) is always popular, and on bold screen and curtain designs braid, ribbon, and chenille can be couched, with great success. Gold can be used for church work.

HEMSTITCHED APPLIQUÉ

A geometric design of straight lines following the warp and weft of the material may be applied by hemstitching (*see Fig.* 8), for working method (*see Fig.* 8 A).

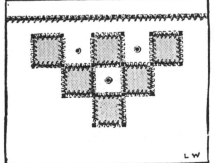

Fig. 8   * = *See* preface   Fig. 8 A

This is particularly effective on fine transparent materials as the coloured patch can be above or below the fabric.

LACE STITCH APPLIQUÉ

Openwork effects are given to lines on the curve by using lace or three-sided stitch (*Fig.* 9), a method used on lingerie materials. No preliminary overcasting is necessary, the motif is tacked in position and the lace stitch worked directly over and as close

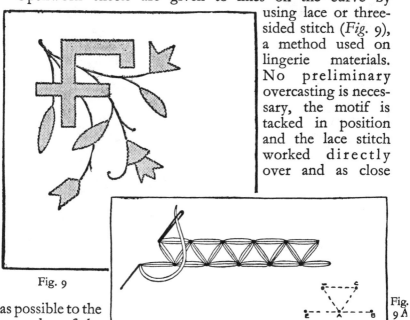

Fig. 9

Fig. 9 A

as possible to the raw edge of the material, which is afterwards neatly trimmed. △ A large punch needle and fine thread must be used to produce the holes which are pulled into tiny patterns by taking each stitch twice into the same hole and pulling the thread tight after each (*Fig.* 9 A).

HEMMED APPLIQUÉ

Ordinary hemming is another method on fine materials. The edges of

Fig. 10

each patch are turned under and neatly hemmed or slip-stitched without any further decorative stitching (*see Fig.* 10). This method shown in *Fig.* 10 A is one which requires some skill, and is frequently seen on Egyptian figure friezes

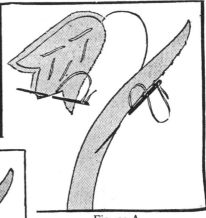

Fig. 10 A

Fig. 10 B

where it has the appearance of a silhouette. An alternative stitch is shown in *Fig.* 10 B, this has two movements given at A and B, the working of which forms a kind of back stitch, and pulls a small hole in the ground material.

FELT AND AMERICAN CLOTH APPLIQUÉ

Felt is a practical medium for Appliqué as it does not fray and looks attractive on coarse linen or canvas. The designs and motifs must be simple in outline (*Fig.* 11) and the method of applying must be suited to the article or

Fig. 11

object being decorated. On cushions, chair backs, and so forth it is necessary to slipstitch all the edges of each motif. to the background, but on firescreens, draught screens, etc. it is sufficient if the motifs are secured with a single stitch.

Fig. 11 A

Flower effects are obtained by placing three circles of felt in graded sizes over each other and securing with a French knot in the centre. *Fig.* 11 A shows in detail the various different methods of applying the motifs. The semicircular band cut with vandyked points is held down with single stitches arranged over the narrowest parts.

Fine leather, suède, American cloth and kid are all suitable for this work, but need careful handling, △ otherwise the thread will cut the leather. Some beautiful examples of applied leather work from the Slav countries are to be found in our museums. The work is of the highest order and generally combined with other embroidery to decorate festive coats and capes.

PICTURE APPLIQUÉ

The making of Appliqué pictures affords a fascinating pastime, as realism is the ruling factor and the worker is bound by no traditions or conventions. Should the picture include children dressed in gingham, then their dresses may be applied in bright checked gingham, or milkmaids in sprigged muslin, fine ladies in brocades, animals in fur, etc., the texture and colours varying the interest and minimising the embroidery work. An amusing Appliqué picture " Punch and Judy " is shown in *Fig.* 12, facing *page* I, into which any number of different materials have been crowded with good effect. An embroidery frame must be used for this work.

As mural decorations for modern rooms, nurseries, shop window displays, commercial posters, etc. Appliqué of this type represents one of the most popular forms of modern embroidery.

APPLIQUÉ ON NET

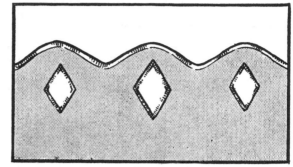

Fig. 13

This form of applied work differs from all methods described, △ as the material is cut away from the motif *after* it has been attached to the ground with embroidery stitches. Both method and effect are similar to the working of Carrickmacross lace, and produce a dainty finish to modern lingerie. Towards the end of the 19th century when the prohibitive tariffs made Continental lace so expensive, this work made an effective substitute. It can be used (1) as a net hem at the top and bottom of a garment with the material carried over to form the Appliqué motif (*Fig.* 13), or (2) as a complete motif (*Fig.* 14).

Fig. 14

Muslin, lawn, cambric, georgette, crêpe-de-chine or lingerie satin are suitable, and it is advisable to use the net double on washing garments and for hems.   Choose a good Brussels net, as the cheap sort tears and renders the embroidery useless.

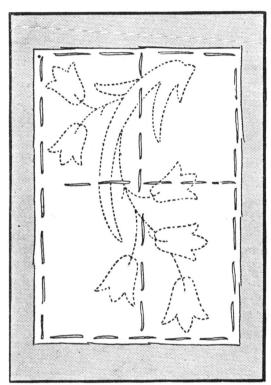

The design is stamped on the chosen material, which is then tacked firmly down on the net, and a running stitch worked through both layers, just inside the outline of the design (*Fig.* 14 A).   This outline is then covered with either buttonhole, slanting satin, fine close stem stitching* or satin couching (*see Fig.* 14 B).   All the stitching △ *must* be taken through both the material and the net, and any surface embroidery on the applied pieces also worked at this stage.   When all is complete, the tacking

Fig. 14 A

threads are removed and the surplus material cut away with care close round the design, using ball-pointed lace scissors (*Fig.* 14).   Any light touches of embroidery on the net are added at this stage.

On fine muslin or cambric the edges are sometimes turned in and hemmed invisibly without any further stitching (*Fig.* 14 C), but skill is necessary to obtain a neat effect.

Fig. 14 B

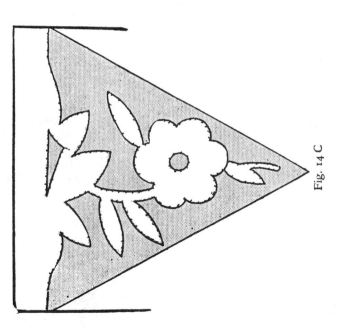

Fig. 14 C

INLAY APPLIQUÉ   Fig. 15

Inlay is rarely used except for church work, carried out in velvet and other rich fabrics.   It differs from the onlay process as the design is inserted.   In mediæval days it was used for inserting the figures of saints or the hands and faces into a large piece of work.

The form of design known as counterchange lends itself particularly well to this type of Appliqué, *see Fig.* 15, as the shaded portion of the design is a replica of the white, and the two fit like a jigsaw puzzle.   The work is carried out on a backing of holland or canvas, which may be removed when completed, or left for additional strength, and the process is shown at *Figs.* 16 A, B and C.

Here the colour scheme is black and white, and the pattern is traced on the white material, which is then laid over the

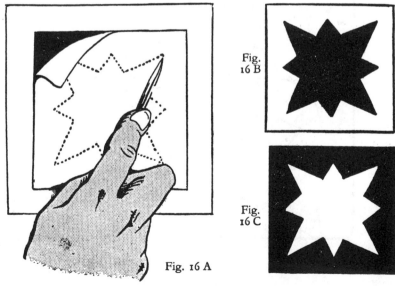

Fig. 16 B

Fig. 16 C

Fig. 16 A

black and the two pinned down to a board. Next, with a very sharp knife, cut round the pattern and through both layers of material at the same time (*Fig.* 16 A). This will produce a black star and a white star. The black is fitted into the white ground and the white into the black, reversing the colours, without wasting a scrap of material (*Figs.* 16 B and C).

The edges of both materials are then overcast together △ without piercing the holland backing, and the join concealed with a couched line of silk, gold or cord, after which the backing material may be removed if desired.

Materials likely to fray are first backed with paper before they are cut. Use a pure paste made from wheat starch and spread over a strong paper or fine holland, and over this smooth the material, taking care to eliminate all air bubbles. The paste must be thinly applied, otherwise it will show through in damp spots, and dry in stains. Both paper and material are then placed under pressure until quite dry, and afterwards cut as described. △ Paper will stiffen and destroys the subtle quality of the material and should be avoided when possible.

MODERN INLAY

A simple form of Inlay is achieved by tacking a linen of contrasting colour to the back of a cloth, mat, etc., and then cutting away the surface material to allow the contrasting colour beneath to show through on the surface. Different coloured patches can be sewn to the back as required or the backing material can serve as a lining to the article, as convenient. △ The design must be simple in outline.

WORKING METHOD

Transfer the design to the material in the usual way, and then pin and tack the patch beneath in position, run stitching round the outline of the shape △ just *outside* the outline of the design. The top material can then be cut away and the edges covered with close satin or button stitches to unite the two materials. If preferred, the button stitches can be worked first, arranging the pearl edge along the outline of the design △ but facing inwards and towards the portions which are later cut away. This form of Inlay is sometimes known as Découpé work.

ASSISI EMBROIDERY

ASSISI EMBROIDERY is a variation of Cross Stitch Embroidery. The stitches are the same but the principle of design is reversed, as it is the background which is embroidered with crosses and the pattern left plain and in outline, like an intaglio (*Fig.* 17). This treatment imparts great dignity to the work, and the designs, which are usually heraldic in character, look effective on banners, ecclesiastical

Fig. 17

or secular, besides forming handsome borders for tea-cloths, bags, etc.

DESIGNS AND MATERIALS

The designs are planned out on graph paper, drawing the birds and beasts in straight lines after the kindergarten principle (*see Fig.* 19). Books on heraldry and wood carving will provide many inspirations for this purpose.

A loosely woven linen of even warp and weft should be used, as the work is done on counted threads, making the unit three or four material threads as in Cross Stitch Embroidery. (Finer materials should be chosen when a transfer is being used.) The ground material is usually white or natural and the embroidery worked in two different colours only, a black, brown, blue, green or red being chosen for the outline, and a lighter contrasting shade for the cross stitch background. The antique effect of the old Assisi embroideries can be obtained by using a rather faded china blue or soft brown for the background with dark blue or black for the outlines. But any two colours are suitable providing a contrast and balance in colour is maintained.

WORKING METHODS

Two different stitches are used; Holbein Stitch for outlining the design and Cross Stitch for the background, and a mixture of both for the little borders.

The method of working Holbein Stitch, which is exactly the same as double running, is shown in *Fig.* 18 A. In Assisi work, this stitch is always known as Holbein stitch. Two journeys are necessary, the first being made all round the outlines of the design, making each stitch and space between

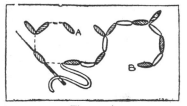

Fig. 18 A

exactly the same in length. The work is then turned and the second journey made along the same line, but filling up the gaps left on the first. At this point refer to *Fig.* 18 B as it reveals the trick necessary to keep the line of the second journey straight. △ Insert the needle above the stitch and

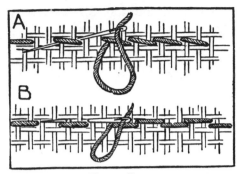

Fig. 18 B

bring it out below as at A. (What happens to the line when this injunction is disobeyed is shown at B.)

The background of Cross Stitch is also worked in two journeys (*see Fig.* 89, *page* 72), as this is the quicker method when filling large spaces, but watch with care that all the top threads of the crosses lie in the same direction, otherwise the even appearance of the background will be entirely ruined.   (See Cross Stitch, *page* 68.)

Commence the first journey of Holbein Stitch at any convenient spot, taking it over and under a unit of three threads which is a good average.   To reduce the whole design by one third, work over two threads, but the size of the stitch and the design will naturally vary on different linens.

During this first journey, work in any little lines or offshoots on the design, carrying the thread out to the end of a branched line and back again to the main outline (*see Fig.* 133, *page* 100). The second journey of Holbein Stitch is shown in progress in *Fig.* 19, which is a close-up of the centre portion of *Fig.* 17. After the first journey, the design looks a muddle, but as the second journey proceeds, the gaps disappear, and the design begins to take shape and form.

When the outlining is complete, fill in the background with Cross Stitch.   *Fig.* 20 shows this in progress.   Notice along the top and down the left of the diagram that several rows of half crosses are shown.   These will be completed as crosses on the return journey.   This " all over " method is often convenient when filling in the smaller odd shapes that occur between the figures.   In larger shapes it is better to complete each row before passing to another.

The embroidery at this stage has a very solid appearance and needs some softening border to merge it gradually into the material, such as that above and below the main design in *Fig.* 17.   Three of these little border designs, A, B and C, are

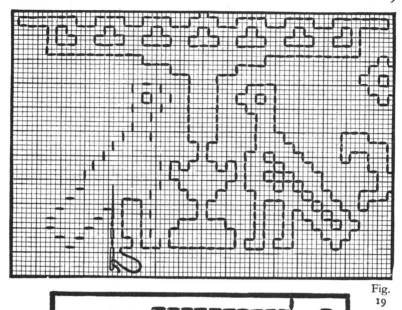

Fig.
19

Fig.
20

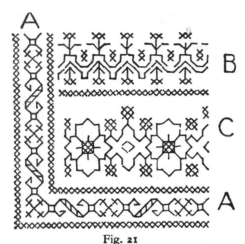

Fig. 21

shown in *Fig.* 21. They are quite easy to construct, and make most fascinating decoration. The only working stitches used are Cross and Holbein.

In *Fig.* 22 is shown the method of adding a few of these filigree stitches to a small isolated motif, which displays a modern toy dog instead of the usual heraldic beast.

FINISHING THE EDGES

The final hem should be narrow and finished with Italian hemstitching as suggested at the base of *Fig.* 17. Two methods of Italian hemstitching are shown on *pages* 90 and 119. Either can be used, according to the size of the article being decorated.

Fig. 22

Another method is to turn down an ordinary hem on the right side of the work and cover the edge with a single line of cross stitch or a tiny border of Holbein and Cross Stitch.

Assisi work can be made to appear alike on both sides by using Two-sided Cross Stitch (*see Fig.* 90), a method particularly recommended for such articles as chair backs, runners, and tray-mats on which the back of the article is often seen, and one consistently employed by the old Italian workers, with the result that it is almost impossible to discern the right from the wrong side. An achievement which should be the ambition of every embroideress.

BLACK WORK

B LACK WORK is a name given to any embroidery worked in black thread on white material and is said to have been introduced into England during the reign of Henry VIII by Queen Catherine of Aragon and her ladies. For this reason it is often called Spanish work, though actually it is of great antiquity, being adopted by the Spaniards from the Moors and Arabs, who in turn borrowed it from the Egyptians and Persians.

Some of the most exquisite Drawn Fabric* and lace stitches are used in this work with fillings such as distinguish the Jacobean embroideries. Like Jacobean and Mountmellick embroidery, it is a work of pure stitchery, but just as refined in quality as these are bold.

An exquisite example of 16th century black work is shown in *Fig.* 23, the following page, worked in black silk on white linen, using Back, Chain, Buttonhole, Braid and Coral Stitches*. The occasional addition of gold thread to produce a richer effect was customary at this period, and the subjects of many famous portraits are depicted wearing shirts, bodices, caps, jerkins and even smocks of white beautifully embroidered with black silk touched in with gold. These earlier specimens favoured floral designs, with long waving stems, leaves, flowers and vines worked in minute and lovely stitchery, and though the popularity of the work declined in the 17th century, it is now again in favour; as the simple black and white colour scheme blends so well with contemporary decoration. The modern aim and interpretation however is quite different; the designs are eccentric and appliqué motifs introduced which considerably speed up the work but coarsen and change its quality. Some striking effects can be achieved, however, providing the stitches are well chosen and well grouped, but

Fig. 23. English pillow-case embroidered in black silk on white linen, 16th century

variety in stitch is essential, since there is no variety in colour (*see Fig.* 24).

The work still has a national importance in Spain, but wool is more often used than silk, this being taken from a black sheep, spun at home and used in its natural undyed state.

Fig. 24

Fig. 25

BRODERIE ANGLAISE

THIS beautiful open form of embroidery is also known as Ayrshire, English, Eyelet, Madeira or Swiss Work, and consists of open worked spaces, varying in shape and size; which are cut or punched with a stiletto and then overcast. The edges of the work are finished with scallops.

The classical period of Eyelet work, to use the old name, belongs to the late 18th and early 19th centuries, when it appeared on dress sleeves, caps, underclothes, baby clothes and house linen in elaborate patterns after the style shown in *Fig. 25*, which is a simple example. At this time no surface embroidery whatsoever was used. The work consisted entirely of little round or oval eyelets, even the stalks of the flowers and the veins of the leaves being rendered in a succession of diminishing eyelets, and in patterns which might extend over a whole skirt or sleeve; worked with such exquisite care that the modern mind is dazed at the thought and labour involved. *Fig. 26* illustrates the modernised version and the introduction of surface embroidery after the manner of Swiss Work. This more than halves the labour, but alas! completely changes the character of both design and work.

Broderie Anglaise forms a charming decoration for dresses, baby clothes, fine house linen, lingerie, handkerchief corners, etc.

24

DESIGNS AND MATERIAL

The designs usually consist of simple or conventional floral motifs, since the circular and oval perforations lend themselves so well to floral formation. *Fig.* 26 contains little more than

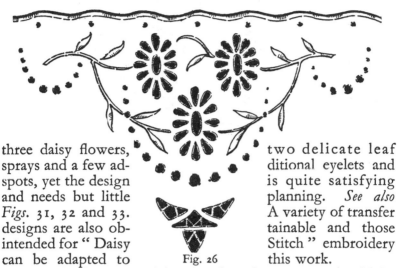

three daisy flowers, sprays and a few ad-spots, yet the design and needs but little *Figs.* 31, 32 and 33. designs are also ob-intended for " Daisy can be adapted to two delicate leaf ditional eyelets and is quite satisfying planning. *See also* A variety of transfer tainable and those Stitch " embroidery this work.

Fig. 26

Only the best materials of a firm fine texture should be used, otherwise the work will fray with constant washing. White cambric, muslin, cotton, lawn and very fine linen are suitable, and fine flannel for babies' garments, or good crêpe-de-chine for lingerie. The working thread should match the material in quality, colour and texture. On cotton materials a linen, cotton or mercerised thread should be used, and for crêpe-de-chine or flannel a fine twisted silk is better.

The older forms of this work were done in white or pale watery blue on white fabrics, but coloured fabrics with matching threads can be used, though the soft paler shades should be chosen, as these are more in keeping with the character of the work. In Czechoslovakia the eyelets are worked in several different colours on the sleeves of national costumes.

STITCHES

Only four elementary stitches are used in this work, Running Stitch*, Overcasting Stitch*, Button Stitch* and Satin Stitch*. A stiletto and fine embroidery scissors are necessary.

WORKING METHODS

Eyelets less than $\frac{1}{4}''$ in diameter should be pierced with a stiletto, as it is impossible to cut them with scissors. First run stitch round the traced outline, then pierce the hole with the stiletto and lastly cover with fine overcast stitch (*Fig.* 27 A).

Eyelets larger than $\frac{1}{4}''$ in diameter must be cut. First run stitch round the outline and then snip from the centre with the scissors, vertically and then horizontally (*Fig.* 27 B). The four points of the material are then turned under to the back with the needle and the eyelet overcast, taking the stitches over the folded edge and the running (*Fig.* 27 C). The points of the material on the back of the work are afterwards cut away as in *Fig.* 27 D.

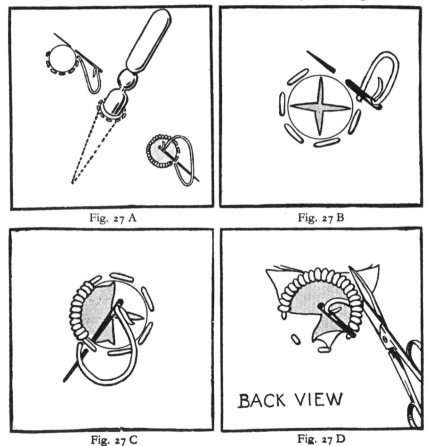

Fig. 27 A

Fig. 27 B

Fig. 27 C

Fig. 27 D

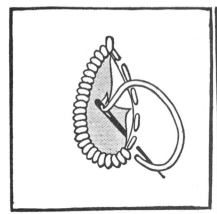

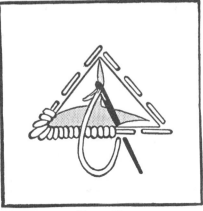

Fig. 27 E   Fig. 27 F

Oval eyelets (*Fig.* 27 E) are worked in a similar way to the round, △ but care is needed to keep the characteristic shape of the oval, well pointed at the top and rounded at the bottom.

For triangular shapes (*Fig.* 27 F) this same care is necessary and the overcasting must be carefully worked, otherwise the angles will develop into curves.

Shaded eyelets (*Figs.* 28 A and 28 B) are derived by first padding the outline with running stitches and grading the length of the overcasting stitches. Notice how the formation of the shading in *Fig.* 28 A gives the round opening an oval appearance. Shaded eyelets are useful when bolder and more solid effects are required.

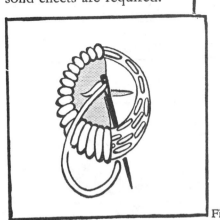

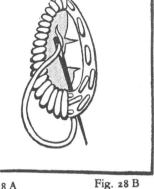

Fig. 28 A   Fig. 28 B

A chain of eyelets as used for the festoons and points in *Fig.* 25 is worked in two journeys (*see Figs.* 29 A to C). *Fig.* 29 A shows the prelimi-

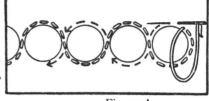

Fig. 29 A

nary running stitches travelling in a "waved" double journey, below one eyelet

Fig. 29 B

and above the next alternately, to the end of the chain, with the needle about to return to the starting point. The overcasting (*Fig.* 29 B) then follows the same path, uniting the two eyelets where they touch and in this way the chain is considerably strengthened. *Fig.* 29 C shows how the same method

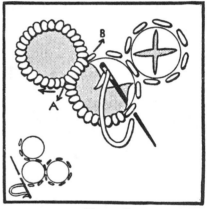

Fig. 29 C

may be employed if the eyelets are arranged in a point or triangle.

The Cucumber Seed Pattern (*Figs.* 30 A to C) is worked in much the same

Fig. 30 A

way. *Fig.* 30 A shows the path followed by the running stitch which this time makes four journeys. The first is outside the eyelets, the second inside as shown by the stitches and arrows.

Fig. 30 B

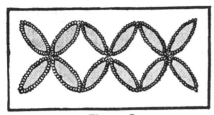

Fig. 30 C

The third journey completes the inner line and the fourth the outer line. The over-casting then follows along over the running stitch (*Fig. 30 B*), but with a slight difference. In order to make each oval appear isolated on the surface, the overcasting is not made in one unbroken line, △ but on reaching the centre of the four ovals, a tiny stitch is taken beneath the material, and then continues on the surface as before. *Fig.* 30 C shows the finished effect.

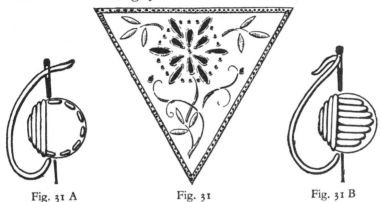

Fig. 31 A   Fig. 31   Fig. 31 B

Surface embroidery as introduced in the modern work (*Fig.* 31) is invariably worked in padded satin stitch with stem stitch for the finer lines as the embroidery must look important to offset the rich appearance of the eyelets. *Fig.* 31 A shows the method of working a small spot and *Fig.* 31 B a bolder effect obtained by padding. First work horizontal satin stitches across the circle, just inside the outline, and over these another layer of satin stitches, vertically this time (*see Fig.* 31 B), so that the padding stitches are completely covered. Either method can be used for working the leaves.

LADDER WORK

What is known as "ladder work" is frequently used in conjunction with Broderie Anglaise (*Figs.* 32 and 33) and the name "ladder" is most descriptive, as the motifs resemble

Fig. 32

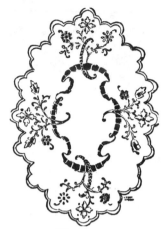

Fig. 33

little ladders composed of buttonhole or overcast bars with the material cut away from beneath them. The ladders may be rectangular or crescent-shaped or follow the outline of a particular shape as shown for the true lover's knot in *Fig.* 32.

Figs. 34 A to E show the working methods. First outline the shape with running stitch, then cut the material down the centre of the ladder and turn back. Over this work the buttonhole stitching, commencing at A and work round to B

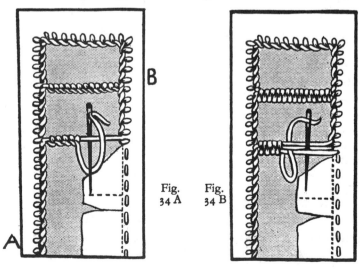

Fig.
34 A

Fig.
34 B

(*Fig.* 34 A) which is the position for the first cross-bar. Here throw a thread across to the opposite side and secure, returning again to B by buttonholing over this same thread. The second

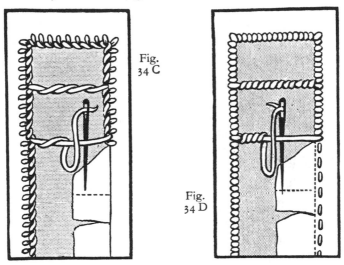

Fig.
34 C

Fig.
34 D

bar is shown in progress, after which the buttonhole edge is continued alternately with the bars until the starting point A is again reached. At *Fig.* 34 B the bars are woven, but the method is the same, except that three threads are thrown across the space and the weaving worked back alter-
nately over two threads
and under one. In *Fig.*
34 C the bars are loosely
overcast to produce a
twisted effect, while in
Fig. 34 D they are closely overcast to produce a
firm rounded bar, and
the edges of the motif are
also overcast, instead of

Fig. 34 E

being buttonholed. Crescent-shaped motifs are shown at *Fig.* 34 E, but here the bars are worked in at the same time as the running stitch, and the buttonhole edge added afterwards. The surplus material is then trimmed at the back.

BEADING

A very narrow ladder motif is known as beading, the working of which requires the use of a stiletto (*Figs.* 35 A to D). First withdraw a thread down the centre of the ladder as a guide, and outline this with two parallel rows of running stitch (*Fig.* 35 A). Then,

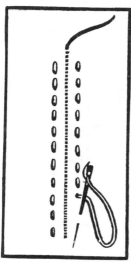

Fig. 35 A

commencing at the top of the ladder, punch a hole with the stiletto on the guide line and another further down, leaving two or three threads of material between each (*Fig.* 35 B). Now overcast the edges of the ladder commencing on the left top corner and work round to the position for the first bar between the two holes, and here throw a thread across to the opposite side (*Fig.* 35 C). Overcast back again, taking the needle over the thrown thread and those of the material beneath, and continue in this way down the whole length of the ladder, until the bottom is reached, and then overcast the other side (*Fig.*

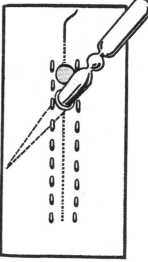

Fig. 35 B

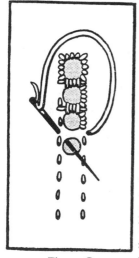

Fig. 35 C

Fig. 35 D

35 D). Beading is used to outline the little motif in *Fig.* 31, and waved beading is seen on the mat in *Fig.* 33 for which type the centre guide line must be pencilled.

SCALLOPING

This is a feature of Broderie Anglaise and of many other types of embroidery, and seven popular designs are given in *Fig.* 36 A to G. *Fig.* 36 A is the simplest form comprised of semi-circular scallops, and is easily evolved by pencilling round a coin, but a great many transfers of these edgings are obtainable, and this after all is the quickest and easiest method. The border should be offset on to the material about ¼″ from the raw edge and the shapes first outlined with running stitch. The scallops are then padded, again using running stitch, and finally covered with buttonhole stitch worked from left to right, keeping the looped edge of the stitch to the outside. △ These stitches must lie close together and completely cover the padding, and the working thread must not be drawn too tight, otherwise the work will pucker. The stitches should be quite small at the points and large at the lower edges in order to retain the symmetrical appearance of each scallop.

Always commence and finish off on the right side of the material, and begin a new thread by taking a few running stitches through the padding, bringing the needle up from below through the loop of the last stitch. In this way an even looped edge is preserved. Finishing-off should be done in the same way.

When the buttonholing is completed, cut away the surplus material close up to the stitches. △ Use very sharp scissors, otherwise the edges will present a frayed appearance and quite spoil the work. The four processes—outlining, padding, buttonholing and cutting—are all clearly shown on *Fig.* 36 A.

Fig. 36 B is a variation of the first but padded with chain stitch to produce a more solid and raised effect. The method and order of working is the same as before, and an example of using it is shown in *Fig.* 33. *Figs.* 36 C to E are all more elaborate versions of scalloping applicable to mats, lingerie, house linen, etc., and it is a good plan to cut these more complicated scallops in cardboard and use as a template for tracing the design.

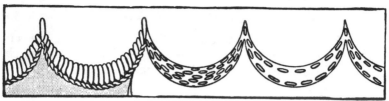

Fig. 36 A

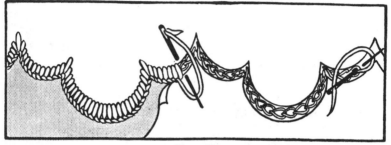

Fig. 36 B

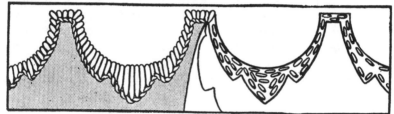

Fig. 36 C

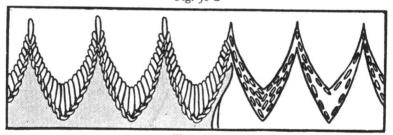

Fig. 36 D

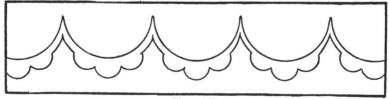

Fig. 36 E

The pear and scroll scallop (*Figs.* 36 F and G) apply particularly to Broderie Anglaise work as *Fig.* 36 F is merely an adjacent row of oval eyelets worked as previously described, with the exception of the lower edges which are buttonholed to allow of the surplus material being cut away. The scroll border in *Fig.* 36 G is worked in much the same way, the lower edges being buttonholed while the open parts are worked as for eyelets. Modern designs are frequently finished with simple wavy lines as shown in *Fig.* 32. These are outlined, padded and covered with buttonhole stitch as before, and make a good finish to work already elaborate enough in itself, without further decoration being needed for the edge.

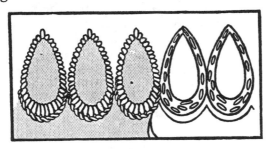

Fig. 36 F

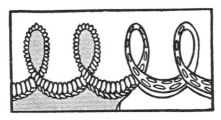

Fig. 36 G

CANVAS EMBROIDERY

"CANVAS EMBROIDERY" or "Canvas Work" is embroidery worked on a canvas background. The stitches cover the entire surface of the material and the finished work presents a woven appearance almost akin to tapestry, which probably explains why the name "tapestry" is so erroneously applied to this form of embroidery. (*See* Tapestry, *page* 265, and Cross Stitch, *page* 68.)

Many stitches peculiar to Canvas Embroidery were in use as early as the Middle Ages and the work occurs at frequent intervals throughout the Tudor and Stuart epochs, but it was during the late 17th and early 18th centuries that it reached the height of its glory; and the great designers of contemporary furniture used it for covering the beautiful chairs and settees of the period. Specimens of this epoch exist to-day in museums and private collections to tell their own glorious story. *Fig.* 37 shows a chair of the early 18th century in tent stitch or *petit point*. During the 19th century, canvas work deteriorated rather sadly into the Berlin wool-work of Victorian days, displaying poor designs and gaudy colourings. From this state it was rescued by the William Morris movement, and to-day takes its place with pride among the most popular forms of embroidery. Workers are happily adapting and reproducing some of the old designs, and still more happily introducing contemporary ideas and designs of their own. An instance of this is shown in *Fig.* 38 on *page* 38, a landscape of extraordinary beauty, measuring 29″ by 23″. So fine and exquisite is the detail that it is difficult to believe it to be a work of the needle.

Canvas Work has a practical as well as a decorative purpose, and is used chiefly for chair seats, stool covers, firescreens, pictures and occasionally hangings, wall panels, card-table tops and book covers. The finer forms are seen on beautiful handbags and pochettes, and the coarser on rugs and carpets done in rug wools and mainly in Tent or Cross Stitch.

By kind permission of the Victoria and Albert Museum

Fig. 37.   Early 18th century Canvas Work in Tent Stitch

Fig. 38   Modern Canvas Work in Tent Stitch by Margaret Vivian

MATERIAL AND TECHNIQUE

Canvas is made of linen, hemp, flax, silk or gauze, and of either single or double weave (*see Figs.* 39 and 40). Single

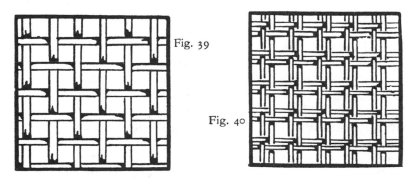

Fig. 39

Fig. 40

canvas is better for work in tent stitch and finer canvas stitches, while double canvas is used for Cross Stitch and other more solid stitches.

A canvas is measured by the number of threads to the inch, and these may vary from 28 (French Canvas) as used for pochettes and fine miniatures, to 3 as used for rugs and carpets. These are the two main types of canvas, though there are others of fancy variety upon which workers can experiment at choice.

A double canvas can be converted into a single by pressing apart the threads with the needle so that they are evenly distributed. This is called " pricking the ground " and is a useful tip for working finer effects, such as the hands and faces, in figure embroidery, as these can then be expressed in Tent Stitch or Rep Stitch, while the dresses and background remain in Cross Stitch. Floral designs can be treated in similar manner.

The embroidery is worked in fine " tapestry " wools, but the thicker embroidery wool can also be used on an appropriate mesh. For smaller articles, silk or mercerised threads are employed, and silk can be mixed with wool to produce a greater effect of light and shade. △ The golden rule in this embroidery is to select a wool or silk bearing a proportionate relationship to the canvas background which must be completely covered by the stitches.

Canvas Embroidery is better worked in a frame, mounting the selvedge edges of the canvas to the braced sides of the frame. (Slate frames are preferable as the tambour frame is apt to pull the stitches.) Blunt wool or tapestry needles are necessary, threaded with short lengths of wool or silk, as a thread of any length tends to fray by being constantly pulled through the canvas. Commence by running the wool in and out of the canvas and cover with the embroidery. Do not use a knot as it breaks away, and finish off on the back of the work. When working a design in many different colours, bring the wool through to the front of the work and lay aside until next required. This obviates the necessity of continually finishing off and also keeps the back of the work tidy. An experienced worker will commence at the bottom left-hand corner and work upwards, leaving the more delicate colours of the sky, flowers or faces until last, but it is quite in order to commence at the top, though in either case the completed embroidery should be covered with a cloth, as progress is made.

DESIGNS

The designs are planned on graph paper, using different symbols to represent the different colours (*see Fig.* 86). or if preferred these can be painted in with water-colours or chalks. Many beautiful designs can be evolved or copied by this method, allowing each line on the paper to represent a thread of the canvas. The finished drawing is called a chart. The size of a design will vary on different canvases according to the number of threads to the inch. The fewer these are in number the larger the squares, the design and the " square " effect of the stitches, and the reverse on fine canvases (*see Fig.* 38) When a design has to fit a certain space, such as chair seat, tray, etc., the number of spaces comprising the design must be counted, and a canvas of proportionate size bought; or the design may work out too large or too small. Commence by finding the centre square on the chart and that on the canvas, and count the squares North, South, East and West on both in order to ascertain that the design will fit the canvas, and leave sufficient margin of border for mounting. △ This is **very** important. In planning a large design it is more convenient to draw horizontal and vertical lines all over the chart spaced, say, 10 or 20 squares apart, and rule up the canvas in the same way (or buy a stencilled canvas on which this is already done).

Any subject, floral, landscape or figure, can be rendered in canvas work, as the colour gamut of modern wools is as full and rich as the paint palette of the artist. The design can be realistic or conventional as desired.

Quite distinct from the popular pictorial designs are those evolved by the use of different canvas stitches, which can be grouped to form repeating and geometrical patterns of great charm and variety, and demand only an elementary knowledge of drawing for their execution (*Figs.* 47, 49, 51).

STITCHES

Cross Stitch or *Gros Point* and Tent Stitch or *Petit Point* are the two most popular stitches in canvas embroidery, so popular in fact that workers often neglect the other two score odd which would bring such lively variety to the work. These stitches are all illustrated and described in the Dictionary, and should be worked out on a canvas sampler in order that their beauty may be appreciated and appropriately used.

Cross Stitch as worked on canvas is shown in *Fig.* 41.

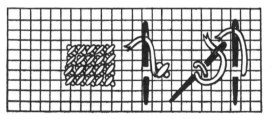

Fig. 41

each cross being completed before passing to the next, and worked in lines from left to right or right to left. The direction of progress does not matter, △ but the top stitch of the cross must always lie in the same direction, i.e. from the bottom left corner to the top right corner, otherwise the work will look irregular and full of mistakes! For working Cross Stitch on articles such as chair seats, rugs, etc., where particular strength and durability is required, the stitches should be worked in diagonal rows.

Tent Stitch is usually worked on single thread canvas and there are two methods. The first and best is illustrated at *Fig.* 42, where it will be seen that the rows are worked diagonally, first down as at A and then up as at B, always taking the

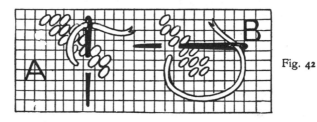

Fig. 42

stitch over one intersection of the canvas. This method is particularly strong and preserves the canvas as it builds up a neat woven effect on the back; and should be used for rugs,

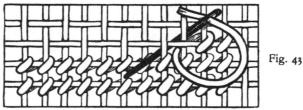

Fig. 43

stools and chair tops, as it will endure for ever. On light articles such as bags, etc., the method shown at *Fig.* 43 can be used. This is worked from right to left.

△ Tent Stitch has a tendency to pull the canvas diagonally

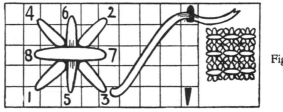

Fig. 44

and is better done in a frame, as it is difficult to correct. *See page* 274.

The less familiar Double Cross Stitch is shown in *Fig.* 44, and the method of planning a design and its worked appearances is shown in *Fig.* 45.

Long-armed Cross Stitch makes an effective background stitch, combined with Cross Stitch for the pattern shapes.

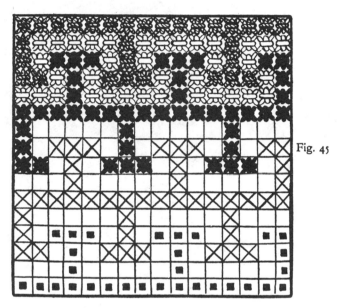

Fig. 45

Another which produces a most effective pattern, is French Stitch (*Fig.* 46), and a method of arranging it into a diaper

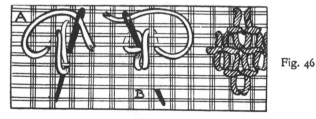

Fig. 46

design is shown in *Fig.* 47. Star Stitch* and Rococo Stitch* are now seldom used but they were great favourites in the heyday of canvas work. Star Stitch is similar to an eyelet on material, and is pretty to use when working flowers on a background of ordinary Cross Stitch. Rococo Stitch, popular in the 18th century for chair seats and stools, was

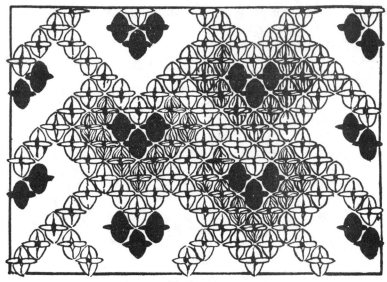

Fig. 47

used for the flowers on the famous Hatton Garden panels in the Victoria and Albert Museum. The stitch is unusual in that it is only worked on each alternate square of the canvas, leaving an open space between each, yet it is so planned that all the canvas threads are covered, the small perforations between each being most attractive.

Another famous group are the Gobelin stitches, named after the famous Gobelin tapestry. These include Simple Gobelin Stitch*, often used instead of Tent Stitch, though its effect is rather flatter and broader. For extra fine effects on

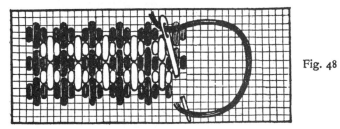

Fig. 48

double canvas use Rep Stitch* (see page 39), as it is worked between the double threads, as well as over them.

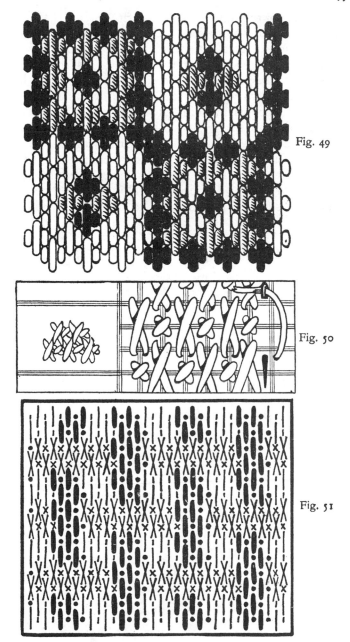

Fig. 49

Fig. 50

Fig. 51

A study of the different canvas stitches in the Dictionary will reveal that many form little independent patterns, needing only the addition of colour to render them exceedingly decorative. Hungarian Stitch, one of the simplest, is shown in *Fig.* 48, while in *Fig.* 49 is a suggestion for working it out in a pattern by means of varying the colours. Others such as Chequer Stitch* or Jacquard Stitch* produce brocaded effects and offer possibilities for backgrounds in one or two different colours.

Double Stitch (*Fig.* 50) is comprised of an oblong and an ordinary Cross Stitch, and a working chart for a pretty pattern in this stitch is given in *Fig.* 51, using three different colours for the working. Experiment along these lines will bring much pleasure and new interest to the work. For *Figs.* 48–51 *see pages* 44 and 45.

CORDS, FRINGES AND
TASSELS

IN LEARNING to make any cord, first experiment with
pieces of string, and though the diagrams may *look*
difficult, and they are difficult to draw, experiment will
reveal that they are surprisingly easy to make. All fringes
are easier to knot and make when the material is pinned
to a board with drawing-pins; and tassels look more interesting when they have a nice " fat " important appearance.

CORDS

Cords can be made of embroidery silks, wools, rug wool,
crochet cottons, macramé string, etc. They can be made to any
thickness by increasing the number of threads, strings or skeins
chosen, and fine cords can be utilised to make a very heavy cord.

Twisted Cord. The simplest form of twisted cord is shown in

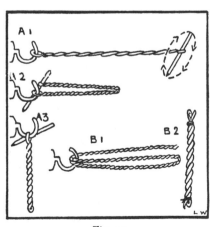

Fig. 52

Fig 52. Several skeins are
often necessary; group
these together and measure
off a length three times as
long as the required finished
cord. Knot a loop at each
end and slip one loop over
a hook as shown at A 1,
and a pencil into the opposite loop. Stand away from
the attached end, so that the
threads are taut, and twist
the pencil round and round
as shown by the little arrows.
When tight enough it will
begin to curl, and then take

the centre (or if it is a very long cord, get someone to hold
the centre), and double the cord back as shown at A 2. Now
let it hang, and it will twist automatically into a tightly coiled

47

cord (A 3). The secret of success lies in keeping the threads absolutely △ taut before allowing them to coil. Should they slacken, the coil will become irregular. It is a good idea to hang a weight in the centre before doubling, and allow it to twist with the weight suspended, though this is difficult when the cord is long, unless you get to the top of the staircase! A three-fold cord is made in the same way (B 1 and B 2 in *Fig.* 52), but after the first twisting, fold into three, keep taut in the process, and then let it drop as before, to coil. A cord of this description can be made to any thickness.

Finger Cord. A " finger cord " is shown at *Fig.* 53, the best results being obtained by using a stiff thick thread. It can be made in one or two colours, but for clearness of construction one of the two threads is shaded in the diagram. Knot two threads or groups of threads together and work upwards, making first a loop with the dark and then a loop with the light. Now insert the light loop into the dark as shown in the diagram.

Fig. 53

Pull the dark loop tight and make another through the light. Now pull the light one tight and make a loop through the dark and so on from side to side. Experiment with fairly thick string, following the instructions with the diagram before you. This cord is very simple to make and most effective when finished. For a softer thread, the fingers may be used as crochet hooks to pull through the loops.

Double Finger Cord. This again is very easy to work, but the instructions and diagram (*Fig.* 54) will be better followed

Fig. 54

If a practical experiment is made with pieces of string when reading. Two of the threads are shaded for clearness of construction, though the cord can be made in one or four colours as required. Use stiff thick thread to get the best result, and knot four lengths together at the top and place round a hook. Contrary to most plaited cords, two of the threads work from side to side and two backwards and forwards, so start by arranging them in North, South, East and Westerly directions. First cross East and West so that they change places from side to side and then North and South so that they change places, but in front and behind. These two movements are repeated, always crossing in the same way. When East and West cross, North and South will be projecting, one in front and one behind. This produces a most attractive and pliable cord which can be made to any thickness.

Greek Plaited Cord. This is a flat handsome cord constructed with five threads, two of which are used as a foundation round which the other three are plaited. These two threads (which are shaded in the diagram *Fig. 55*) act as drawstrings on which the finished plait can be drawn up or extended to produce a tight or loose effect as desired. It is easier to work with thick threads, and the cord when complete is very pliable and easily adjusted at corners, for cushion decorations. Knot all five threads together at the top and

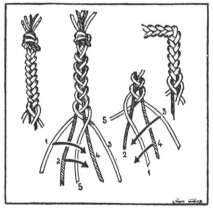

Fig. 55

secure over a hook. The plaiting process is quite clear in the diagram and shows how the outermost thread is always brought over *two* others into the middle again. This process will take one of the foundation threads to the outside which is then brought back again to position over *one* thread. These two movements are continued first on the right and then on the left, all the way down the plait.

FRINGES

There are three kinds of hand-made fringe: (1) those knotted into the edge of the material, (2) those formed from the frayed-out ends of the material itself, (3) those darned into the material. The first is used when the material is closely woven and difficult to fray into a fringe, and the second when the material is of a soft open texture, perhaps too easily frayed. The third is worked in darning stitches (straight or diagonal direction) into the material either end for about the depth of 1½". Cut a strip of cardboard 1" or so wide; and upon reaching the edge of the material loop round the cardboard and then darn into the fabric again. The loops are cut when the fringe is completed. Additional coloured threads can be added to a frayed fringe by this same method.

"Knotted-in" Fringes. The simplest knotted-in fringe is shown in *Fig.* 56, and applied with a crochet hook. Cut a

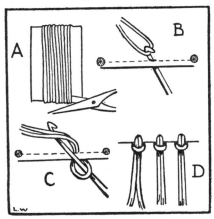

Fig. 56

piece of stout cardboard a little deeper than the required depth of the fringe to allow for the knot, and round this wind the thread forming the fringe. Cut along one side, as at A in *Fig.* 56 to produce equal lengths, ready for fringing. Roll the edge of the article being decorated into a tiny hem, a few inches at a time (it can be slipstitched if preferred but this is not necessary) and fasten the material down with drawing-pins to a board. This keeps it taut (B in *Fig.* 56). Double a length of thread in half and push the crochet hook through the edge of the material from below upwards and hook the thread as at B. Draw through and hook the two ends as shown at C, and tighten them up as at D. This completes one unit of the fringe, and the process is continued along the edge, placing each unit quite close to its neighbour.

Fig. 57 shows this same fringe attached to a preliminary

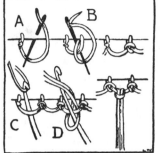

edging of Knot Stitch which is first worked all along the edge of the material. This method is more convenient when fringing fine material such as crêpe-de-chine, etc. First turn down or roll a narrow hem and then work the Knot Stitch as shown at A and B, *Fig* 57, leaving a loop

Fig. 57

between each knot. The cut length is then knotted in as before, but over each loop and not through the material (C and D in *Fig.* 57).

A more elaborate decoration is obtained by knotting and re-knotting the ends as shown in *Figs.* 58 and 59. After securing the first row of knots, the

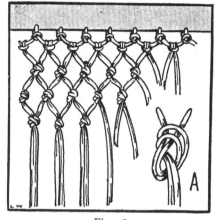

Fig. 58

strands are divided and knotted together in the manner shown at A, *Fig.* 58. This process of knotting can be continued for several rows, providing the threads are cut long enough in the first place. A good length of loose fringe must be left below the knots in order to obtain a pleasing balance. *Fig.* 59 shows how to knot this fringe when attached to a scalloped edge. The bunches which

Fig. 59

accumulate at the points of the scallop are just tied into one large knot.

Frayed Fringes.   Fig. 60 shows the method of making a fringe frayed from the material.   First ascertain the length of the fringe *before* fraying out the material. 8″ makes a pleasing decoration. △ Withdraw two threads of the material 8″ from the edge, and work a row of hemstitching, picking up an equal number of threads. After this, unravel the material up to the hemstitching. (A short fringe of 1″ may be left at this simple stage, but a wide fringe needs further control and decoration). The threads may be knotted together in bunches as shown in *Figs.* 58 and 59,

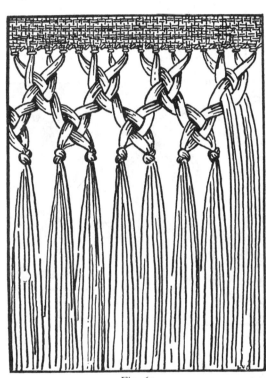

Fig. 60

but *Fig.* 60 suggests a more elaborate finish.   The threads are first plaited in groups of four and again sub-divided into other groups of four, and finally knotted in twos.   This method of fringing and knotting is an ancient work and the predecessor of lace into which it developed.   Ancient garments were fringed, knotted and reknotted with the addition of gold and coloured threads, and ultimately after many centuries these were separated from the clothing and made as independent decorations.

TASSELS

The simplest of all tassels is that made by knotting one end of a cord and fraying out the threads below the knot. The result is rather amateurish and the more professional looking tassels are very little more trouble to make, and much more pleasing in appearance.

SIMPLE TASSEL WITH BUTTONHOLE TOP

Fig. 61 illustrates the making of a useful tassel for attaching to the end of a cord or the corners of a cushion. Cut a piece of cardboard the required depth of the tassel, and round this wind the thread some forty or fifty times. △ (Be sure and make a good " fat " tassel as a skimpy one looks mean and uninteresting.) Next, cut the threads along one edge of the card as at A in *Fig.* 61. Keep the threads folded in half and prepare a needle threaded in the manner shown at B. Pass the loop round the group

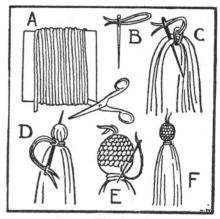

Fig. 61

of threads at the middle as shown at C, and down through the middle of the bundle where the ends are lost. This loop holds the threads together while the tassel is being made. Thread the needle again in the same manner, and, after padding the head of the tassel with a small pellet of cotton-wool, secure it with a looped thread as shown at D, pull tightly, and pass the needle up through the head and out at the top of the tassel. These two ends of thread should be left uncut, as they are used later for attaching the completed tassel to a cord or cushion. The tassel head may be decorated with a covering of detached Buttonhole stitch*, commencing at the top and working round and round as shown at E. The finished tassel is illustrated at F.

Heavy Tassel. A heavy tassel needs to be more firmly attached than that just described, and an excellent method is suggested in *Fig.* 62 A. The threads are cut and tied in the middle as before (*Fig.* 61 A), but a thick cord is also included. The threads are then folded back over

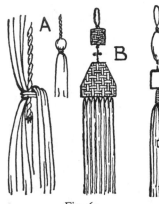

C the first binding and bound again to form the tassel head. The first binding and the end of the cord are thus completely encased and a neat tassel firmly suspended.

Flat Tassel on Buckram. The flat tassel illustrated in *Fig.* 62 B is made of threads attached as a fringe to two shaped pieces of buckram, the edges of which are turned in and whipped together. The shape thus formed may be

Fig. 62   afterwards embroidered or covered with material as desired.

Bead Tassel. The tassel at 62 C has a narrow tightly-bound head, the threads of which are then passed through a square wooden bead and again through an oval bead and so on, producing an oriental effect. Many variations of this tassel can be easily evolved with different shaped beads.

Turk's Head Knot for a Tassel Head. No article on the subject of tassels would be complete without the description of a Turk's Head Knot, which makes a jolly tassel head or decorative dress button. The working method is clearly illustrated in *Fig.* 63 and is surprisingly easy. Use a stiff thread or cord, and when the first three loops have been made, the thread repeats the first journey all over again as shown by the arrows. It is easier to work the knot fairly loose and flat, then ease round the threads until they tighten up and take a neat rounded shape, to which a tassel may be attached as shown in the diagram.

Fig. 63

COUCHING, LAID WORK
AND GOLD EMBROIDERY

I N " Couching " the embroidery threads are laid upon
the surface of the material and fastened down with
small stitches, using another independent thread. (The
name is derived from the French word " coucher," to lie
down.) When one or several threads are grouped as an
outline the process is known as " Couching," but when many
threads are laid side by side to fill a space, it is known as
" Laid Work." It is an economical method of using expensive
silks, or gold and silver, and all Gold Embroidery is carried
out in this method. An embroidery frame must be used for
this type of embroidery.

COUCHING

Couching is excellent for (1) working a bold unbroken line,
(2) covering the edges of applied motifs, or (3) for working
raised effects. It is also useful on a fine fabric, as the heavier
couched threads are only laid on the surface and not forced
through the fine material.

THREADS

Any cotton, wool, silk or cord can be couched, and very
fine threads are grouped in six or ten strands and " couched "
with two strands. The tying-down thread can be of a matching or contrasting colour according to the effect desired; but
for outlines, subordinate to the rest of the design, a fine
matching thread renders the stitches almost invisible. On the
contrary, if the couched line forms the chief decoration,
then a thicker thread in contrasting colour is effective. Keep
two sizes in needles handy, one to carry the thicker and the
other, the finer thread.

Fig. 64 illustrates a bold unbroken line in couching as used
for borders or to outline a design. The laid threads are

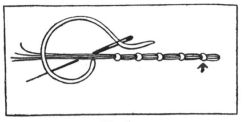

Fig. 64

brought from beneath
on the right and tied
down with a single
thread brought through
at the arrow. The
ground thread lies
fairly loose upon the
surface and is guided
along the design with
the left hand. The overcasting stitches are placed at
regular intervals and pulled fairly tight, △ but in following
a curve they need to be closer, and any angle or point must be
clearly defined by placing a stitch at the apex.   See the flower
petals in *Fig.* 68.

This simple method of couching can be varied by arranging
the tying-down
stitches in pattern
formation.   Three
suggestions are
given in *Fig* 65,
where chevrons,
pairs and crosses
are used, and ex-
periment will pro-
duce many others.
Several different
embroidery stitches
can be used as tying
stitches, *see Fig.* 66.
These produce a
broader effect, and
make pretty decora-
tive borders.
Blanket stitch is
used at A, herring-
bone stitch at B,
open chain stitch
at C, while at D
Cretan stitch is
worked over two

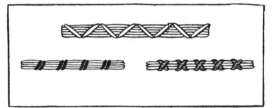

Fig. 65

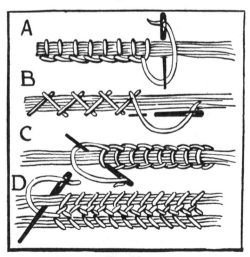

Fig. 66

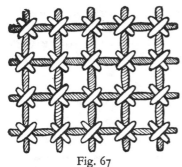

Fig. 67

groups of threads to form an extra wide border.

Fig. 67 shows a couched open filling, the charm of which can be appreciated by studying *Fig.* 68. Such fillings are found in Jacobean embroideries and in modern work where large fruit, flowers, leaves, etc., need a light dainty treatment. The threads are first laid across the shape vertically and horizontally, and secured with a cross stitch worked in matching or contrasting colour, over each intersection of the threads. A single slanting satin stitch can also be used in the same way. The floral design in *Fig.* 68 gives some idea of the different

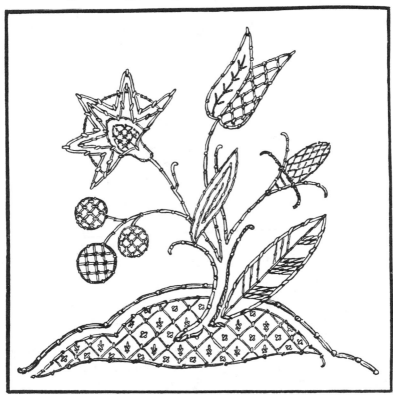

Fig. 68

ways in which couching can be used to work out an entire design. The couched filling shown in *Fig.* 68 is set both straight and diagonal, and the lattice base, being quite wide, shows small Cross stitches and Ermine filling stitches arranged within the spaces.

LAID WORK

Laid Work is really but an elaboration of couching, and a useful means of filling large shapes such as the flower in

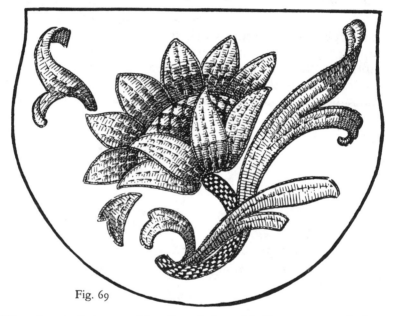

Fig. 69

Fig. 69, and is notably found in old Portuguese, Indian, Japanese and Chinese embroideries. Its decorative qualities are best offset on curtains, blotters, fire-screens or such articles not frequently in the wash!

Designs. The designs should be large, bold and important. Flowers, leaves and birds, etc., lend themselves particularly well to this treatment, as do bold conventional patterns (*see Fig.* 69). Entire backgrounds are often covered in laid work, as the large expanse of ground encourages a pretty play of lights in the silks.

Threads.   All luxury threads are mainly used, such as floss silk and gold, though mercerised cottons and embroidery wools can be used if desired.   △ When laying floss or silk, it is particularly important to see that it does not get twisted in the process, and a frame should be used to keep the long laid threads taut until secured in position.   Laid work may be embroidered on any material, the choice of which must govern the thickness of the threads used.   Threads which are too thick to pierce the material are " turned " upon the surface and a finer thread used for tying down.   Some very beautiful colour schemes can be evolved, as the laid threads can be graded from one colour to another with comparative ease as shown in *Fig.* 69.   For " turning " *see page* 64.

Laying the Threads.   The method of " laying " is more convenient when performed in two journeys (*see* A and B in *Fig.* 70), as a stitch can be taken on the circumference of the form, while in the second journey (B) the needle pierces the first thread and fills in the vacant spaces.   △ The outline must be kept even and the stitches close to cover the material as shown in the leaf beneath in *Fig.* 71.   When worked in a frame the needle would of course take an upward and downward movement.

The next process, that of " tying down " the laid threads, is done at a contrasting angle and affords great scope for individual treatment.   The petal at C in *Fig.* 70 is secured by three couched lines arranged to suggest the petal markings of the flower.   The tying-down stitches on the large flower stem in *Fig.* 69 are grouped to form a chequered pattern while an open lattice effect is given to the central portion of the flower. In order to show how individual and varied the methods can be, *Figs.* 71, 72, 73 and 74 depict the same leaf treated in four different ways.   In *Fig.* 71 five straight lines are couched at right angles, while in *Fig.* 72 the couched lines are placed fan-wise.   In *Fig.* 73 single running stitches are arranged in " brick " formation, and in *Fig.* 74 the laid threads are secured with single stitches and Fly stitches. △ Care must be taken in arranging fan lines, otherwise the curve will run parallel to the laid threads and their purpose lost.   See next page for *Figs.* 70–74.

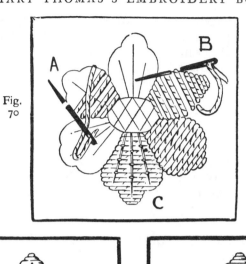

Fig.
70

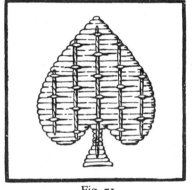

Fig. 71

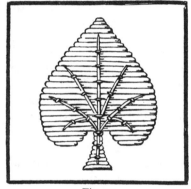

Fig. 72

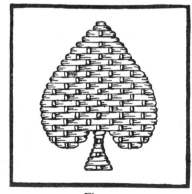

Fig. 73

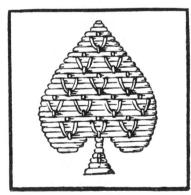

Fig. 74

BOKHARA AND ROUMANIAN COUCHING

There are two forms of laid work which combine the laying and tying of the threads in one process. The first is known as Bokhara Couching, *Fig.* 75, for which a long stitch is thrown loosely across the space to be filled, and tied down with small stitches on the return journey. These stitches are all made at a slant, and arranged to form a decorative diagonal line across the surface of the laid threads.

Fig. 75

The second is Roumanian Couching, *Fig.* 76. The working is exactly the same as for Bokhara Couching, but the result aimed at is different, as the tying-down stitches are not meant to form a pattern on the surface. For this reason, they are made longer on the surface, picking up but a small piece of material with each stitch and

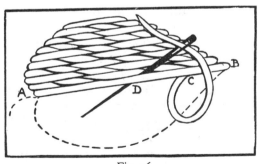

Fig. 76

kept fairly loose, and when the space is filled, it is almost impossible to distinguish between the laid and the tying-down threads. Roumanian Couching is often used to fill in a solid background for such subjects as skies, grass and lawns in picture embroideries.

GOLD EMBROIDERY

Embroidery worked with gold dates back to Biblical days, and its records and technique alone would be sufficient to fill a volume! To-day it is rarely seen, except on church embroidery, ceremonial regalia, military uniforms and so forth, and perhaps on a college or club blazer in the form of a badge or monogram.   The subject is here treated in its simplest and most practical form in order that the work can be appreciated, and used by those who wish to work banners, etc., for their church or guild.

There are three types of gold work, 1. Outline, 2. Flat, 3. Raised.   The same methods as described for couching apply also to gold work in outline, the other two forms are described separately.

Threads and Materials.   There are a number of different gold threads, passing, bullion, purl, plate, etc., but for the purposes of this brief article Japanese gold is the most suitable medium, as it is more adaptable and easier to handle.   All gold must be couched with fine twisted silk of strong and good quality, to hold the springy, metal thread in place; cotton or mercerised thread look cheap and out of place.   In flat gold work, a coloured silk may be used with good effect for tying down the stitches, as this accentuates the pattern, but for raised gold work, where the pattern is formed by the light and shade on the embossed motifs, a fine twisted silk in matching gold colour should be used, as this is then almost invisible.

A padding thread such as thick embroidery cotton or wool is needed for raised gold work, and a fine good quality white string or macramé thread for gold basket work.   Gold embroidery can be worked on silk, satin, velvet, linen, leather or fine kid, as it is always backed with a coarse linen or holland. Only the best materials should be chosen, and for preference the amateur should begin on a strong linen backed with a second of coarser weave.   The method of working the gold on linen and transferring it, using a couched outline, and per-haps softened with a lighter couched thread, in filigree patterns, is recommended for velvet.

The choice of material will, of course, be governed by the type of design and embroidery worked, but the richer fabrics are used particularly for church embroidery, while a silk brocade offers a good choice as the brocaded pattern may be used as a design basis for the embroidery.   All loosely woven fabrics should be avoided, as these make the work more difficult. If the entire background is to be covered with embroidery, choose a firm natural coloured linen.

Needles with wide eyes are required to take the gold thread and finer ones for the silk, △ and all gold work must be done in a frame. Mount the foundation linen first, sewing upon this the upper fabric, which must be stretched taut and secured firmly in position.

Gold thread is always used double, that is, two strands at a time, and straight from the skein. △ *Never* pull it out in lengths and thread straight into the needle as in the usual way, since this would unravel and damage the precious metal. An examination of a new skein of gold thread will reveal a loose protruding end from either side of the skein. Both these should be gently pulled out at the same time to the required length △ (only a short length at a time, just sufficient to cover the immediate row upon which you are working), place both ends together to form the double thread. Gold thread tarnishes very easily, so great care should be taken to handle it as little as possible, keep it wrapped with the ends only exposed; and keep the work covered up as much as possible and never store it in a damp place.

FLAT GOLD EMBROIDERY

The method illustrated in *Fig.* 77 is used when filling a small clearly defined shape demanding a neat outline. Commence on the left side by pushing a wide-eyed needle through on the outline, leaving only the eye above the surface, and thread in this the double gold as shown at A, only about $\frac{1}{2}''$ from the ends. The needle is then pulled through to the back unthreaded and removed. The gold threads are then couched down with silk, making the first stitch

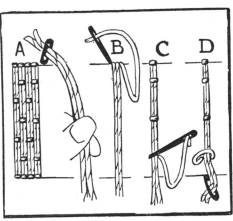

Fig. 77

close up to the outline of the shape as at B, in order to secure both ends of the gold under the material. The couching continues at regular intervals down the double line as shown at C, making two distinct movements, *up* to the right of the threads and down on the *left*. △ Don't try to make the stitch in one movement, and when entering the material, the needle should be inserted well under the threads of the previous row, by which means the double lines of gold will lie closely together when the stitch is pulled tight. This is important, otherwise the lines of gold will lie in "waves" over the surface and the material beneath show through and spoil the effect. On reaching

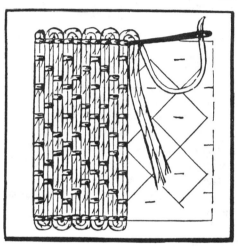

Fig. 78

the opposite side the gold is cut, allowing an extra half inch and taken to the back as shown at D, being finally secured by the last couching stitch. When the filling is complete, the gold ends are trimmed neatly on the back, and the shape left at this stage, or finished with a couched outline of gold.

A quicker and more convenient method for filling larger shapes is shown at *Fig.* 78, where the gold is " turned " on the surface of the material. This diagram also shows how the couching stitches can be arranged to form an all-over diaper pattern, and to accentuate the pattern a silk of contrasting colour may be used. The diapers must be traced beforehand upon the foundation material as shown in *Fig.* 78. The first pair of gold threads are secured as before (*see Fig.* 77) and the couching worked in the same way, but the spacing between the stitches is governed by the lines of the pattern beneath. Upon reaching the opposite edge the gold is neatly turned (*see* diagram) and the work continued. When the shape is completed the outline can be neatened if desired by couching down a line of thicker gold or cord over the looped edges.

Fig. 79 contains suggestions for three different diaper patterns, each simple in construction, while *Fig.* 80 shows how to work an initial in much the same way. This is also first traced on the material beneath and a bright coloured silk, say emerald, is used for the tying-down stitches. Couch

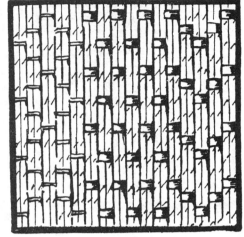

Fig. 79

the gold threads as before, but on reaching the outline of the initials, the stitches are worked closely together, completely covering the gold, and so produce an initial in green on a " field of gold."

RAISED GOLD EMBROIDERY

The foundation for this work is made by first padding the shape with satin stitch, using a thick cotton or wool thread to produce an effect of high relief. Felt or cardboard is sometimes used for the padding; especially for crosses and other large shapes (*see Fig.* 81). The gold threads are then couched across the shape as before, using a matching gold-coloured silk as the contrast is achieved by the light and shade on the raised gold. Carry the couching stitches well up to the edge of the design, the last stitch being

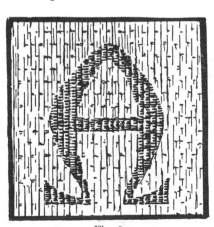

Fig. 80

Fig. 81

made on the outline. After this the gold thread is passed over the motif and the couching silk beneath, to come up on the opposite side and continue the work. It will be noticed that the couching stitches in *Fig.* 81 get closer together as they approach and recede from the motif. This flattens the background and accentuates the contrast of the embossed parts.

GOLD BASKET-WORK

This is another form of embossed gold work obtained by couching down the gold thread over a padding of fine string or macramé thread. The method produces a basket-like weave as shown in *Fig.* 82. The string is first cut into the required lengths and placed at right angles to the direction in which the gold is to be worked, and each end is firmly secured with several stitches (*see* A, *Fig.* 82). The spaces must be evenly arranged, and the first gold thread is then carried over two strings and tied down as at B, but in

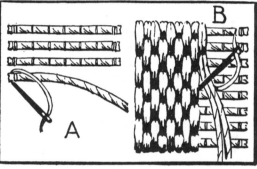

Fig. 82

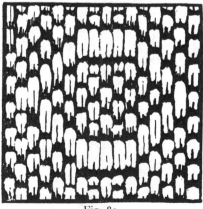

Fig. 83

order to get the basket effect the next line commences over one string and continues over two as before. *Fig.* 83 shows how a pattern may be made in basketwork. The stitches forming the pattern are taken over three strings instead of two. This necessitates an occasional stitch being worked over one string in order to keep the basketwork background regular.

The most fascinating way of using string as a padding is shown in *Fig.* 84. The design is first traced in double outline on the linen background, and the string couched down between the lines. These foundation strings must not cross over or under each other, but be cut off and secured as shown in *Fig.* 84, in order to keep the padding regular throughout. The gold is laid at right angles to the string, and couched down in the usual way, always working the final stitch close up to the string on both sides to accentuate the pattern. A contrast can be obtained by couching the background in gold silk and using a coloured silk to secure the gold thread on either side of the string pattern.

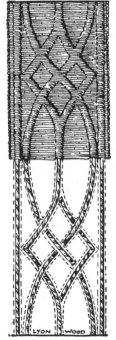

Fig. 84

CROSS STITCH EMBROIDERY

ROSS STITCH EMBROIDERY must not be confused with Canvas Embroidery. The two types of work are very similar and stitches from both are interchangeable, but Cross Stitch is worked upon a material while canvas embroidery is, as its name implies, worked upon canvas, the stitches completely covering the ground, while in Cross Stitch Embroidery they form a pattern only on the material.

The embroidery is as its name implies based on a stitch made in the form of a diagonal cross and is the simplest of all embroideries. Perhaps this explains why it is often so carelessly worked, its beauty being marred by irregular crosses and top threads slanting in contrary directions.

The best examples of Cross Stitch Embroidery hail from the Slavonic countries of Eastern Europe—Roumania, Bulgaria, Russia, Jugoslavia, Czechoslovakia and Macedonia, where the adornment of clothes and household linen with this form of work has been a peasant industry for hundreds of years. The designs and colour combinations are manifold, each country— and sometimes each district—claiming its own characteristic colours and designs, which are worked on counted threads without the guide of either graph or transfer. The European peasants are aghast at the suggestion of transfers!

Cross Stitch can be worked on almost any article—clothes, household linens of all types, curtains, cushions and so forth. It is used for ecclesiastical and heraldic embroideries and was employed to work parts of the Syon Cope and the curtains of the Tabernacle. In Victorian days Cross Stitch was used to make little pictures which became widely misnamed " samplers." (*See* " Samplers " on *page* 239.)

Materials and Threads. Only materials of even warp and weft should be used, such as embroidery linen, voile, hessian, hopsac, etc., and providing this principle is adhered to, almost any material is suitable, some of the new furnishing

fabrics being particularly successful. △ (A warp and weft
of uneven thickness com-
pletely changes the appearance of a pattern as the
crosses work out elongated
in shape.) Check materials
of an uneven weave can be
used, as the principle of
work is different, the size of
the crosses being regulated
by the size of the squares; and
not by counting the threads.
Cross Stitch can be worked on
fine materials and on those of
diagonal weave by working over
canvas (described further on) or
by using a transfer.

Any thread, mercerised, silk,
wool or linen, can be used providing a balance is maintained
with the background material.
A coarse material necessitates a
coarse thread and vice versa.
Stranded cottons are useful, as
they can be divided. If embroidery wools are used, the stitches
should not be pulled quite so tight
as when using cotton threads.

Fig. 85

Design and Colour. Fig. 85 shows a beautiful Roumanian cross
stitch design which explains the manner of grouping and mas-
sing the stitches to form geometric shapes and repeating
motifs. The zigzag line and method of turning the corner
are characteristic of Slavonic patterns. The shape of the spaces
left between the embroidered masses are as important as those
filled by the grouping of the stitches, and a well-spaced background is essential for a good design. Other treatments are
shown in *Figs.* 87 and 92.

Colour must be considered in groups and shapes, and not as

individual stitches. Bright basic colours have more character than delicate half-tones, and one, two or twenty different colours can be used on one design with good effect. The designs are planned out on graph paper using different symbols to represent the different colours (*Fig.* 86).

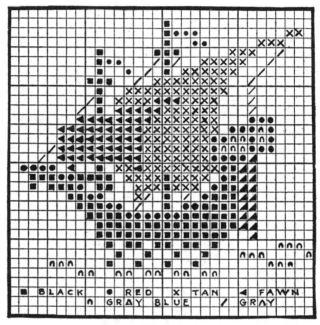

Fig. 86

Method of Work. In working from such a chart as *Fig.* 86, each square must be considered a unit and a unit may consist of one or more threads (the number being governed by the texture of the material and the size of design required), and must remain the same throughout the whole design. A unit of three threads is a good average for which each cross would be made by counting three threads along and three threads up. By increasing or reducing the size of the unit a design can be enlarged or reduced accordingly.

A transfer obviates the necessity of counting threads, but in offsetting see that the lines of crosses are laid along the weave of the material, otherwise the finished work will look awry.

It is quite possible to work regular cross stitches on fabrics of uneven or diagonal weave without a transfer by following the method employed for working on very fine silks, etc. (*see Fig.* 87). A fine single-mesh canvas is first tacked over the material, and the design then worked upon the canvas (counting the threads) and taking the stitches through both canvas and material at the same time. When completed, the threads of the canvas are carefully pulled away. △ Each stitch must be pulled tight in working, otherwise they present a loose

Fig. 87

untidy appearance when the canvas threads are pulled away. It is advisable to cut away the canvas close up to the embroidery, by which means only short threads of canvas are pulled through the stitches and the work not unduly disturbed (*see* Fig. 87).

Technique. In working Cross Stitch Embroidery there are two simple but important points to remember: (1) The crosses must be regular in shape and size; (2) the stitches *must* cross in the same direction.   △ The latter is important and tradition says that the upper stitch should slope from the left upwards to the right as in handwriting.

There are two working methods illustrated in *Figs.* 88 and 89.   Both diagrams show how the stitch can be commenced from the right and worked to the left or vice versa, but in either case the upper stitch always lies over to the right.   In

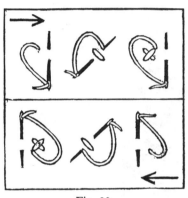

Fig. 88

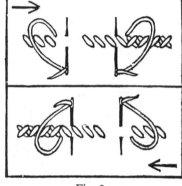

Fig. 89

Fig. 88 each cross is completed before the next is commenced. This method produces the most even effect and is considered by expert workers to be the better.   *Fig.* 89 shows a quicker way for covering large patterns and long border lines, the first half of each stitch being worked along in a row, and the second half added on the return journey.

VARIATIONS OF CROSS STITCH

Both methods of Cross Stitch as shown in *Figs.* 88 and 89 produce irregular effects on the back of the work, but, by using " Two-sided Cross Stitch " (*see Fig.* 90) the work is alike on both sides, the crosses on the back being as perfect as those on the front.

Commence at the arrow and work from left to right and right to left alternately in four journeys, making two auxiliary or half stitches at A and E.   The first at A is made at the end of the first journey.   B shows the return journey from right to left, and C and D the method of turning and ending the third journey.   The second auxiliary stitch is shown at E, and the final journey given at F. The dotted lines show the progress of the stitch on the back of the work. The thread forming the cross on the right (*see* E) takes a contrary direction which is

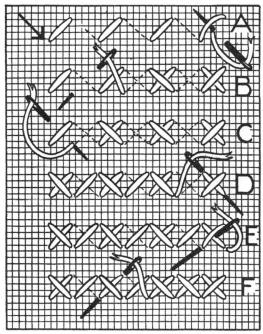

Fig. 90

corrected by making an extra stitch before commencing the journey, shown at F.

Marking Cross Stitch (*Fig.* 91) is employed for purposes of marking linen, or working monograms, etc. This has the appearance of ordinary cross stitch on the front and neat little squares on the back, achieved by covering some of the stitches twice. Commence at A and work the first three movements. The second stitch at B is shown completed at C with the needle in position

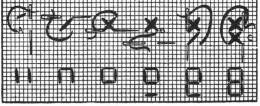

Fig. 91

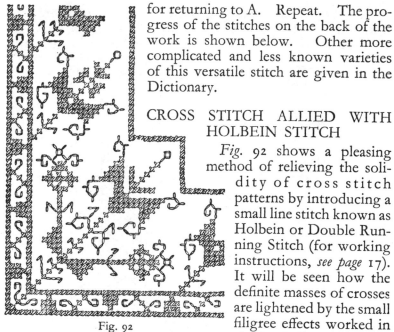

for returning to A. Repeat. The progress of the stitches on the back of the work is shown below. Other more complicated and less known varieties of this versatile stitch are given in the Dictionary.

CROSS STITCH ALLIED WITH HOLBEIN STITCH

Fig. 92 shows a pleasing method of relieving the solidity of cross stitch patterns by introducing a small line stitch known as Holbein or Double Running Stitch (for working instructions, *see page* 17). It will be seen how the definite masses of crosses are lightened by the small filigree effects worked in single stitches, each stitch being the same length as the crosses. This method has the effect of drawing together and co-ordinating the design, and is frequently seen in Bulgarian and Roumanian embroideries worked out in black.

Fig. 92

VOIDING

A certain majesty is given to cross stitch designs by drawing them on the stencilled principle as shown in *Fig.* 87. This is technically termed " voiding," and can be successfully applied to heraldic shapes, quaint and often humorous figures of birds, beasts and nursery objects, or conventional floral designs. In all cases the markings of the bird or animal or petal markings of the flower and leaves, are left unworked or " avoided," leaving spaces of the material to show between the stitches and suggests these details. " Voiding " is a favourite treatment in Chinese embroidery, and the term is applied to all forms of embroideries worked in any stitch, but on this principle of design.

CUT WORK

"CUT WORK" is a name given to those forms of embroidery where portions of the foundation material are "cut" away from the background of the design; and the title embraces (1) Simple Cut Work, (2) Renaissance, (3) Richelieu and (4) Italian Cut Work. The work has a distinct air of grandeur and rich lace-like effects can be obtained by increasing the number of "cut" spaces until its appearance almost resembles Venetian or Reticella lace.

In Simple Cut Work the spaces are quite small, but in Renaissance work they grow larger and are decorated with bars, while in Richelieu work the addition of picots to the bars makes the work still more elaborate, but the most ornamental of all is the Italian Cut Work, which is built up round small open squares, filled with needlepoint stitches. Cut work is suitable for all household linens, though the delicate and more elaborate forms are better used on articles such as table runners, luncheon sets and so forth and the simpler and less delicate forms on sheets and pillow-slips.

Designs. The designs need careful planning as the shape of the cut spaces and the position of the bars are just as important as the embroidery and the outline. The favourite subjects are floral, either naturalistic or conventional in character, and *Figs.* 93, 96, 104 and 105 are all very typical, *Fig.* 96 being rather reminiscent of the old lace patterns. △ When planning or adapting a design for Cut Work see that the shapes "tie up" securely at the vital points, otherwise the work hangs loose, when the background is cut away. This refers in particular to the points and tips of leaves, scrolls, etc. All the main outlines of any Cut Work design are drawn double to act as guide lines for the running and buttonhole stitching (*see Fig.* 94).

Materials and Threads. Only a stiff, firm linen is suitable for this work, otherwise the material frays after the spaces are cut. White or natural coloured linens with matching threads have been the tradition of the past, though moderns are experimenting with coloured linens and different coloured threads. △ This is quite permissible but it needs care and discrimination as the work is so easily spoilt by bold or blatant colours. Actually, the charm of the work lies in the design and the technique, which does not call for the addition of colour to enhance its own natural beauty. When coloured linens are chosen it is better to use a matching thread. Linen, cotton or mercerised threads are all suitable, and a thick crochet cotton makes a useful padding. A pair of very sharp embroidery scissors are essential for cutting away the background.

SIMPLE CUT WORK

The type of design used for Simple Cut Work is shown at *Fig.* 93. Here the cut spaces are so arranged that no stray

Fig. 93

leaves or petals are left detached in any part. The embroidery consists of running stitch covered with button stitch.

After transferring the design to the linen, work two rows of running stitch just inside all the double lines of the design (*see* A in *Fig.* 94). △ These stitches must not be pulled tightly at any angle, otherwise the work will pucker. When the run stitching is complete, cover the double line with buttonhole stitch as at B in *Fig.* 94. Work each stitch close to the next, arranging the looped or " corded " edge of the stitch to face toward those parts of the design to be later cut away.

Fig. 94

Fig. 95

When the buttonhole stitching is completed, cut away the spaces (*see Fig. 95*). △ This can be done on the right or the wrong side of the work, cutting the material away close up to the buttonholing, otherwise the edges will "fluff" up and spoil the appearance of the work. Letter A in *Fig. 95*, shows how dreadful a badly cut space can look.

RENAISSANCE EMBROIDERY

This form of cut work progresses one step beyond Simple Cut Work. The preparation and embroidery is the same, but the cut spaces being larger need to be strengthened with bars, or "brides." This gives the work a very rich and lacy appearance as seen in *Fig. 96*. Bars are *the* feature in

Fig. 96

Renaissance Embroidery and may be (1) buttonholed, (2) woven or (3) twisted, and of these, buttonholing is the most durable and weaving better for spanning larger spaces. The foundation of the bar and the running stitch outline are both accomplished in one journey.

Start the embroidery at any point on the design by working the outer row of running stitch as before (*Fig.* 94 A), but upon reaching the position for the first bar, the thread is carried across to the opposite side as at A in *Fig.* 97. Here

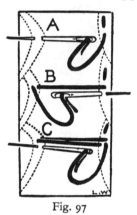

Fig. 97

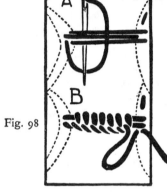

Fig. 98

make a tiny stitch, return and make another as at 97 B and yet a third time as at 97 C. The three threads now thrown across the material are closely covered with buttonhole stitching, keeping the bar quite firm but detached from the material beneath as at A in *Fig.* 98. Upon reaching the starting point again continue the running stitch as before until the next bar is thrown. When all the bars are completed in this way, the inner row of running stitching is worked, and finally the design is buttonholed as directed in Simple Cut Work. The final task is cutting away the background. △ Do this with care, cutting beneath the bars which are left to form a lace-like filling and strengthen the cut spaces.

BRANCHED BARS AND " SPIDER WEBS "

It is not convenient to cross every space with a straight bar and an examination of *Fig.* 96 will show how " branched "

and " spider webs " can be used with good effect. *Fig.* 99
shows a simple branched bar. The first group of threads

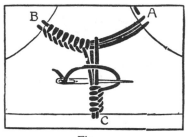

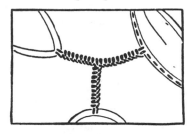

Fig. 99   Fig. 100

are thrown across from A to B, and these are buttonholed
back from B to the centre, and from thence three more
threads are thrown at right angles to C. The buttonholing
is then worked back to the centre again, and then on to A.
The finished bar is shown at *Fig.* 100, together with the running stitch which then continues round the design.

A Four Branched Bar is shown at *Fig.* 101. The working
method is the same as before and easily followed from the
diagram.

" Spider Web " filling is shown in *Fig.* 102. Here a single

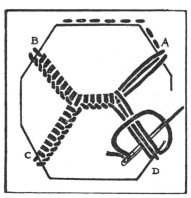

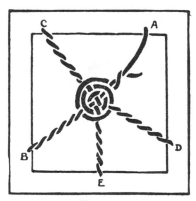

Fig. 101   Fig. 102

thread is carried across from A to B, and then twisted back
to the centre, from whence the three other twisted bars,
C, D and E, are thrown out and back in the same way. All
five bars are secured in the centre by weaving under and

over the intersections, after which the first bar is completed by twisting back again to A.

Fig. 103 shows how to work " Ring Spider Web." First

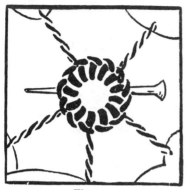

make the small detached ring by winding the thread six or seven times round a pencil. Slip this off and cover all round with buttonhole stitch. Now break off the thread and pin the ring into position on the material (*see Fig.* 103). Ordinary twisted bars are then worked, out from the design to the ring and back again. Four or five such bars are sufficient to hold the ring in place. When these are completed the

Fig. 103

pin is removed and the " Ring Spider Web " complete. Both ring and bars are, of course, quite detached from the material beneath, as this must be cut away as in *Fig.* 104. This pretty

cut work motif shows how effective " Ring Spider Webs " look set in fairly large spaces.

△ When working any type of bar, branch or " Spider Web," the fixed ends of the foundation threads must be placed well inside the double outline. This not only ensures that all untidy ends will be well covered by the final buttonholing, but that the " pull " of the bar will be removed beyond

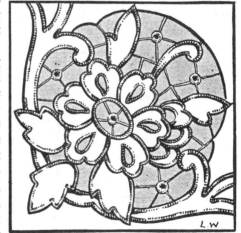

Fig. 104

the edge when the background is cut away.

RICHELIEU WORK

Richelieu work advances two steps beyond Cut Work and

the embroidery grows still more open and " lacy " by adding picots to the bars already introduced in Renaissance Embroidery. A study of *Fig.* 105 will reveal how rich in ap-

Fig. 105

pearance these bars become with the addition of picots. This being the only difference between Renaissance Embroidery and Richelieu Embroidery, the two are frequently confused.

Since the working of Richelieu Embroidery is the same as that described for Simple Cut Work and Renaissance Embroidery it only remains to describe the working method of picots. These are added in with the process of working the bars. The easiest is a " Loop Picot " illustrated at *Fig.* 106. After buttonholing to the centre of the bar, a pin is inserted into the material as shown in the diagram; and the working thread slipped under the head of the pin from left to right, then up over the bar and out beneath it. Examine *Fig.* 106

carefully to see just how the needle is slipped under the loop

Fig. 106

on the pin, and the working thread twisted once round the needle point before it is pulled through. The thread must be pulled tightly to secure the picot, after which the pin is removed and the button-holing continued. A finished picot is shown to the right of *Fig.* 106.

Bullion picots as shown in *Fig.* 107 are a little more elabo-rate. All the bars and buttonhole stitching is worked as before and the needle then taken back into the looped edge of the last buttonhole stitch (or the upright part of the stitch if preferred). △ The working thread is then twisted five or six time round the body of the needle which is then

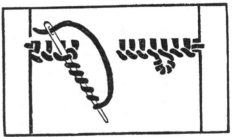

Fig. 107

pulled through. To set the picot well into position, make the next buttonhole stitch firmly and close up to the last.

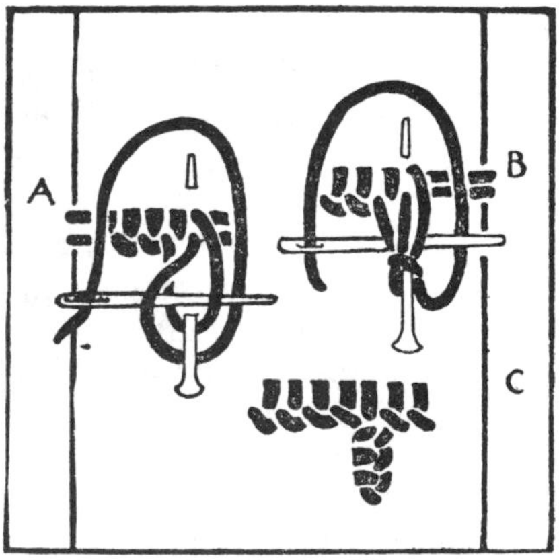

The Buttonhole Picot (*Fig.* 108) is the most elaborate member of its family, and here again a pin is employed. The thread is slipped under the head of the pin from left to right, then taken up over the bar and out again beneath it. The thread is now slipped once more under the pin head from

Fig. 108

Fig. 109.   16th Century Italian Cut Work

left to right and the needle inserted into the two loops as shown in *Fig.* 108. △ This is now pulled through and a knot thus formed at the head of the picot (*see* B), after which button-hole stitch is worked up the picot to the bar again and continued along the bar in the usual way.   The pin is now removed and the picot complete (*see* C).

VENETIAN CUT WORK

Each different form of cut work just described can be further enriched by padding the embroidery, as shown in *Fig.* 95. The padding process may consist of a row or rows of chain stitch worked between the double lines of running stitch before the buttonholing is worked, or of a thicker thread or threads, such as crochet cotton, couched down with the buttonholing as it proceeds.   Any surface embroidery must be likewise padded and covered with satin stitch.   Embroidery of this description is sometimes referred to as Raised Cut Work or Venetian Cut Work.

ITALIAN CUT WORK

All forms of cut work are indelibly associated with Italy, but this form in particular is known as Italian Cut Work, the style of which bears a striking resemblance to Reticella

Fig. 110   LYON WOOD

lace. The work consists of small squares cut and drawn from the linen into which little geometrical patterns, quaint figures or birds are added chiefly in buttonhole stitch. The surface of the material is decorated with raised stitches such as bullion knots*, detached stem* stitch and so on, and the work reached a standard of great magnificence in the 16th century as shown in *Fig.* 109 (*page* 83). This is a portion of a long table runner, from which it will be seen that the idea of cutting out small squares has developed into quite a long open border. The work to-day remains the same though considerably simplified, and *Fig.* 110, a small sachet, is a popular example of its modern presentation. This contains but a single cut and decorated square finished with the characteristic raised stitches on the surface of the material and the particular hemstitching round the border. Little square motifs of this kind make charming corner decorations for tray-mats, luncheon sets, tea-cloths, etc., with light touches of surface embroidery to soften the outline.

Designs. These are based on the pleasing distribution of the small squares varied by fillings of simple lace stitches. *Fig.* 111

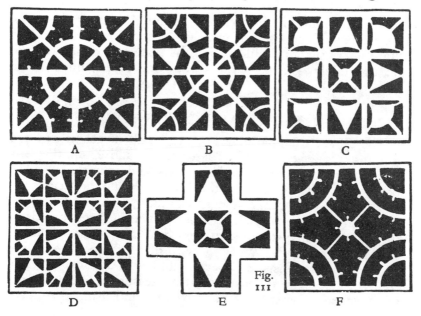

A   B   C

D   E   F

Fig.
111

gives six different suggestions for filling these small squares, that at A being the same as that shown on the sachet in *Fig.* 110. Such decorations are formed by leaving two or more vertical and horizontal " bars " of the material when cutting the squares, and adding diagonal lines, circles and arcs worked in buttonhole stitch. Squares A and B, *Fig.* 111, are based on a single vertical and horizontal bar of linen threads left in cutting, while in the pattern at C two vertical and two horizontal bars are left. D has three vertical and three horizontal bars, while E actually consists of five small squares arranged in the form of a cross, with four bars of material surrounding the inner square. F shows yet another method where all the threads are cut away and arcs of button stitching added as a filling. Other squares of this type will be seen on studying the ancient example in *Fig.* 109.

These squares can be arranged to form a repeating border or grouped in chessboard fashion all over a table cloth for an elaborate decoration, the divisions being made by lines of hemstitching. The surface embroidery takes the form of tiny scrolls, whirls and spirals, with bullion knots grouped to give the appearance of an eyelet, as in *Fig.* 110.

Materials. Only the best natural coloured linen of close firm weave should be used as the looser kinds will fray. The embroidery thread should match the material exactly, both in texture, thickness and colour, and a good quality linen thread is the best choice.

CUTTING AND PREPARING THE SQUARES

The typical example given on the small sachet in *Fig.* 110 is chosen as the basis for description, and from this any number of other squares can be worked and understood. The position of the square on the article should be accurately marked and then outlined with running stitch (*see Fig.* 112), which shows the material, then cut to within three threads of the running stitch (the method of withdrawing the threads is shown in *Fig.* 112). When bars formed of the material are left, these must consist of an even number of threads. △ The edges of the square are next closely overcast all round as shown in *Fig.* 113. The stitches must be neat and firm, to prevent

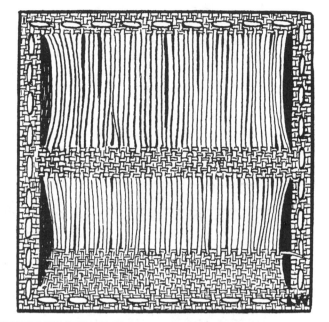

Fig. 112

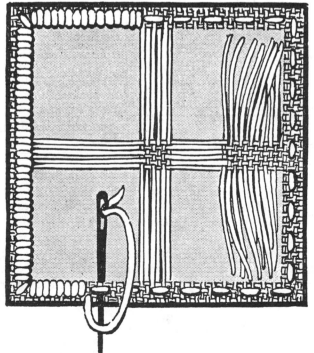

Fig. 113

the material from fraying, and made to cover the running stitch. If extra strength is required, use buttonhole stitch. The square which now looks like a little window, with a horizontal and a vertical bar left across the middle, is ready for the filling. An "open" square will of course contain no bars, otherwise the process up to now is the same.

WORKING A FILLING

Figure 114 gives the process of throwing and working the bars, arcs and circles comprising the motif on the sachet in *Fig.* 110. The bars of material are first woven, as shown in

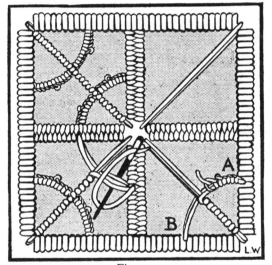

Fig. 115. The diagonal lines are next added, commencing from the centre and throwing a long stitch out to each corner and back again to the centre, finishing off securely at the back of the little middle square. The diagonal lines are now closely overcast, commencing from one corner of the square and working until the

Fig. 114

position for the first arc is reached. Here the thread is thrown across into the edge, as at A on *Fig.* 114, then right across in a curved line to B and back again to A, and the threads covered with buttonhole stitch. The tiny points shown on the buttonholed bars are picots, the addition of which is optional, but the simplest and that most frequently used is the Loop Picot (*see Fig.* 106). (Others more rarely used are the buttonhole, woven, ring and bullion picot.) The picot is worked in with the buttonholing process, and when completed the buttonholing is continued to the centre of the arc where the diagonal line intersects; and from here the thread is again thrown over to B and the second half of the arc worked back again to the middle. The overcasting then continues down the dia-

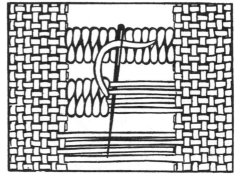

gonal bar until the position for the second arc is reached. This is actually part of the centre circle, but the process is the same as shown in the left-hand lower corner of *Fig.* 114. When this is finished, the remainder of the diagonal bar is overcast and one quarter of the square completed as shown in *Fig.* 114.

Fig. 115

On this simple basis, any number of different fillings can be built. The solid triangles and shapes at B, C, D and E on *Fig.* 111 are all formed by working close rows of lace filling stitches, usually buttonhole stitch. The work is commenced from the widest part of the triangle by throwing across a double thread as for the arc in *Fig.* 114, and over this the first row of buttonhole stitch is worked. Each subsequent row is worked into the looped edge of the previous row, gradually diminishing the number of stitches until the point of the triangle is reached and fixed into the material.

SURFACE EMBROIDERY

The two stitches most frequently used for this are bullion

Fig. 116

knot or stitch (*see Fig.* 116) and detached overcast stitch (*see Fig.* 117). To work bullion knot, bring the thread out at the arrow and put the needle in at A, and out again at the arrow, twist the thread firmly round the point of the needle, hold the end with the left thumb and pull through. For detached over-

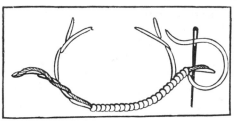

cast stitch, make two rows of long loose stem stitches. The first, shown in white in the diagram, alternates with the second row (black). These are then over-cast together without taking the needle

Fig. 117

through the material. The little eyelets surrounded by bullion stitch arranged to form a square in *Fig.* 110 are formed by taking every stitch into the same central hole, a method which draws the ground material aside to form a pro-nounced perforation. Detached overcast stitch is used for the longer lines and the bullion stitch for any short lines or motifs.

FINISHING THE EDGES

Most of the old Italian Cut Work was finished with an edging of needle point lace, but modern work is finished with a border, as shown on the little sachet in *Fig.* 110. Allow sufficient material for a tiny hem and then with-draw three bands of threads as in *Fig.* 118. Two or three threads only are drawn for the narrow strips, and five or eight for the wider middle portion, four threads of the

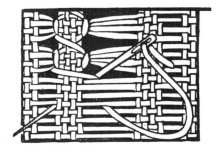

Fig. 118

material being left between each. The hemstitching is worked as shown in the diagram, the left side first. After this the work is reversed and the opposite side worked (*see Fig.* 119). Here it will be seen that this second row has an additional movement to it. After dividing and tying the loose threads into bundles as before, the needle is carried to the central line where two bundles are united with a single stitch. The long white arrow shows where the needle will next be inserted. These two simple journeys build up the charming threefold border shown on the little sachet in *Fig.* 110.

Fig. 119

DARNING ON FABRICS

E VERY STITCH HAS ITS DAY, even darning stitch, and in the 18th century it was the fashion to make a sampler in darning stitches, and these works to-day form a fascinating study. Contemporary embroideries of that period were frequently carried out in this one stitch, which, if carefully and intelligently used, can be as distinctive as any of its more elaborate relations. Darning Stitch, used as a decoration, has a history as noble and ancient as Cross Stitch.

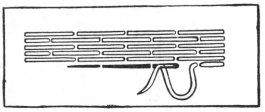

Fig. 120

The working method as used in embroidery is shown at *Fig.* 120, and consists of a long stitch taken over the surface of the material, picking up a thread or two of the ground material between each This type of embroidery demands a material of defined weave, as the threads can then be counted and the stitches kept an even length.

Fig. 122

The most popular method of using Darning Stitch is as a background, leaving the design more or less plain, as in *Fig.* 121. Here a soft indefinite effect without further outline is shown on the leaf to the left, and a bold pronounced effect, outlined with stem stitch, on the centre flowers. The darning is arranged in " brick " formation, but quite another effect is obtained in *Fig.* 122, where

Fig. 121

Fig. 123

the darning suggests form and contour as a background, throwing the duck outlined with stem stitch into bold relief.

This process can be reversed with good effect and *Fig* 123 shows the same motif as *Fig*. 121, but this time the darning stitch forms a filling instead of a background. Three different treatments of the stitch are shown. The leaves to the left are darned vertically and horizontally following the weave of the material, and disregarding any interior markings; while

to the right the same vertical and horizontal method is combined on one leaf to emphasise the centre vein and contrast of light and shade. The flower shows the stitch worked at right angles to the outline of each petal, and this again induces a contrast of light and shade. This play of light on the different angles of the stitches is akin to a change of colour in other forms of embroidery. Yet another " filling " is

Fig 124

shown in *Fig*. 124. The darning is commenced on the outline of the flower petals, and each subsequent row is worked parallel to and within the last, until the shape is filled. The left leaf follows the same method but worked in two different shades, while to the right an impression of the centre leaf vein is achieved by working each half in a different colour. Both stem and tendril are darned while the centre of the flower is darned in radiating lines.

Pattern Darning is the most fascinating method of using darning stitch, either as a background or a filling. The stitches are arranged to form little all-over diaper patterns, the numbers of which are legion. Four of the most familiar are shown in *Figs*. 125 A to D, and will serve as an inspiration for working out many others, while the old samplers and mediæval embroideries will also prove a rich source of inspiration in this respect. The method is exactly the same

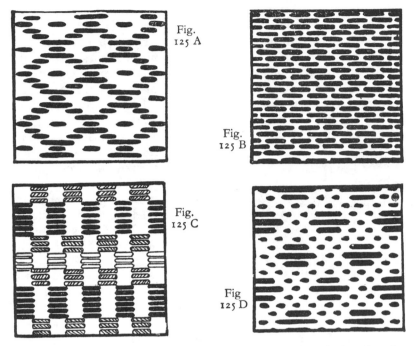

Fig. 125 A

Fig. 125 B

Fig. 125 C

Fig 125 D

as in any other darning, △ the only variation being in the different lengths of the stitch and the quantity of ground material picked up in each successive row. A material of which the threads can be easily counted is essential, as absolute regularity of stitching is the first and only consideration in pattern darning.

Damask Darning is illustrated in *Fig.* 126. This is intended to stimulate the effect of damask fabrics; and if worked in two shades of one colour, produces a delightful " shot " effect. It is equally attractive in one colour only, as

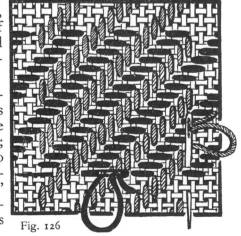

Fig. 126

the different direction of the stitch invites a contrasting action of light and shade. The stitching in the diagram has been drawn in two different colours for clearness of construction. All the horizontal rows should be worked first, then the vertical, or vice versa, and the darning taken under and over an equal number of threads (three in this case) with each row commenced one thread in advance of the previous row.

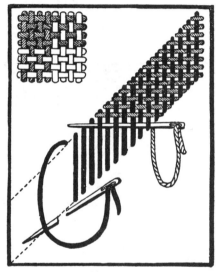

This particular pattern gives the illusion of diagonal lines worked in alternate vertical and horizontal stitches.

Surface Darning. An ordinary darn such as used for stocking mending forms the filling in *Fig.* 127. This is quite detached from the material, except at the sides of the shape, and is known as Surface Darning. At the top of the diagram is shown a little square worked in two different colours, and arranged to form a small diaper of checks. Surface Darning makes an attractive centre filling for large flower shapes, etc., and the arrangement given in *Fig.* 127 shows how it can be used as a diagonal line.

Fig. 127

HUCKABACK DARNING

A form of darning popular in Denmark is worked on huckaback towelling. This material which is woven with tiny loose loops at regular intervals all over the surface invites the addition of darning stitches which are threaded under the loops to form borders on towels, etc. On a fine huckaback the rows of darning can be placed so close together that they completely obscure the background.

The weave of the material obviously limits the scope of

design to the geometric variety as shown in *Fig.* 128, but the successive lines can be worked out in different colours or several shades of one colour, ranging from dark at the bottom to a pale at

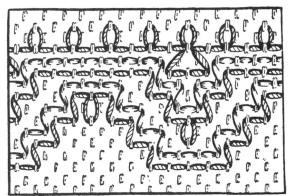

Fig 128

the top, with good effect. Care must be taken to see that the weave of the huckaback is correct for this particular work as it is manufactured in two ways—(1) with the loops lying parallel to the selvedges and (2) with the loops lying at right angles to the selvedge. For border ends on small towels, the first type of weave is essential.

The working method will be clearly seen from the illustration, since the thread is merely slipped under the loops

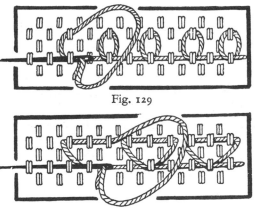

Fig. 129

Fig 130

without taking it to the back of the material. To start or finish, run the thread in alongside a previous line of darning. A study of *Fig.* 128 will show that the lines of darning are broken by looped and triangular shapes to give interest to the pattern. The method of working the loops △ is shown at *Fig.* 129, and the triangles at *Fig.* 130. In both cases the auxiliary decoration is worked in continuously with the darning, carrying the thread first round the shape and then again under the same little loop to continue with the main outline of the design.

DOUBLE RUNNING OR BACK STITCH EMBROIDERY

THIS EMBROIDERY which is worked entirely in Back Stitch or Double Running, is so popular in Roumania, that it is often called Roumanian Embroidery, but English samplers dating back to the 17th century show that the work was known in this country, while fragments of ancient Egyptian and Coptic embroidery taken from the tombs would indicate that its origin is ancient and obscure. Double Running Embroidery is characterised by its delicacy of line and design, there being no solid forms on the embroidery, and only one stitch is used throughout, namely Double Running (*page* 17, *Fig.* 18 A) or Back Stitch. These stitches, though alike in appearance on the front of the work, are different in construction and appearance on the back. A design worked in Double Running will appear exactly the same on both sides of the material, an advantage on articles such as tray-mats, luncheon sets and so forth; whereas a design in Back Stitch will show cut corners on the reverse side which renders it more suitable for cushions or articles finished with a lining. The embroidery is most pleasing and fascinating to do, as the stitch is simple and the design of great interest, being worked out by means of counted threads.

Designs. The designs are planned on graph paper as shown in *Figs.* 131 and 132. Each square represents a unit of say three threads, the number varying with the texture of the material. All designs are based on some simple fundamental line or shape, which in *Fig.* 131 takes a "V" formation. This zigzags through the whole border, embellished with little sprig motifs branching off at regular intervals, and is characteristic of Roumanian design (*see* Cross Stitch, *page* 69). *Fig.* 132, an English design, is based on a square to produce an all-over pattern of Tudor roses. The artist could experiment on a series of parallel diagonal lines, a " battlement "

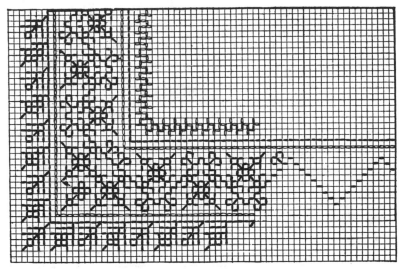

Fig. 131

line, or a simplified version of the Greek Key pattern with good effect, and from these arrange the little offshoots and motifs as suggested in *Fig.* 131. This embroidery is so simple in stitchery that the design must be important and lacy looking, otherwise the charm of the work is lost. Pictures of wrought iron work or fine filigree jewellery will inspire many beautiful ideas for double running patterns, and

Fig. 132

of course, the old samplers are a never ending source of inspiration.

Materials. These are important as the warp and weft must be of even degree and loosely woven in order to count the threads without undue eye-strain. White, cream or natural coloured linens are best, and the working thread used for the embroidery should be about equal in thickness to the warp or weft of the material, and is better made with a loose cable twist. Work with a blunt-pointed needle in order not to split the ground threads.

Colours. The embroidery can be worked in one or many colours, Roumanian patterns following the peasant tradition of gay colouring in reds, greens, blues, yellows and black judiciously blended. English designs are more often planned for one colour only and it is surprising how very effective

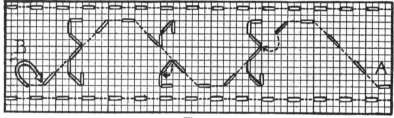

Fig. 133

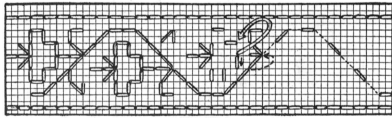

Fig. 134

this monotonous colour scheme can appear, providing △ the design is a good one. Such colours as china blue, leaf or bottle-green, or dull red on white or cream linen are all beautiful, while a dark brown thread on natural linen, or black on white produces the rare and unusual effect of an etching.

WORKING METHODS

Before commencing this embroidery it is necessary to study the design from which you are working and discover the fundamental lines (*see Fig.* 131), as these must be worked in first. *Figs.* 133 and 134 illustrate the method of working designs in double running, and if the stitch is worked in this way throughout it should be practically impossible to tell the right from the wrong side. Two journeys are necessary, the first being shown in *Fig.* 133. Commence at A on the right and run over the whole outline, making each stitch and space of equal length. The dotted lines show where the needle is taken beneath the material. Upon reaching the spot for an " offshoot," work right to the end of the branch and return again to the main outline. The dotted arrows indicate the procedure, while at B the white arrow indicates the commencement of the second journey, which is shown in detail in *Fig.* 134. This is always the most exciting as the spaces left on the first journey are filled in to make a continuous line, each stitch fitting into its place like the final pieces of a jig-saw puzzle! *Fig.* 134 shows that further " offshoots " are added on this second journey, but whether these are worked in on the first or second journey or some on both must depend on the construction of the design. The great thing to remember is that the back of the work must look just like the front, and when working these secondary motifs the thread must keep to the outline of the design on the back, and not be carried across a space or allowed to " cut " a corner; otherwise an unwanted stitch alien to the design appears and spoils the whole effect. The best method to commence and finish off is to run in the end of a new thread on the right side, weaving it under and over single threads along the outline for a short distance, and cover this with the double running stitches. An important point to remember when working the second journey is to insert the needle in the hole just above the stitch made on the first journey and bring it out below, or vice versa, as this makes all the difference between a good and bad line. *See* A in *Fig.* 18 B, *page* 18, which also shows the wrong method at B.

Ordinary Back Stitch, accomplished in one journey, can be used instead of Double Running, but only on articles finished with a lining, or cushions. This stitch may be worked regardless of its appearance on the back and so allowed to " cut " across corners; or, to make a neater effect, be worked in the special method shown in *Fig.* 135. This is a useful little drawing, as it shows both the front and the back of the stitch; the dotted lines on the back view represent spaces. To work, it becomes necessary to cover every other stitch twice

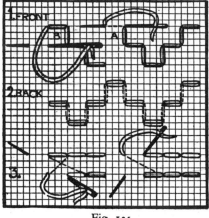

Fig. 135

on the back, as at A, while B shows the surface stitch. This method lends itself to geometric patterns and simple repeating borders, but is a little complicated on isolated motifs and more elaborate patterns. At the bottom of *Fig.* 135 is shown the quickest way to work a border of double parallel lines. This is accomplished in one journey, by carrying the thread across at the back as shown by the dotted lines, and is technically known as Crossed Back Stitch.

Fig. 136 suggests a clever method of decorating the edge of a mat. The stitching is arranged to imitate a lace or crochet edging, but the material of course is carried beyond the edging, and turned under to A and here secured by a line of running stitch with good effect. An ordinary turned-in hem can also be used and the stitching disguised on the right side by a line of back stitches. Simple hemstitching as a finish is also effective and often used.

Double Running Stitch when used with other types of work is known as Holbein Stitch. *See* Cross Stitch and Assisi Embroidery.

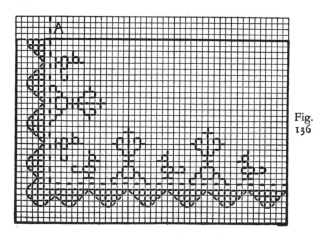

Fig. 136

DRAWN FABRIC WORK

D RAWN FABRIC WORK must not be confused with Drawn Thread Work, as the material threads are not withdrawn from the fabric; the perforations, as shown in *Fig.* 137, being obtained by working certain stitches in such a way that the threads of the material are " drawn " or " pulled " aside to form an open-work pattern. The name " Pulled work," by which it is sometimes known, is perhaps more explanatory (*see* Frontispiece).

This lovely embroidery has a history of several centuries, and in some countries developed into lace, but withal it is of peasant origin. Beautiful works of this type were done in the Greek Islands, but in the 17th and 18th centuries, Flanders, Denmark and Germany became interested and here it developed into an exquisite form of embroidery closely allied to needle-point lace. Several fine museum pieces prove, too, that in England the work reached a very high standard about this time.

Drawn Fabric Work holds an irresistible fascination for all embroideresses, and its charms to-day are becoming more and more appreciated as its delicate " lacy " appearance in no way impairs its strength since the threads of the material are not withdrawn to weaken the fabric.

This work lends itself best to such articles as luncheon sets, tea-cloths, tray-mats, bedspreads, curtains, etc., worked on linen, though the accomplished worker will find that small motifs can be worked on the finer lingerie fabrics.

MATERIALS AND COLOURS

Select hand-woven linen, when possible, or linen scrim, as the threads of both can be more easily counted. The warp and weft must be of even degree. Coarse muslin and voile are sometimes used for curtains.

The working thread should be of the same colour, texture and thickness as the thread of the ground material. If anything

By courtesy of the Victoria and Albert Museum

Fig. 137. Drawn fabric work forming part of a bedspread worked by the late Mrs. G. Newall
(*See also* Frontispiece)

a little finer, as it is not meant to show since the stitches are but a means of " drawing " different shaped spaces in the material. For the surface stitches and outlines, a thicker thread is better. For use on linen, a linen thread of good quality is much the best choice. Use blunt-pointed needles in order to avoid splitting the material threads, and an ordinary fine needle to finish off the ends.

Monotone colour schemes show off the work to its best advantage, white on white, natural on natural, and so on, though a working thread in pastel colours is occasionally introduced when the simpler stitches, such as punch stitch, are used on lingerie.

DESIGNS

Each stitch forms its own pattern, and the work is mainly used as " fillings " for shapes and forms as shown in *Fig.* 137, and only occasionally as all-over backgrounds (*see page* 177). Little flower sprays with the petals embroidered in satin stitch and each centre and leaf filled with drawn fabric stitches, make a most effective decoration. *Fig.* 137 gives a portion only of an exquisite bedspread showing a flowing classical design of formal shapes each filled with a different drawn fabric stitch. The reproduction is very small, but the close-up on the Frontispiece reveals a story almost magic in beauty. From this example it will be seen that almost any shape (providing the right material is used) can be filled with drawn fabric stitches. Geometric forms and borders, vandyke, etc., can be worked out on graph paper, and these make handsome decorations on mats, etc. Some stitches are worked horizontally, others diagonally, and this should be remembered when planning a design.

In using the work as a background, see that the design is bold in character and simple in outline, as fine lines would be lost.

THE STITCHES

Each country specialises in its own particular drawn fabric stitches, and fifty-four of these have already been published in the Dictionary in diagram and photographic form, so there is no need to reproduce them again in this volume,

though one explanatory diagram, " Punch Stitch " (*Fig.* 138)
is repeated for reference.　The stitches are all worked upon
counted threads represented in the diagram as vertical and
horizontal lines, each line representing a thread of the
material.　Each stitch is taken twice into the same hole and
pulled quite tightly, which causes the finished result to be
totally unlike the appearance of the working diagram, as
will be seen by referring to the Dictionary.

All the drawn fabric stitches contained in the Dictionary
were perforce arranged in alphabetical order which somewhat
alienated their grouping, but they may be roughly divided into

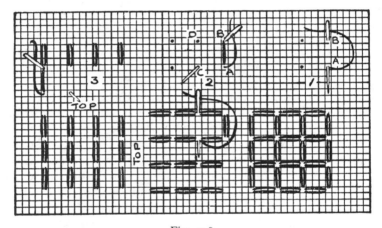

Fig. 138

the following categories, according to the method of work:
(1) Stitches worked horizontally and vertically.　(2) Stitches
worked diagonally.　(3) Stitches worked by means of back
and double back stitch.　(4) Surface stitches.　(5) Isolated
stitches.　(6) Border stitches.

(1) *Stitches Worked Horizontally and Vertically* are possibly
the easiest group and comprise the following, of which
Punch Stitch is the best known and most frequently used as
a background, and when thus employed it may be known as
Punch Stitch or Rhodes Work:

Cobbler Filling Stitch, Framed Cross Filling, Double Stitch
Filling, Four-sided Border Stitch, Honeycomb Filling Stitch,

Maltese Filling Stitch, Mosaic Filling Stitch, Octagonal Filling Stitch, Punch Stitch, Squared Ground Stitch, Three-sided Stitch (as a filling), Wave Stitch, Window Filling and Double Window Filling.

(2) *Stitches Worked Diagonally* are those which produce a particularly " lacy " effect and comprise the following:

Drawn Buttonhole Stitch, Chequer Filling Stitch, Diagonal Chevron Stitch, Chevron-Cross Stitch, Diagonal Drawn Filling, Diagonal Raised Band, Crossed Faggot Filling, Drawn Faggot Filling, Double Faggot Stitch, Reversed Faggot Stitch, Single Faggot Stitch, Greek Cross Filling Stitch, Indian Drawn Ground Stitch, Net Filling Stitch, Diagonal Overcast Ground, Ridge Filling Stitch, Rosette Filling Stitch, Russian Filling Stitch, Detached Square Filling, Open Trellis Filling.

(3) *Stitches Worked by Means of Back and Double Back Stitch* are fewer in number and include the following:

Ringed Back Stitch Filling, Braid Stitch Filling, Cushion Stitch, Diamond Filling Stitch, Eyelet Stitch Filling, Festoon Filling Stitch, Ripple Stitch.

(4) *Surface Stitches* actually comprise the different groupings of ordinary satin stitch and produce a more solid effect, and as a rule these are not drawn so tight in working as the others. They include:

Algerian Filling Stitch, Open Basket Filling, Chessboard Filling Stitch, Gobelin Filling Stitch, Lozenge Filling Stitch, Mosaic Diamond Filling, Step Stitch Filling.

(5) *Isolated Stitches* are comprised mainly of eyelets which may be grouped to form an all-over pattern, a filling, or used singly to express small spot motifs. These are:

Drawn Square, Algerian Eye Stitch, Detached Eyelets, Barred Buttonhole Wheel, Bullion and French Knots.

(6) *Border Stitches* include Chained Border Stitch, Four-sided Stitch, and Three-sided Stitch, though the latter is used as a filling as well as a border. It is advisable to work out a sampler of all the different drawn fabric stitches, arranging them in the order as detailed above.

WORKING HINTS

△ It is possible to work all drawn fabric stitches in the hand. To use a frame, however, is a wise precaution against puckering. If a rectangular frame is used the material should first be stretched tightly in the usual way (*see page* 271), taking great care that the warp and weft threads are parallel to the sides and top of the frame respectively. △ Then before the embroidery is started the frame should be slackened, leaving no strain on the linen in either direction. This slackness is essential if the proper " drawn " effect of the stitches is to be obtained. The frame may be tightened for working the surface stitches. A small circular frame may be used, △ and when mounting it is important to see that the warp and weft of the linen are placed truly vertically and horizontally across the frame. Again the linen must not be tightly stretched. These little points make all the difference, and should the material be mounted crooked the finished work will remain crooked and unsatisfactory.

Another good idea is to work with a dark cloth in your lap which shows up the holes and threads in working and helps to " spot " a mistake instantly.

First offset the design on to the material. △ This accomplished, the next process is to work all the drawn stitches, whether they act as a filling or a background does not matter, they must be worked first, and before the design is outlined, △ carrying each line of stitching close up to the traced line. In working these stitches, remember to pull the thread tightly after each stitch or movement forming a stitch, so that the ground material is drawn up into little bunches and a pronounced hole left in the surface. The exception to this rule occurs in some of the surface stitches as previously detailed, the object being to obtain contrast and more solid effects, Even so, the stitches should be pulled tighter than in ordinary satin stitch.

Accuracy in counting the threads forming each stitch is essential as the openwork depends on the " pull " of the stitches and a miscount would upset the pattern. This applies in particular to " isolated stitches " worked over a different number of threads. On the contrary a whole filling, not just part of a filling, can be surprisingly varied by repeating an irregularity, working *every* stitch over more or fewer threads than are indicated. Different patterns are also obtained by varying the number of threads left between the rows. This often produces a surprisingly different result.

A number of the stitches may be effectively combined to produce different patterns, especially the diagonal stitches. For instance Diagonal Raised Band alternating in rows with one of the various Faggot Stitches is effective (*see Fig.* 137), and once the different stitches have been mastered, quite a number of exciting experiments may be embarked upon in this way.

Finishing off the stitches at the end of each row, in order to maintain the correct " pull " before passing to the next, often requires " wangling." A good plan is to take the thread under a previous stitch at the back of the work, to " pull " it from the last hole, then thread along the outline to a spot just *past* that where the needle will next emerge. The method will vary according to each stitch but the principle is quickly grasped after a little practice. When all the drawn stitches are completed, the surface embroidery is added and the fillings outlined and co-ordinated into pleasing designs. As previously mentioned, all stitches are carried well up to the outline of the design, and at this point any irregularity in finishing off the stitches can be conveniently covered with any outline or surface embroidery. For this purpose, and to provide contrast, the outline embroidery should be of the raised variety and worked with a thicker thread. A study of *Fig.* 137 will show this point clearly. Any of the whipped and threaded stitches are suitable, also Raised Chain Band, Raised Stem Stitch Band, Portuguese Border Stitch, Rope Stitch, Coral Stitch (with the knots very close together) or Close Herringbone Stitch, all of which are described and illustrated in the Dictionary.

DRAWN THREAD WORK

"DRAWN THREAD WORK" is of a delicate lace-like nature, necessitating the removal of certain weft or warp threads of the material and adding decorative stitchery upon those which are left. This classification should embrace Needleweaving, Hardanger and the older form of Hedebo embroidery, but since all three bear such distinctive characteristics and are so widely known by their "local" names, a separate section to each is given in this book. Drawn Thread Work is used chiefly in the form of borders from which the threads have been withdrawn, in one direction only. The more elaborate versions show threads drawn out at intervals in both directions (*see Fig.* 139).

MATERIALS AND COLOURS

A good quality linen should be chosen, and one on which the weave is fairly distinct, otherwise the drawing process is trying to the eyes. Use a working thread of similar colour but a little coarser than the material, with a finer for the hemstitching and buttonholing.

The work is used as a decoration for sheets, pillow-slips, bedspreads, duchesse sets, runners, towels, tea-cloths, luncheon sets, table napkins and so on, and is found in church needlework on altar cloths, chalice veils, etc.

PREPARING THE MATERIAL

A border running the full width of the article is a simple preparation. Allow sufficient material for the necessary hem and then slip the point of a pin under the first thread which marks the commencement of the border (quite near the edge of the material). Ease out an end long enough to be firmly gripped and then withdraw across the full width of the material. This process is continued until a border the

Fig. 139   Elaborate border in drawn thread work embroidered by Mrs. A. C. S. Benning

Fig. 140 A

required depth is obtained. Next turn up the hem close to the edge of the drawn border and tack, and the work is then ready for the decorative stitching.

Borders arranged on all four sides of a square present a problem at the corners and make the drawing process a little more complicated. First plan the depth of the hem as before and then mark the four spots where the four outer corners of the border will fall. These points represent the limit to which the threads are withdrawn. The first drawn thread should be cut two to three inches away from the marked point at both ends, and then pulled out from the corners (see Fig. 140 A). Here it is left for the moment and the remaining portion of the thread across the centre is withdrawn. The threads are withdrawn in this way round all four sides of the square until a border the required depth is achieved. The loose hanging threads as shown in Fig. 140 A are then tidied up in either of the following ways: (1) by cutting them off close to the edge and covering with buttonhole or overcasting stitch, or (2) by securing the ends between the hem. This is a much better and stronger method (see Fig. 140 B). The threads are first cut to an even length and tacked. Later when the hem is turned they will be completely hidden.

TO MITRE A CORNER

Any article square or rectangular in shape should be mitre-joined at the corners

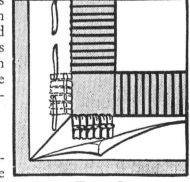

Fig. 140 B

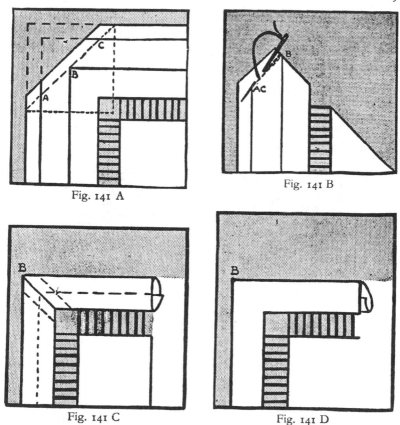

Fig. 141 A

Fig. 141 B

Fig. 141 C

Fig. 141 D

(*see Figs.* 141 A to 141 D). The hem is first turned up and the folds are creased (*see Fig.* 141 A). Now mark spot B on *Fig.* 141 A which indicates the corner of the cloth *after* the hem is finished, and fold the corner over so that it falls along the dotted lines and mark the crease A, B and C. Unfold the material and cut away the corner just beyond the creased line as shown. Fold the corner together as in *Fig.* 141 B, so that A and C meet, and back stitch firmly down the crease mark from B to AC. Finish the stitching at AC as the portion beyond is left for turnings. The seam is now opened out and the corner reversed. Turn under the raw edges and the hem will automatically fall along the drawn thread border as in *Fig.* 141 C, and here it is tacked. The dotted lines on the diagram represent the raw edges of the linen which are hidden within the folded hem. The professional appearance of a mitre-joint corner is shown in *Fig.* 141 D, no stitching being visible at all on the right side.

HEMSTITCHING

Most drawn thread borders are first hemstitched along the top and bottom edges. This serves the triple purpose of (1) securing the hem, (2) strengthening the edges, and (3)

Fig. 142 A

Fig. 142 B

tying the loose threads together in convenient little bunches which facilitate the working of the decorative stitches later.

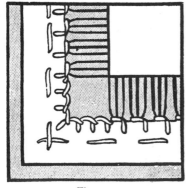

Fig. 143

The best method to hemstitch along the folded edge of the material is shown in *Figs.* 142 A and B. These two movements tie the bunches of threads firmly together. Upon arriving at the open space in each corner, change to buttonhole stitch which is worked close together over both edges of the hem, until the loose threads are again reached (*see Fig.* 143). In hemstitching along the inner side of the border see that these same bunches of threads are again tied together (*see* Ladder Hemstitch)*. At this point the work is ready for the decorative stitching, which may

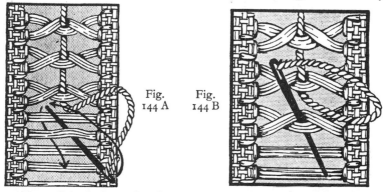

Fig.
144 A

Fig.
144 B

consist of twisting the bars in various formations, or of gathering them together with different embroidery stitches.

TWISTED BORDERS

These are explained in *Figs.* 144 A and B, where for clearness the working thread is distinguished by a corded effect. First

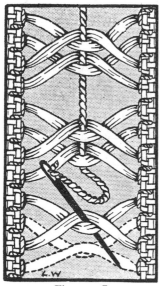

secure in the middle of the button-holed corner (*see Fig.* 150) and then take over the intervening space to form one spoke of the " wheel " (worked later). The needle then proceeds over the first two bars (a "bar" being one tied bundle of threads) and is slipped back under the second bar, and over the first bar as shown by the arrows in *Fig.* 144 A and hooked forward as in *Fig.* 144 B. The thread is then pulled through and the process repeated all along the border.

This is the simplest twist, but the method can be elaborated as shown in *Figs.* 144 C and D. In *Fig.* 144 C the twists are made in overlapping pairs, with four bars to each

Fig. 144 C

Fig. 144 D

completed twist. Before commencing this decoration, first ascertain that the border contains a number of bars divisible by four. To commence, pass the needle under the third bar and back to the first bar, which is hooked over and twisted. The same process is repeated with the fourth and second bars and so on along the whole border.

Fig. 144 D shows a double twisted border and comprises the same twisting process as in *Figs.* 144 A and B, but worked in a double row. The first row is placed one-third of the border width from the hem, while the second divides the twists by taking a bar from each and uniting them in a criss-cross fashion.

LATTICE BORDER

The working method of this is clearly seen in *Fig.* 145

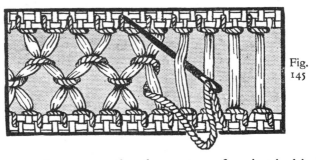

Fig. 145

The bars are drawn together by means of a simple binding stitch, taking the first and second bar above, then the second and third below, next the third and fourth above and so on. The needle should be passed behind the bars from right to left, with the working thread below the needle for the lower stitch and above for the upper.

BARS CLUSTERED WITH CORAL STITCH

Ordinary Coral Stitch can be employed to tie the bars into clusters as in *Fig.* 146 A, where the needle is shown in the process of forming the knot. The working thread should be held down with the left thumb while the needle is passed under three bars and drawn out through the loop formed. The last completed knot is shown in loosened form to explain the construction and the method may be used on the back or front of the work.

Fig. 146 B is an elaboration of the previous figure. The Coral Knot is made in the same way but picks up four bars to a cluster in order that two bars may be taken from one cluster and two from the next to form the second row.

KNOTTED LATTICE BORDERS

The Lattice Border shown in *Fig.* 147 A where pairs of bars are tied

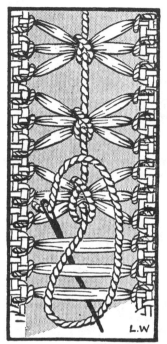

Fig. 146 A

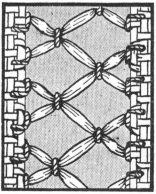

Fig. 147 A

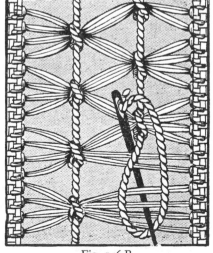

Fig. 146 B

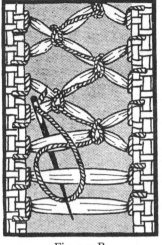

Fig. 147 B

together and divided for the second row, is a particularly neat method achieved by working Coral Stitch as just described on the *back* of the work. In this way, both rows are worked in one journey, since the thread does not show as it passes from one side to the other. *See Figs.* 147 B and C, which gives the two movements and shows the knots drawn loosely so that their construction may be seen. Actually they are pulled quite tight as the needle travels from side to side, knotting together the first and second bars on the left, then the second and third bars on the right and so on.

The same method of working from the back is used for the handsome D o u b l e K n o t t e d Lattice border shown in *Fig.* 147 D. Here the bars have been clustered and divided along each edge, and left straight down the middle. The edges are not hemstitched, since the outer rows of knots serve the same purpose. The border is achieved by

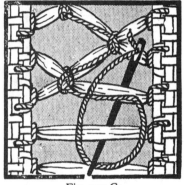

Fig. 147 C

working two rows of Coral Stitch on the back in the method shown in *Fig.* 147 E, two journeys only being sufficient to build up the four rows of stitches seen on the right side.

A further development of this border is shown in *Fig.* 147 F, which combines *Figs.* 144 A and 147 D. Notice in particular

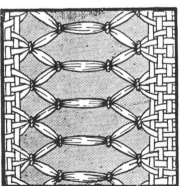

Fig. 147 D

the bars as shown in *Fig.* 147 D, as these are divided when twisting in the centre line, taking half from the upper and half from the lower in each case.

DOUBLE BORDERS

Particularly wide borders may be handled as in *Fig.* 148, where **a** narrow strip of solid material is left between two strips of drawn threads to act as a strengthening agent. The extreme upper and lower edges are hemstitched in the usual way, but those in the middle are secured together by various decorative stitches. Either of the Coral Knot methods is applicable, but the easiest idea is illustrated in *Fig.* 148, where ordinary herringbone stitch is worked round the bars of the upper and lower border. Cross stitch worked in two journeys also serves, and this same method can be applied to a border of any width.

What is known as Italian Hemstitching is shown

Fig. 147 E

Fig. 147 F

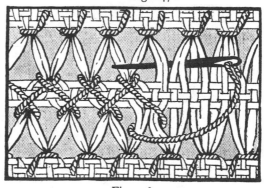

Fig. 148

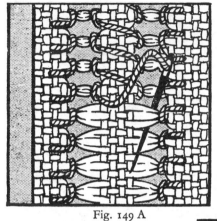

Fig. 149 A

in *Figs.* 149 A and B. The stitch is worked downwards as illustrated and the two movements can be clearly followed in the two diagrams.

DECORATIVE WHEELS

Any square or rectangular article decorated on all four sides with borders of drawn thread work needs some motif to fill the open spaces left in each corner, such as a "wheel." This may be worked in a variety of ways. The Woven Wheel in *Fig.* 150 is the simplest, and is worked in the same process as the borders and not added afterwards as most other wheels. To the right of *Fig.* 150 is shown the final twist of a long border

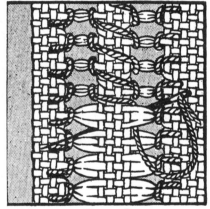

Fig. 149 B

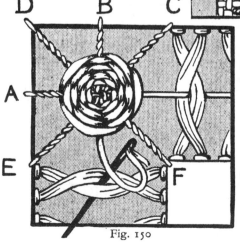

Fig. 150

and from here the thread is secured in the material at A and twisted back on itself to the spot which will form the centre of the wheel. From here it is carried to B and twisted back to the centre and the four diagonal "spokes," C, D, E and F, are then added in the same way.

Since an uneven number of spokes is better for weaving, the sixth and last spoke is not added until the wheel is completed. This causes a larger gap between E and F, but the space is not noticeable when the dummy spoke is added. The next process ties the " spokes " together with a stitch in the centre and

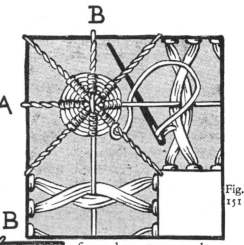

Fig. 151

from here weave alternately over and under each spoke until a wheel the required size is made. The thread is then darned in and out at the back to the centre and then down again to emerge as shown in the diagram forming the sixth spoke and in position to continue the border.

Fig. 152

The pretty little wheel shown in *Fig.* 151 is worked in back stitch after the borders are completed. The spokes A and B are formed in process of working the border, A being secured into the material and twisted back upon itself to the centre of the wheel and then carried up to B and twisted again to the centre, after which the border is continued in the usual way. On returning to the wheel, four extra diagonal spokes must be added and twisted, and then secured in the centre with a single stitch. The back stitching is then worked, round and round until the wheel is wide enough when the thread is slipped in at the back and secured.

The Knotted Wheel as illustrated in *Fig.* 152 is better used in larger corners.   This contains sixteen plain spokes, twelve of which are already in position when the border is completed. To add the four remaining spokes, bring the thread out at A, carry it across to B and from here slip it down through the knots of the border to C, from whence it is carried over and secured at D.   The spokes are then tied in the centre with a single stitch and the thread woven in and out for the first round, after which it is tied to each spoke with a Coral Knot in the form of an ever-widening spiral, until the edge of the material is reached and the thread finally secured.

A Knotted and Woven Wheel is shown in *Fig.* 153 worked on twelve spokes, eight of which are already in position,

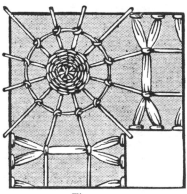
Fig. 153

Fig. 154

the remaining four at the diagonals being added as previously described.   The weaving is commenced from the centre outwards for about six or seven rounds, after which the thread is carried invisibly behind any one of the spokes and secured in position for the first Coral Knot by piercing the spoke. The remaining knots are worked in the usual way and the circle is completed by securing the thread behind the first Coral Knot and then carrying it up behind the spoke into the material and finishing.

An elaboration of this same wheel is illustrated in *Fig.* 154. The weaving and outer ring of knots are first worked as described after which the knots are further enriched by weaving round them again as shown in the diagram.   An enlarged view of the weaving process appears in the bottom right corner.

Fig. 155

The Woven Cross, shown in *Fig.* 155, is something quite different as a corner filling. Twenty spokes are necessary and these are already in position from the method of working the borders. If a narrower border is used then the additional spokes should be added as previously described. The spokes are first tied together in the centre, after which the thread is woven backwards and forwards through four of the diagonal spokes until these are almost covered, when the weaving is continued on two only. To finish, slip the thread invisibly through the weaving to the centre and from here work the other three arms in a similar way.

BORDERS WITH THREADS WITHDRAWN IN BOTH DIRECTIONS

Wheels and crosses can also be used as all-over patterns (*see Fig.* 139), the working method of which is shown in *Fig.* 156.

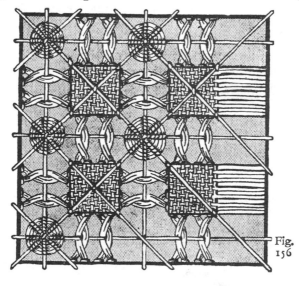

Fig. 156

This necessitates the withdrawing of threads in both directions. The work looks rather complicated but once the principle is grasped it becomes fairly simple. The threads are withdrawn in groups, both horizontally and vertically, drawing and leaving an equal number along the entire length and depth of a border or article. This will result in rows made up of open squares and loose threads alternating with rows of loose threads and solid squares of material (*see Fig.* 156).

The border is next hemstitched and it is advisable (though optional) to hemstitch round the edges of each small solid square. Next the long horizontal threads are twisted in as shown in *Fig.* 144 A, carrying them across each open square to the border. When these are all complete, the vertical threads are worked in the same way. The next process is to add the diagonal threads. These are commenced from the border in the top right corner of any open square and then carried across an open space and secured with a coral knot into the top right corner of the small solid square and another in the diagonal corner opposite. This process is repeated diagonally across the border until the lower edge is reached. After working in several of these diagonal lines it is advisable to add some of the other diagonals which will lie at right angles. These are commenced at the top left corner of any open square along the border and added the same way except where they cross the first set of diagonals and here the two are knotted together, both in the open squares and above the solid squares, though in the latter case the thread must not pierce the ground material.

As this web of horizontal, vertical and diagonal threads is built up, the open spaces are automatically filled with eight spokes which may be converted into any one of the wheels previously described. The backstitched wheel has been employed throughout in *Fig.* 156, but any other wheel would look as well, and different wheels can be set in each alternate square if preferred. A close study of *Fig.* 139 will show a variety of different wheels used with brilliant forethought. The beginner is advised to commence with a simple border such as shown in *Fig.* 156, and afterwards proceed to the more elaborate patterns such as *Fig.* 139, which necessitates the addition of many extra horizontal, vertical and diagonal threads as a foundation for the various wheels.

RUSSIAN DRAWN THREAD WORK

The particular type of Drawn Thread Work found in Russia has a background which is cut and drawn leaving a bold solid design in the linen as in *Fig.* 157. The grotesque little horse and his owner, rather reminiscent of a Cossack, are

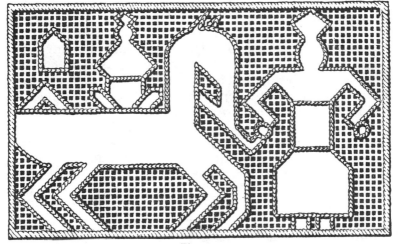

Fig. 157

taken from an old Russian peasant design. The solid parts of the design are outlined and the surrounding border worked in buttonhole stitch, after which the background, which consists of drawn threads, is overcast. Such backgrounds may be treated in many various different ways.

The work is usually done in white on white linen, or in natural colour, though a few of the old Russian pieces are found with the design outlined in colours. The linen should be closely woven and not liable to fray and a matching linen thread used for the embroidery.

The designs are bold and simple in outline with no fine offshoots as these make the drawn thread background difficult to manage.

The design itself is first traced upon the linen and outlined with Heavy Chain Stitch (*see Fig.* 57 Dictionary). In conventional floral patterns, etc., the petal markings and centres are sometimes introduced and such internal stitchery should be worked in before the shape is outlined, and in accordance with the weave of the linen, that is, in vertical, horizontal or diagonal lines. Satin stitch in broad bands and geometrical borders, herringbone stitch, four-sided stitch,* etc., may all be used for this purpose. These patterns perforce are of a geometrical nature, and providing the outline of the design is of sufficient interest, the fillings may easily be omitted.

Russian Drawn Thread Work is generally used as square motifs set at each corner of a tea-cloth or mat, but any motif such as the horse and his rider could very easily be repeated along a whole border. This is purely a matter of choice, but in either case both border or motif must be outlined in close buttonhole stitching or overcasting.

After outlining the design with Heavy Chain Stitch and enclosing it in a buttonhole frame as described, the next step is to cut and draw the threads. This is done in groups, usually cutting two and leaving two threads alternately both horizontally and vertically. The threads must be cut with care close up to the outlines of the design and border and the alternate principle of cutting two and leaving two adhered to throughout. This finished it only remains to overcast the resulting mesh of material threads. To produce a heavy solid effect, the overcasting may be done as shown in *Fig.* 158, where it will be seen that the stitching is worked diagonally in " steps " across the shape working two stitches to each bar and two over each intersection. A lighter background is obtained by working only one overcasting stitch to a bar as shown in *Fig.* 159. This again is worked diagonally, the thread being carried once behind each intersection. This diagram also reveals how a woven filling may be worked upon the overcast mesh, a method sometimes used to work out a whole design instead of leaving it in the linen as just described. The procedure is a little different. The entire shape, square, oblong or border, is first outlined in buttonhole stitch, after which the threads are cut and drawn in groups of two or three as previously described, but no linen is left at all to form the pattern. The mesh is then overcast with either the light or heavy stitching, and the design, which must first have been worked out on squared paper, is woven in after the manner shown in *Fig.* 159.

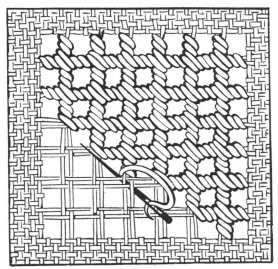

Fig. 158

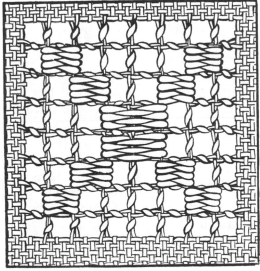

Fig. 159

FILET DARNING

ILET DARNING or "lacis," the old French name, consists of patterns woven or darned upon a net of square mesh known as filet net and is, in reality, a simple form of filet lace.

During the mediæval period, this work was produced in the convents of Italy, France, Spain and Portugal. Later, during the Renaissance, it developed into a product of most elaborate nature, and was mounted on linen, which was decorated with cut work, and used for bed hangings and curtains.

The work used to-day is of a much simpler nature and found chiefly on mats, luncheon sets, d'oyleys or window hangings, or as small squares inset upon linen bedspreads or tea-cloths (*see Fig.* 160).

Designs. The patterns may be of the conventional geometric type, but many show floral designs and even figures, cherubs, and heraldic beasts, and which, owing to the square form of the foundation net, can all be conveniently planned out on squared paper. In planning these patterns, small isolated spots should be avoided as the darning must flow continuously from form to form with as few breaks as possible.

Materials. The net used for the basis of this work must be square, and in the old days it was made by hand in a process known as netting, and many workers still follow this method. Hand-netted filet can now be bought from the shops, and industry has also provided us with a machine-made substitute. The size of the mesh varies considerably from four to six squares to the inch, and this of course governs the ultimate size of the design and should be taken into consideration when planning the work. The traditional colours are white, cream or natural, embroidered with a matching thread of good quality linen. For unusual effects, a coloured thread

Fig. 160.   Filet Darning in " Cloth Stitch "

may be used for the darning, and this, in a thick variety on a wide-meshed net, is often very effective for window curtains, etc.   The thickness of the embroidery thread is governed by the size of the mesh, but generally two lines of thread should fill a mesh when working in " Cloth Stitch " and four or six when " Weaving " or " Reprise " stitch is used.   A long blunt-pointed needle is necessary.

PREPARING THE WORK

This work is better done in a frame, especially motifs of complicated pattern, and a special metal square into which the net is sewn can be obtained.   △ The mounting must be done with care and the lines of the net kept strictly perpendicular and horizontal, otherwise the work will be crooked. An ordinary circular embroidery frame can be used as a

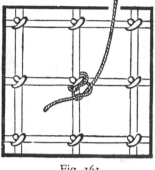

substitute if these points are heeded, but the net should be arranged to " give " a little on the frame as the needle darns in and out. To commence, the end of the thread should be secured with a reef knot to one corner of a mesh as in *Fig.* 161, and afterwards trimmed off neatly. All good Filet Darning should be tidy alike on both sides of the work, and when a join is necessary in the middle of the work the new thread

Fig. 161

is reef-knotted to the end of the other and the ends trimmed off later.

THE STITCHES

Two simple stitches are used in modern Filet Darning. The first, a simple darning or weaving stitch, technically known when connected with this work as " reprise " or " point de reprise," is shown in *Fig.* 162. This may be used to work out whole patterns or judiciously combined with the second stitch, and it can be worked horizontally throughout the entire design, or both horizontally and vertically. The latter gives a pleasing change of light and shade to the work. Each movement takes the thread over one bar of net and under the next, the process being reversed on the line beneath, making the thread pass over those bars which it previously passed under, until a closely woven and well-packed section is achieved.

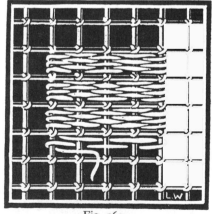

Fig. 162

The second and most popular stitch is illustrated at *Fig.* 163 and known as cloth or " toile " stitch. This is a simple darning stitch worked both horizontally and vertically over and under the mesh as in stocking darning. In order to keep the corners and edges of each shape well defined the thread should be carried round an intersection of two bars and △ not just over a single bar.

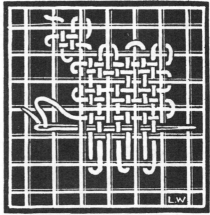

Fig. 163

The method is shown in *Fig.* 163 and is very important, otherwise the threads will merely hang over the single bars and the pattern sag and lose most of its shape when washed.

This applies particularly to any corner or angle in the design as shown in *Fig.* 164, which gives the correct method of turning a corner. This diagram represents two sides of a small square which when completed will have an open space in the middle. For such, the work is commenced at A. Should, however, the right angle as shown in *Fig.* 164 be the complete motif, the work should be commenced at B.

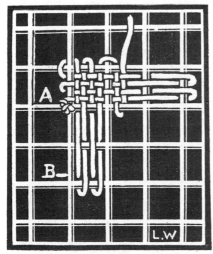

Fig. 164

WORKING THE PATTERNS

It is almost impossible to make any definite rules concerning the best spot to start a design in this kind of work, especially those worked out in cloth stitch. △ Each different design must be carefully studied before the work is

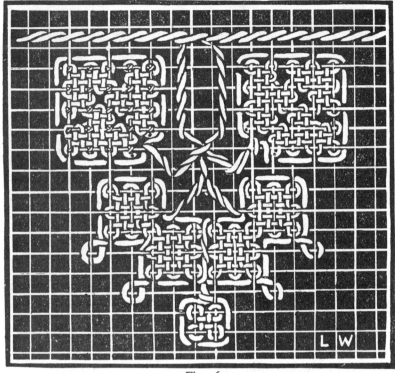

Fig. 165

commenced in order to find the best spot from which the darning can be arranged continuous and regular throughout. This
will invariably mean that the stitch, at some point or other,
will have to be " wangled " in one of the following ways: (1)
Side-stepping in order to keep the darning movement correct.
(2) Looping two threads in the middle of a shape in order to
change the direction of the thread. (3) Twisting round a single
bar of net in order to pass from one square to another which is
not immediately linked up to its neighbour. These three
points will be better appreciated by referring to the explanatory
diagrams. *Fig.* 165 shows a very simple motif in which the
pattern is outlined in a thicker thread, and an impression of
stems given to the shapes. This is known as Filet-Richelieu,
but the method of working the design is identical, the outline
being optional and added afterwards. At *Figs.* 166 and 167

small portions of this same motif are shown on a considerably larger scale in order that the various "wangles" necessary to work out the design may be seen. *Fig.* 166 is the top left-hand portion of *Fig.* 165 and shows clearly the little "side-step" necessary to make the darning continuous throughout. The stitch is commenced at the knot in the bottom right corner

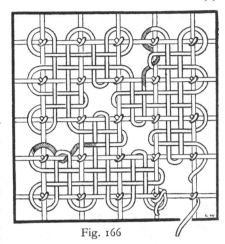

Fig. 166

and the process of working can be clearly followed. The shaded portions of thread indicate where the regular order of the stitching deviates in passing from one mesh to another, but in actual working this will be practically invisible, and will not show on the finished work, as experiment will prove.

In *Fig.* 167 one of the lower squares from *Fig.* 165 has been enlarged and the shaded portion again shows how it is necessary to change the direction of the thread with a "loop" in order to make the square begin and end in

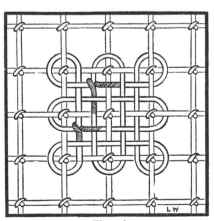

Fig. 167

one corner and so pass to the next without a break. The entrance and exit is from the top left-hand corner and the journey can be traced with a pencil on the diagram. The four small squares on the lower part of *Fig.* 165 are arranged in groups of two and must be worked continuously in this way and without a break at the corners.

The simple filet pattern given in *Fig.* 168 is worked

continuously without a single break, commencing in the centre square at A and finishing at B.   In order to do this, the thread occasionally " side-steps " over a bar already covered, as in *Fig.* 166, or " twists " round an uncovered bar in passing to the next square as shown at the top centre of the diagram.

A beginner should commence by working out these two simple motifs (*Figs.* 165 and 168), noting with care the particular methods prescribed.   These will with practice soon become automatic, and new patterns planned out with ease.

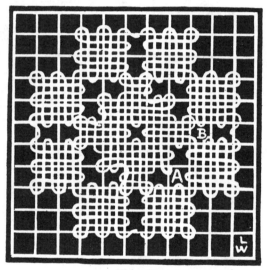

Fig. 168

FLORENTINE WORK

FLORENTINE EMBROIDERY, known also as " Flame Stitch," " fiámma " and " point d'Hongrie," is of rather vague origin, but legend has it that one of the Medici married a Hungarian bride who brought this work with her to Italy in the 15th century. Whether or not this be true, such work has been found at Florence in great abundance ever since, the peculiarly distinctive patterns being used alike for embroidery, woven fabrics and brocades. The embroidery is done on a canvas background, and strictly speaking should come under the heading of canvas work, but so distinct in form and treatment are the stitches and the designs, and so widely is it known under this local name, that it merits a complete section of its own in this book.

Fig. 169 (*p.* 136) shows an exquisite example of Florentine Embroidery, an Italian altar frontal of the 17th century, worked in coloured wools and white silk, from which it will be seen that the alternative name of " flame stitch " is very descriptive, since the characteristic zigzag lines bear a close resemblance to leaping tongues of flame.

Colours. The most beautiful feature of this embroidery is the shading and blending of colours. In the old Italian work, so much used for chair seats, stool covers and screens, the favourite colours were dull pinks, greens and browns, but modern workers have waived this tradition, introducing the more brilliant colours and violent contrasts as an attractive foil to modern furniture decoration, or even handbags, pochettes, etc. Such adventures, however, are rarely attempted on a first effort. △ As a rule it is better to use but two or three colours on any one piece of work, with as many intermediate shades of these same colours as desirable, working each succeeding line in a lighter or darker tone than the last, and so shading gradually from one basic colour to another. In this way the characteristic colour effects of Florentine Embroidery are obtained. One colour only, graded in a variety

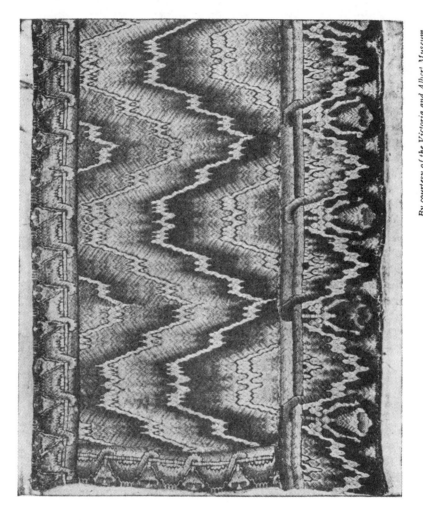

Fig. 169.   Italian Altar Frontal (17th century) in Florentine work

of different shades is surprisingly attractive, while a pattern worked out in black, greys and white, blending the grey tones gradually from dark to light between the black and white, is unusually smart in a modern room or for handbags and pochettes.

Any successful colour scheme can be evolved for a particular room by taking the dominant colours of the carpet, a porcelain vase or the cretonnes, and with suitable intermediate shades, work them into the design. Before commencing the embroidery, lay the skeins of wool out on the table and grade them carefully from one basic colour to another, and buy extra intermediary shades if necessary to form a really successful colour "palette." Number each shade 1, 2, 3, in this order with little tie-on labels, or record the shade number of the wool, to ensure no mistakes in the process of working. This applies in particular when 7 or 8 intervening shades are used, the fine gradations of which might defy detection by evening or artificial light.

MATERIALS

Use a single thread canvas with embroidery wool of proportionate thickness to the mesh of the canvas and to cover the background completely. Tapestry and embroidery wools, because of their wonderful colour range, are most frequently used. Silk can be used on a much finer canvas.

Florentine Stitch. One stitch only, known as Florentine Stitch, is used to work out any Florentine

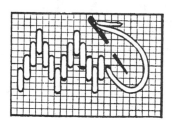

Fig. 170

design. This, in its simplest form, is shown in *Fig.* 170. The thread is taken vertically over four canvas threads and back under two ready for the next, which again mounts over four threads, making each stitch two threads higher or lower than its predecessor. The needle in the diagram shows how to pass from one stitch to the next.

Florentine Patterns. This method of grouping the stitches up and down in zigzag lines forms the basis of all Florentine designs. The different pinnacle patterns are achieved by augmenting or diminishing the number of threads over which a stitch is worked, while by grouping the stitches in " blocks "

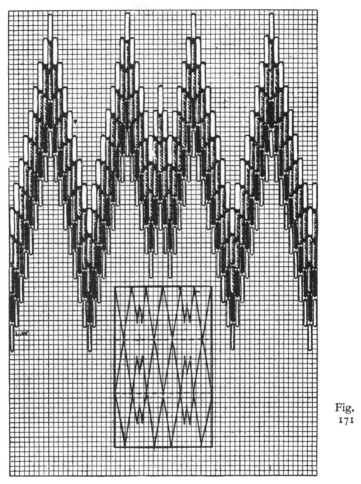

Fig.
171

or " steps " a more gradual " arch " or curve is developed. Compare *Figs.* 171 and 176.

A very simple Florentine design could be worked out as in *Fig.* 170, passing each stitch over four threads and back two, which for brevity's sake will be described as the 4/2 principle. The easiest way to change this would be to vary the height of the stitch, and *Fig.* 171 shows what happens if the stitch is taken up over six canvas threads and back one every time (6/1 principle). The contrast between six and one produces

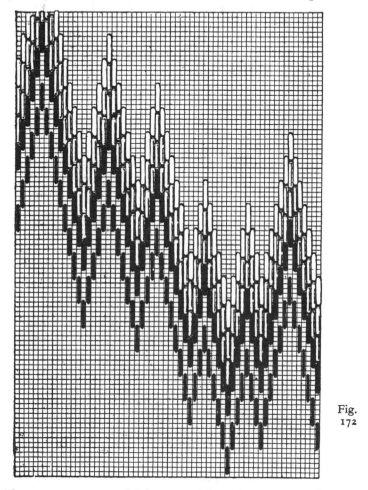

Fig.
172

a sudden steep ascent which to avoid monotony may be converted into pinnacles of varying height. Each successive colour follows the first original line over the entire surface, or the pattern can be inverted, as suggested, by the inset at the bottom of the diagram. In this case it will be necessary to fill the intervening spaces with similar shaded colours. The dotted lines on the inset denote the division between the pattern lines.

This same 6/1 principle can be varied in endless different ways, one being illustrated in *Fig.* 172. Here a bold zigzag line travels diagonally from corner to corner in great " lightning " zigzags, each pinnacle being a different height from its neighbour as fancy pleases. Once this first irregular line has been worked (and this has been divided in *Fig.* 172 to show its construction), all the succeeding lines fall quite easily into position. This exaggerated type of design looks best on screens and other large articles, to show off its somewhat startling beauty.

Both designs in *Figs.* 171 and 172 are worked on the 6/1 principle, but either could, of course, be worked on a 5/1 or 4/1 principle and accordingly reduce the height of the pinnacles. The next progressive development is to convert the point of each pinnacle into an arch by doubling the stitches at the top in step formation. The method is shown in *Fig.* 173, a

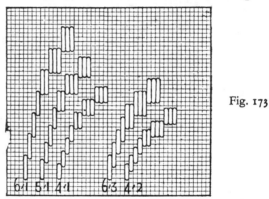

Fig. 173

valuable little " key " diagram from which any number of designs can be evolved. Five different arcs are shown of different heights and different curves, yet each contains exactly the same number of stitches. The difference is obtained in the first three arcs by reducing the height of the original stitch. That is, the first is worked on the 6/1 principle, the second over five and back one (5/1), and the third over four and back one (4/1). The fourth and fifth arcs show quite a different principle, as the stitch is taken over six threads but steps back three (6/3) instead of one to produce a very pronounced curve, while that at five is taken over four threads and back two (4/2). Each arc can of course be joined to form an arch or inverted as shown in *Fig.* 174, which is built on the

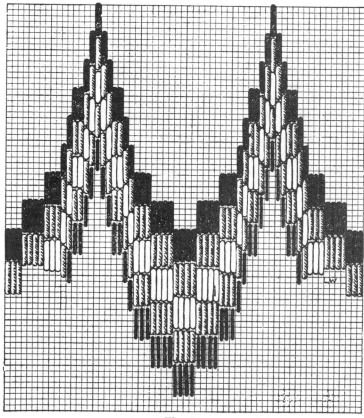

Fig. 174

6/1 principle with the " steps " now arranged at the bottom.

The construction of *Fig.* 175 is really quite simple, yet most effective. Each stitch is the same length—over five threads—but in forming the sharp ascent it steps back only one thread (5/1), while in the shallow curve, consisting of seven grouped stitches, it steps back four threads (5/4). By now it will be realised that while the original length of the stitch must remain the same throughout, its appearance can be varied

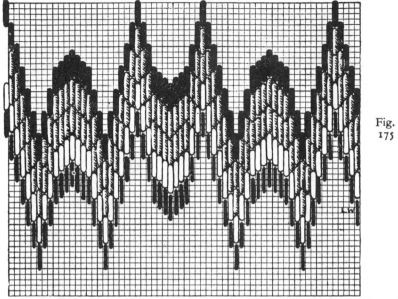

Fig.
175

considerably by stepping back beneath a varying number of threads, but with some comprehensive plan in view.

The more gradual curve shown in *Fig.* 176 is achieved by

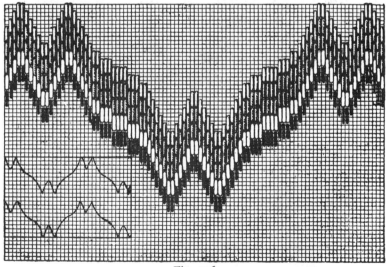

Fig. 176

doubling the middle stitches in the wavy line instead of those at the beginning or the end. This produces a graceful, gradual curve worked on the 4/2 principle. A further reference to the key in *Fig.* 173 will reveal that this long waving line is none other than a continuation of the 4/2 arc shown in that diagram!

Fig. 177 is yet a further development of this same 4/2 arc but this time it is reversed, also repeated above to form the popular repeating Medallion design. Each stitch is taken over four threads and back two (4/2 principle) and the basic line is from A to B. Where the lines touch, a stitch or group of stitches will be common to both and the resulting spaces must be filled in, shading to a darker colour in the centre as suggested.

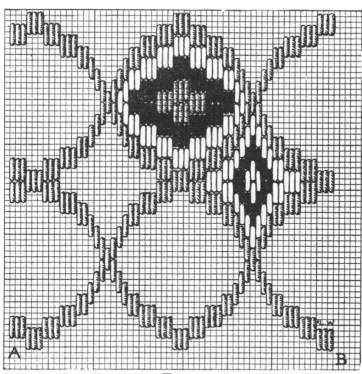

Fig. 177

HARDANGER EMBROIDERY

THE PEOPLE OF HARDANGER, a mountainous district in Norway, at the head of the lovely Hardanger Fiord, are famed all over the world for a beautiful openwork embroidery, known as Hardanger Embroidery. This is characterised by little rectangular groups of satin stitches, known as " kloster " blocks, arranged to outline the cut spaces and build up the major portion of the design. An example of Hardanger work is shown in *Fig.* 178, where it will be seen how these blocks are arranged to build up a pattern of squares and rectangles following the warp and weft of the material.

DESIGNS

Hardanger designs must of necessity take some geometrical form, such as a square, triangle, oblong or diamond, and the method by which these can be planned out on squared paper is shown in *Fig.*

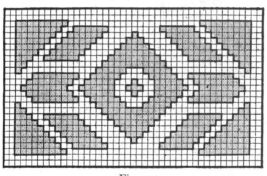

179. The main outlines of the designs are simple, but the pattern develops into one of great interest as smaller shapes are gradually built up round and within the larger outlines.

Fig. 179

Materials. This work being somewhat heavy in appearance, necessitates a background of heavy linen with coarse regular weave so that the threads can be easily counted. Hardanger linen or canvas woven with double warp and weft should be used, since it is strong and does not fray in cutting. The

Fig. 178

LYON WOOD

working thread should be a little coarser than the threads of the linen for working the kloster blocks and a little finer for filling the open spaces.

The process of working Hardanger Embroidery falls conveniently into five divisions, under which headings it will be described:

1. Outlining the spaces and design with kloster blocks.
2. Working in any additional embroidery motifs, lines, borders, etc., on the surface of the material.
3. Cutting and drawing the threads for the open spaces.
4. Decorating the bars of the larger open spaces.
5. Addition of lace stitch fillings, wheels, etc.

1.   THE KLOSTER BLOCKS

A kloster block is composed of an irregular number of stitches enclosing a regular number of linen material threads as in *Fig.* 180.   Here the block comprises five stitches taken

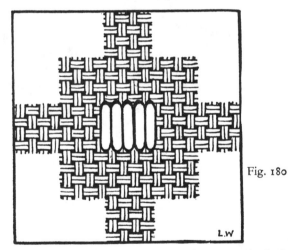

Fig. 180

over four horizontal threads to enclose four vertical threads, top and bottom.   (It is these vertical threads which are cut later at the head or foot of the block to form the open spaces.)

Five stitches to a block is the usual size, but the number may vary from nine stitches enclosing eight threads (*see Fig.* 182), seven stitches enclosing six threads or three stitches enclosing two threads.

Klosters may be grouped (1) vertically or horizontally to outline the spaces as to the right of *Fig.* 181 which leaves a space of four threads between each group, or (2) in steps to

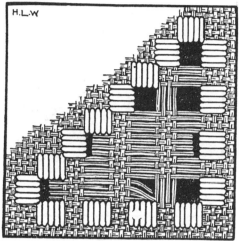

Fig. 181

make a diagonal line across the material for the purpose of outlining a triangle or diamond-shaped motif (*see Figs.* 178 and 181). Notice how the head of each stitch, in *Fig.* 181,

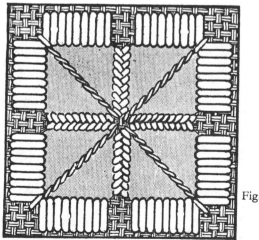

Fig. 182

always faces towards a cut space, and in this way the cut ends of the material are protected and kept from fraying.

Kloster blocks can be varied in height as well as in length (*see Fig.* 183). Here a little square is cleverly worked to simulate a diamond, achieved by making the three centre

Fig. 183

klosters on each side of the square twice the usual height. The last stitch in each longer group is carried up to form the first stitch of the next group, which helps to create the illusion of the diamond. (The filling is explained later.)

2.   ADDITIONAL DECORATION

In addition to the kloster blocks which outline all the shapes, further decorative embroidery stitches are added to the work as in *Figs.* 184 A and B. These surface stitches greatly enrich the design and still adhere to the geometric principle of following the weave of the material. In *Fig.* 184 A the long arms of the cross are worked in chain and back stitch,* ending in satin stitch and Algerian eye stitch.* This motif could be repeated in

Fig. 184 A

each corner of a tray-mat as a beginning effort. *Fig.* 184 B shows a simple yet decorative way of working satin stitches of varying length from a centre line, very much after the style of kloster blocks. These likewise form a cross with a tiny cut square in the centre, and the design suggests a centre decoration or one which could be extended in repeats to cover an entire cushion.

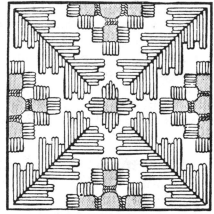

Fig. 184 B

A variety of other stitches may be used for this surface embroidery, such as Back, Star, Cross, Close Herringbone, Eyelet, Four-sided, and Interlacing stitch,* to name but a few, the latter being particularly effective with Hardanger work. A further reference to *Fig.* 178 will show isolated kloster blocks attractively finished with three small straight stitches, while satin stitches grouped to form small squares or diamonds is another idea.

3. CUTTING AND DRAWING THE THREADS

In most cut and drawn works the threads are first removed and the decorative embroidery worked afterwards, but Hardanger work is the exception to the rule, Δ as all the embroidery is completed before the threads are cut or drawn.

At this third stage of the work, the thrilling part of Hardanger Embroidery begins. Should the work up to this point have been done in a frame, it must be removed and completed in the hand, as material cut while stretched will cause the edges of the kloster blocks to sag. The method of cutting and withdrawing threads within a triangle is shown in *Fig.* 181, but in a square, diamond or rectangular shape the method is the same. Four threads are cut and four left alternately, the number being one less than the number of stitches contained in the kloster block. Use very sharp scissors and cut the threads close up to the satin stitches, and it is advisable on a large piece of work to cut and complete one motif at a time. The correct method of cutting is important. △ First cut and remove all the horizontal threads and then the vertical, or vice versa, but do not mix the process. When the cutting is complete, there will remain an open mesh of squares within the outline of kloster blocks, and these must be strengthened and decorated. Small isolated blocks such as those in *Figs*. 184 A and B may be cut on all four sides of the square and just left.

4. DECORATING THE BARS

The material threads left after cutting as in *Fig*. 181 are strengthened with overcasting or weaving stitches to bind them into a firm foundation for the lace filling stitches.

Fig. 185 shows the method of overcasting in progress, which is always worked diagonally across any shape, whether

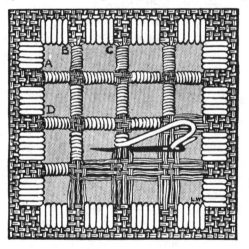

Fig. 185

square, diamond or rectangular, in order to keep the right "pull." The diagram shows the overcasting commenced at A and worked up to B. Here the thread is taken under the kloster block to C and travels down in "steps" to D and so on. Make each twist firm and cover each bar completely. At the intersection of the mesh carry the thread behind the work to the next bar, and allow the little square of foundation material to show.

A woven bar which produces a flatter and heavier effect is shown in *Fig.* 186. The weaving, like the overcasting, is done diagonally, and to commence bring the thread through

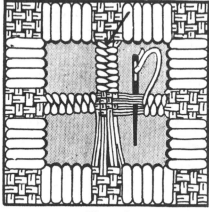

to the surface at the arrow, and weave in and out as shown in the illustration, passing diagonally beneath the centre square from bar to bar in order to maintain the correct " pull " of the threads. △ Always work with a thread of sufficient length to complete the weaving of any bar or bars. It is not advisable to mix woven and overcast bars on any one piece of work, as their effect

Fig. 186

is so different that used together they would look and be irregular.

At this stage of the work, simple Hardanger patterns or those already highly enriched with surface embroidery are regarded as finished, the overcast or woven bars being sufficient decoration. *Fig.* 187 examples a simple yet beautiful

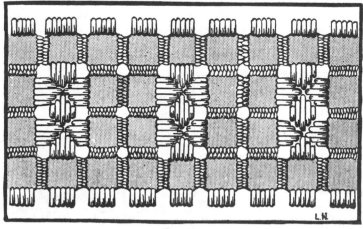

Fig. 187

border of this type, while *Fig.* 188 shows how little picots may be added to the woven bars as further decoration in lieu of lace stitch fillings. These picots are worked in the centre on either side of the bar and the thread is twisted

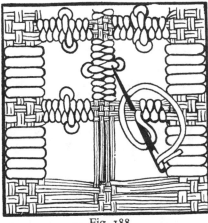

once round the needle to make the picot, after which the needle " weaves " to the opposite side and repeats the process. △ Practice is necessary before picots can be made neatly and evenly. Bullion picots are also used but it is advisable to experiment with both bars and picots on an odd scrap of linen first, before introducing them to a large piece of work. The addition of small picots greatly

Fig. 188

enhances the bars, and should a square such as that in *Fig.* 185 be made with woven bars enriched with picots, the effect would be enchanting, almost lace-like.

5. LACE STITCH FILLING

Most of the lace stitch fillings are worked in at the same time as the bars are over-cast, so at the end of stage three it is necessary to decide whether the work is to be finished with plain bars, bars with picots, or bars with lace stitch fillings. Lace stitches greatly enrich the work as shown in *Figs.* 178, 182 and 183, but *Fig.* 189 gives the most popular and simple lace filling stitch set straight, and worked in each alternate space. This filling may be incorporated

Fig. 189

with either a woven or overcast bar, and the illustration shows how it is worked in one journey with the process of overcasting as the bars are being covered. Commence at A in *Fig.* 189 and work round to the centre of bar B, and here the filling is worked as shown by the needle in the centre. When the fourth loop is completed, the

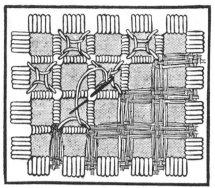

Fig. 190

needle returns again to bar B and completes the overcasting. The next row is commenced at C and an ordinary row of overcasting is worked diagonally up to D. The next row begins at E, in the course of which another filling is worked in the top right corner, and the needle is shown working the next centre filling after which the overcasting will be continued and another filling worked in the bottom left corner. The last two bars and filling will then be worked diagonally in the bottom right corner to complete the square. (The same method applies when the bars are woven.) △ It is very important to get the " unders and overs " of this stitch in their correct order, otherwise the fillings will look irregular. The trick is to pass the needle under each bar first in making the loop. A study of *Fig.* 189 will show the object of this.

In *Fig.* 190 the same filling stitch is shown but set diagonally. Here again the filling is added in as the bars are worked, but from each corner of the square instead of from the centre of the bars. The method is clearly shown by the needle in the diagram.

Both the fillings shown in *Figs.* 189 and 190 may be given an extra twist by slipping the needle again under each loop as it is made, and before proceeding to the next to produce a closer, tighter effect.

On articles not subject to much wear and tear, such as table runners, it is permissible to leave the mesh without weaving or overcasting, and just add a filling of interlocking

Fig. 191

lace stitch. This is shown at *Fig.* 191 and is not nearly as complicated as it looks! Commence at A in the top left corner and follow the arrows along to the opposite side at B. Here the stitch turns back along the dotted line, and interlocks with the first row and at the same time loops round the mesh of horizontal threads, returning again to A. The next line is worked in the same way, but looped into the first line of filling and round the mesh at the same time.

Fig. 192 A shows the same filling set in alternate squares. The working method is a little different in order to pass invisibly from space to space. It is better to work vertically, making a complete filling,

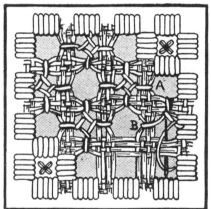

Fig. 192 A

first a stitch to the right and then to the left. That at A is commenced and finished at A, after which the needle is slipped under the thread of the first loop at the back to get the correct " pull," and from here it is carried to the position for the next stitch by catching it lightly into the

Fig. 192 B

back of the material with a darning movement. The whole
process on the back of the work is shown in *Fig.* 192 B.

A little " spider web " filling is given in *Fig.* 193, and looks
most effective when worked in alternate squares. The bar
is first overcast down to A and a stitch thrown diagonally
across the square, and twisted back again to A. This is the
first movement after which the overcasting is continued as
at B, and the opposite diagonal stitch is thrown across and
twisted back to the centre, and a buttonhole stitch worked
over the intersection of the threads as shown. The needle
then weaves under and over the four threads and completes

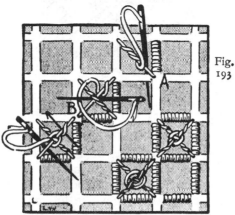

Fig.
193

the filling by twisting round the fourth " arm " to the bottom
left corner. Two completed fillings are also shown.

For larger isolated squares, such as that in *Fig.* 183, a more
elaborate decoration is possible. The horizontal and vertical
bars are first woven and to these are added two twisted bars
worked from each corner to the centre, as shown in *Fig.* 182.
These form the foundation of *Fig.* 183. The centre of the
wheel is woven but in the diagram this is left unfinished so
that its construction may be clearly seen. Further decorative
loop stitches are then carried twice round the square. The
stitch is commenced at the arrow and the needle is shown on
the second journey, which interlocks with the first. Upon
reaching the arrow, again pick up the two rather loose loops
and give the thread a final " pull," and then take it through
the material to the back and finish.

Another wheel filling is shown at *Fig.* 194, which has a ribbed effect, produced by working back stitches over each of the bars.   Other wheels suitable for use in Hardanger Embroidery will be found in the section devoted to Drawn Thread Work (*see pages* 121 and 122).

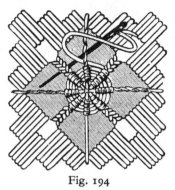

Fig. 194

FINISHING THE EDGES

The edges of most articles decorated with Hardanger work are finished with a single line of hemstitching as the embroidery is rich and elaborate and needs but a simple hem decoration.   Sometimes a narrow border of needleweaving is used, and sometimes the edges are left flat without a hem and finished with a pattern of vandyke points or " battlements " worked in close buttonhole stitching after the manner of scalloping.

HEDEBO EMBROIDERY

EDEBO EMBROIDERY is a Danish form of cut and drawn work, in white on white linen, and flourished chiefly in the 18th and 19th centuries among the peasants who lived on the flat tract of land known as " Heden " (the heath), which lies between Copenhagen and the former capital Roskilde. " Bo " means to live, and the name " Hede(n)bo " is derived from this source, being the work of the people who lived on the heath. Originally Hedebo Embroidery was a simple peasant art used to decorate the men's shirts, women's underclothing, sheets, etc., and the workers wove their own linen and designed their own patterns.

DESIGNS

There are three very distinct forms. (1) The oldest, for which the designs were adapted by the peasants from wood carvings found on their old furniture, etc., consisted of conventional floral shapes with but a few open spaces in cut and drawn thread work. The surface embroidery in chain stitch considerably outweighed the openwork portions, yet the whole effect was one of exceeding grace and charm, being the unspoilt expression of the peasant's desire to beautify her home. An example of this type is shown in *Fig.* 195 (p. 158).

The second form which came about 1840 somewhat changed the character of the work. The conventional floral shapes with their drawn fillings were retained but further cut and drawn spaces, similar to those found in Italian cut work or Reticella, were added in the form of squares. This caused the designs to become more geometrical and formal, as shown in *Fig.* 196 (p. 159).

The third form, dated about 1850, coincided with the " discovery " of Hedebo Embroidery and its exploitation by dealers, with the result that its simple peasant qualities were quickly lost. The shapes became highly conventional and

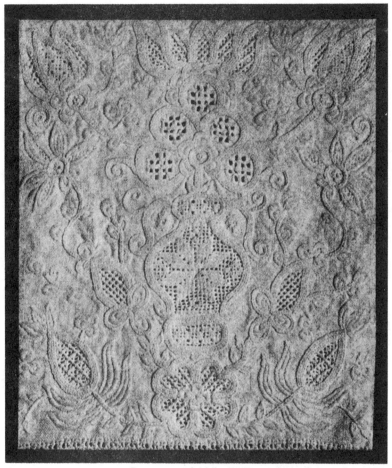

By courtesy of Selskabet Til Haandarbejdets Fremme, Denmark

Fig. 195. Old Hedebo embroidery, 18th century

the spaces were cut, instead of drawn and cut, and filled with elaborate lace stitches, while the surface embroidery sank to insignificance (*see Fig.* 197). This third form, which survived but a short time in Denmark, was taken up in other countries and became widely and generally known as Hedebo Embroidery.

This commercial movement had a devastating effect on " Hedebo-syning " (the Danish name) in its own country, and by 1870 it was almost forgotten. Happily of late years a strong

Fig. 196

movement has been made by various societies to revive the work in its older and purer form, and as such it is again being worked in Denmark.

In order that the difference between the three forms of the work can be better appreciated, they are treated separately under the headings Old Type, Intermediate Type, Third Type, using *Figs.* 195, 196 and 197 as working examples, since each is typical of its own period.

WORKING METHODS, OLD TYPE

Old Hedebo as illustrated in *Fig.* 195 was worked with linen thread of medium thickness on a closely hand-woven linen. The larger shapes were filled with cut and drawn work,

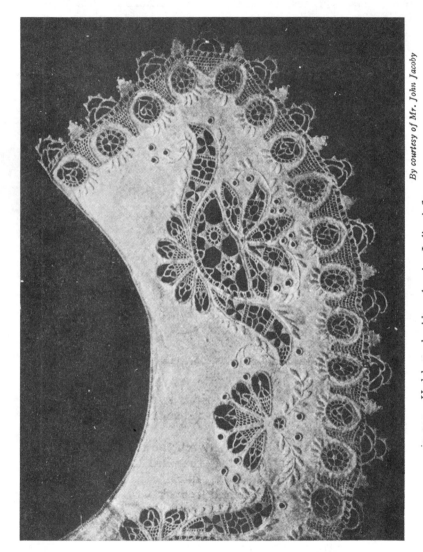

By courtesy of Mr. John Jacoby

ig. 197.   Hedebo embroidery showing Italian influence

cutting two and leaving two threads alternately, both vertically and horizontally. This was done from the back of the work. The edge of the shape was then secured with overcasting stitch, and an overcasting stitch was then worked over the mesh as shown in *Fig.* 198, working first horizontally with two stitches to each bar, and then the vertical. *Fig.* 199 shows the method of weav-

Fig. 198

ing in patterns in these overcast bars, though this lighter mesh as shown in the diagram was rarely used.

Each space was first prepared as described and then further enriched with other stitches, as will be seen from a study of *Fig.* 195. The centre star pattern is woven after the manner shown in *Fig.* 199. The leaf shapes at the top left and right corners show an uneven surface of square holes set diagonally,

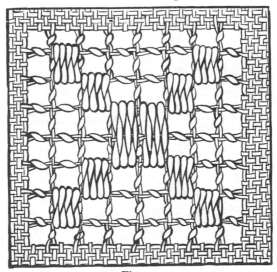

Fig. 199

and *Fig.* 200 shows how these ridge effects were achieved on a mesh as in *Fig.* 198. The stitch is similar to a drawn fabric stitch, only worked through the spaces of the bars, each line being completed in two diagonal journeys. (The overcast stitches are omitted on all bars in the diagram to avoid confusion.) For the first journey, shown by the dark thread, bring the needle out at the

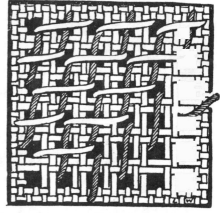

Fig. 200

bottom edge of the shape and pass over an open square and one bar. From here carry it diagonally behind the intersection of the bars to emerge one square to the right and one down, after which it passes over a bar, a square and a bar and repeats the process. These stitches on the upward journey are all vertical, those on the downward journey, shown in white, are worked horizontally, and across those of the first journey to form a diagonal row of crosses. Both stitches are taken into the same holes and each must be pulled tightly in the working, both for the first and second journeys, so

Fig. 201

that the mesh is drawn up into a marked ridge. The bunch of leaves at the top of *Fig.* 195 is the same over stitch, but the alternate rows only are worked and over a mesh background as in *Fig.* 198.

The method of working the three lower fillings in *Fig.* 195 is shown in *Fig.* 201. The same diagonal rows of crosses are worked as before, but spaced further apart, leaving two or

Fig. 202 A

three bars between each, and on a mesh as at *Fig.* 198.

The five window shapes in the centre top are worked as at *Figs.* 202 A and 202 B. *Fig.* 202 A shows how the threads are first cut and drawn for the foundation, and *Fig.* 202 B how the edges of the shape were then overcast and the broad bars across the centre woven. After this the remaining narrow bars are overcast with two stitches to each bar, leaving the intersections of all bars uncovered.

Having completed all the openwork part of the embroidery, the shapes were then outlined with a double row of close small chain stitches. The method is shown in *Fig.* 203. This is a close-up of the top left and right motifs in *Fig.* 195, and shows very clearly this double outline of chain stitch, so characteristic of old Hedebo work. Chain stitch, in both single and double lines, was also used for stems, scrolls and other details, with buttonhole stitch and satin stitch for the small leaves, calices, etc. The centre spot of the conventional calyx shown in *Fig.* 203 is formed of French knots.

INTERMEDIATE TYPE OF HEDEBO

For the second and intermediary type of Hedebo illustrated at *Fig.* 196, the formal flower and leaf shapes with their fillings of overcast bars were retained, the working being exactly the same as in the older type; but the addition of cut and drawn squares very much

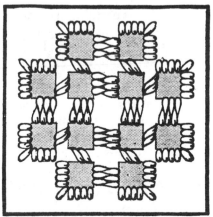

Fig. 202 B

after the style of Reticella lace, gave the work a very different appearance. A little " grid " of material threads was left when cutting and drawing the squares, and upon this weaving and overcasting stitches were worked to make different patterns of geometrical form. The squares themselves were usually arranged in diagonal lines to form large diamond shapes, interspersed with floral shapes and surface embroidery.

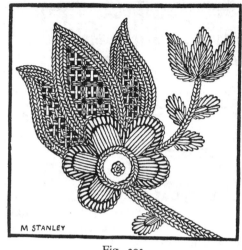

Fig. 203

THIRD FORM OF HEDEBO EMBROIDERY

The elaborate collar, a portion of which is shown at *Fig.* 197, illustrates the third and better known form of Hedebo work. The embroidery mainly consists of cut spaces filled with lace stitches, interspersed with motifs in satin stitch and eyelets rather reminiscent of Broderie Anglaise, and finished with an edging worked after the manner of needlepoint lace.

It makes a charming decoration for collars and cuffs, tea and tray cloths, luncheon sets, etc., or on any article worked on white or cream linen.   Although so very open and fragile-looking, it wears surprisingly well and will stand a lot of washing.

DESIGNS

The designs are built of small circles, larger semi-circles, ovals, pear-shapes, long flowing leaf shapes and so on, as shown in *Fig.* 197, which includes all the most characteristic shapes, and shows how these are arranged in groups to form attractive patterns.

MATERIALS AND THREADS

Only a firm, closely-woven white or cream linen should be used with a strong fine cotton or lace thread for the fillings.

The surface embroidery provides a delightful contrast, being worked in a softer but thicker and lightly-twisted linen thread. It is quite permissible to work this form of embroidery throughout in thick threads, but the effect, of course, will not be so delicate.

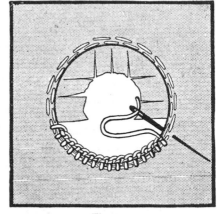

Fig. 204

WORKING METHODS

First offset the design on to the linen and then work a double row of running stitches round all the outline (*see Fig.* 204). The material within the shape is then cut away, cutting along the grain of the material. After this the space is outlined with buttonhole stitch as shown. In all Hedebo Embroidery the buttonholing differs from ordinary buttonhole stitch, and to avoid confusion will be referred to throughout as Hedebo buttonhole. (It is similar, but not the same as loop edging stitch.) The working method is shown in *Fig.* 205. Two separate movements are necessary, and the material is held and the stitch worked away from the

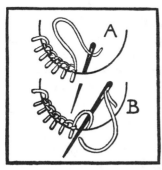

Fig. 205

worker, leaving a small space between each. Insert the needle into the edge of the material downwards as shown at A and draw through until a small loop remains. The needle is then slipped through the loop as shown at B and both stitch and loop pulled tight with a little jerk.

Turn the material under with the needle all round the shape in working and take each stitch through the two thicknesses. Any surplus material is then cut away on the back, close up to the stitching, when the outlining is complete. This is the only stitch, together with a

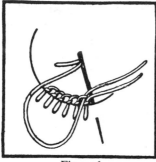

Fig. 206

whipping or overcasting stitch, used in working out all the seemingly complicated lace fillings shown at *Fig.* 197.

All the different shapes shown in the subsequent diagrams are first prepared in this way before the fillings are worked.

The method of joining a new thread is shown in *Fig.* 206. Slip the new thread under the last loop and lay it alongside the old. Both ends are then held and six or seven stitches, worked over both ends which are then cut close to the work and the resulting join, practically invisible.

FILLING STITCHES

The worked effect of the following fillings can be seen on the collar in *Fig.* 197. That at *Fig.* 207 shows an inner circle of Hedebo but-

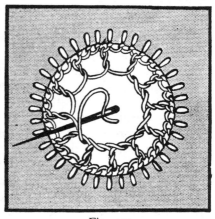

Fig. 207

tonhole worked loosely within the first. The inner circle is worked into every third stitch of the outer, and to get the loose effect avoid giving the final jerk to each stitch. When the circle is completed, the looped edges are whipped as shown in the diagram.

In *Fig.* 208 the filling is commenced at A with a little loop made by taking the thread backwards and forwards two or three times into

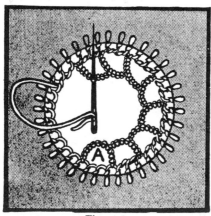

Fig. 208

the edging and then covering with Hedebo buttonholing. The needle then whips along two edging stitches and three more threads are thrown from the edge to the first loop as shown in the diagram. This loop is then covered with Hedebo buttonhole back to the edge again and so on to the next loop. This makes a very solid inner ring.

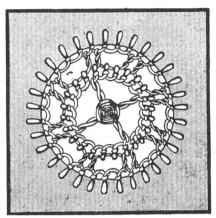

Fig. 209

The filling at *Fig.* 209, one of the border circles in *Fig.* 197, consists of an inner circle similar to *Fig.* 207, but arranged in groups of two stitches with a space between each. The loops are further covered with a close row of Hedebo buttonhole and the circle finished with four twisted bars and a woven centre.

At *Fig.* 210 the inner circle of open Hedebo buttonhole is only carried round half way, the remainder of the circle being finished with closely covered loops similar to those in *Fig.* 208.

PYRAMIDS

Little pyramids of closely worked Hedebo buttonhole as set into the collar edge in *Fig.* 197 are a characteristic feature in this form of Hedebo Embroidery. Other uses for pyramids are shown in *Figs.*

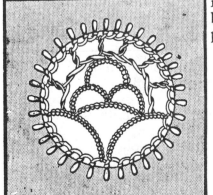

Fig. 210

Fig. 211

212, 215 and 218. The stitch is the same Hedebo buttonhole and the method is shown in *Fig.* 211. The edge is first prepared with Hedebo buttonhole as usual, and the pyramid is commenced at A by overcasting from right to left over the required number of stitches. The Hedebo buttonhole is then worked back from left to right, but with one stitch less at the end of each row; and this process continues until the top of the pyramid is reached. From here the needle whips down the left side and is ready to continue the next. Pyramids make an effective filling within a circle, particularly if a large pyramid is alternated with a small one and so on.

Fig. 212

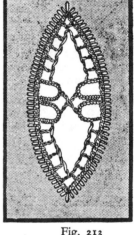

Fig. 213

Fig. 212 shows how the favourite pear-shaped motifs in *Fig.* 197 are worked. The method can be easily followed since it combines those of other fillings previously described. Note the very tiny pyramid at the top of the shape.

Fig. 213 shows the method of filling an oval shape. This is also based on previously described methods, except for the centre, which is formed of two little twisted bars worked across from the loops.

Fig. 214 shows two different methods of working bars in a circle. The upper bar is constructed on a foundation of two or three threads thrown across the space and closely covered with the Hedebo buttonhole. The lower bar commences in a similar way along the base after which the needle whips back to the left side and works a second and more open row, taking each stitch into every third of the previous row. This again is whipped back (or the thread merely carried across if preferred) and the upper bar is completed with a final row of close Hedebo buttonhole. This makes a wide double bar and is also used for the beading on the collar in *Fig.* 197.

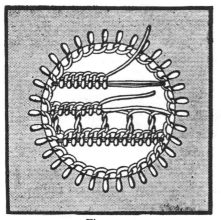

Fig. 214

Fig. 215 is one of the more elaborate fillings from *Fig.* 197, but again built up by methods previously described. Two of the double bars shown in *Fig.* 214 are thrown across the middle while four little pyramids are arranged on the outer sides of each double bar. In working these pyramids, each must be completed as previously described and the thread whipped round

to the position for the next, but after the fourth and instead of whipping down the side, the four points are joined in the middle with little twisted bars.

On studying *Fig.* 197 it will be seen that the large semi-circular

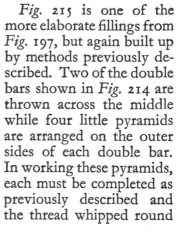

Fig. 215

shape is filled with two small six-pointed stars, a pretty filling to set in a circle or any other suitable shape. The method of working is shown in *Fig.* 216. The thread is twisted several times round a stiletto or a pencil and secured with a stitch as at A. The ring is then slipped off as at B and covered with Hedebo buttonhole. With this as a foundation, a further row

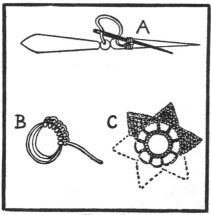

Fig. 216

of open Hedebo buttonhole is added all round as at C. Upon this little pyramids are worked as previously described to form a six-pointed star. The stitches must be

Fig. 217

portioned out carefully before commencing the pyramids so that each point is equal. The star is then used as a filling by securing it with a single stitch at each point.

SURFACE EMBROIDERY

Any surface embroidery chiefly consists of satin stitch and eyelets, arranged as leaf sprays. This will be clearly seen in

Fig. 218

Fig. 197, and in more detail in *Fig.* 215. Any fine stems are worked in stem stitch.

FINISHING THE EDGES

The edges are finished in characteristic fashion with needle-point lace (*see Figs.* 217, 218, 219), all of which are worked like the various fillings previously described. The same Hedebo buttonhole stitch is used throughout, arranged as loops, pyramids, and little rings (*Fig.* 219), made in a similar way to that

Fig. 219

shown at A and B in *Fig.* 216.   The more elaborate edging
seen on the collar in *Fig.* 197 can also be worked out from the
diagrams previously described.   The linen has been cut into a
deep scalloped formation, and each point filled with a pyramid
of open Hedebo buttonhole stitch.   This is worked before the
scalloping and before the linen is cut away, and makes a particularly effective finish to a beautiful piece of work.

INITIALS AND MONOGRAMS

A LMOST EVERY TYPE of embroidery enumerated in this book can, with a little ingenuity, be adapted to the working of Initials and Monograms.

At one time the linen chest of a young bride overflowed with snow-white house-linen, exquisitely embroidered with her initials or monogram, and a charm still lingers about a " best " sheet and pillow-slip hand-embroidered with its owner's initials or monogram. Clothes frequently favour a modernised initial on blouses, scarf ends and handkerchiefs, and for this purpose all kinds of interesting modern methods are employed and quickly imitated.

Padded Satin Stitch. The old English letter " B " in Padded Satin Stitch (*Fig.* 220) is a type

Fig. 220

still used a great deal on bed linen. The thicker parts of each letter are first outlined with fine running or chain stitches and then padded with a bold running or chain stitch. Should a highly embossed letter be required a second layer of chain stitch is worked over the first and possibly a third line or two down the centre. △ All padding stitches should follow the outline of the letter, working round and round within until the centre is reached. The covering satin stitches are then added and to prevent puckering are better worked in an embroidery frame. Make each satin stitch slant as in the diagram and cover the finer lines of the letters with closely worked stem stitching. Ordinary crochet cotton gives a firm solid padding for large letters with the satin stitch worked in a good quality linen thread. A complete alphabet of Old English letters is given in *Fig.* 221 and readers can pick out their own initials.

A modernised version of a monogram ("B. H.") is shown in *Fig.* 222, worked on the same principle as just described, and any number of initials can be arranged in this way, making one upright stroke do duty for two letters. This distinguishes a monogram from a cipher. In the former one upright stroke serves two letters (*Fig.* 222), while in the latter both letters are complete but arranged ornamentally over each other (*see Figs.* 225 and 227).

Fig. 221

The old English letter "W" looks splendid in *Fig.* 223, where the outline is first worked in stem stitch and then filled in with herringbone stitch. This treatment is smart in a dark

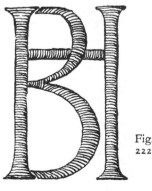

Fig. 222

Fig. 223

thread such as brown worked on beige.   The method is quick
as there is no preliminary padding.   Another effect is obtained
by filling in the bold parts of any letter with French knots
after first outlining with stem stitch.

Cross Stitch.   The most popular method of working initials on
sheets, etc., for identification purposes is in Cross Stitch.   No
preliminary outline or transfer is required as the linen threads
can be counted to form each letter.   Ordinary Cross Stitch
can be used for the purpose but it is more professional to use
Marking Cross Stitch which, if properly worked, builds up
neat squares on the back, making both sides of the work
decorative and sightly.   The working method will be found
in the chapter on Cross Stitch (*Fig.* 91, *page* 73), but requires
a little care to master.

Cross Stitch lettering is usually worked in red or blue, as the
stitches are not bold enough to show up effectively worked

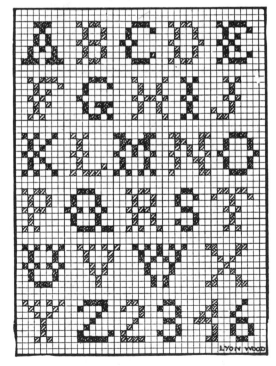

Fig. 224

in white on white material. An alphabet in Cross Stitch is given at *Fig.* 224, from which any initials may be worked.

Appliqué. An attractive cipher in Appliqué is shown in *Fig.* 225. This looks effective on a scarf or handbag and should be carried out in a material of contrasting colour. The initials "A.N." are not actually interlaced, though the ingenious way in which the couching thread is laid gives this impression. First plan out the cipher on paper and then transfer to the material for application. Cut out the whole design, pin in position and tack. The edges are then oversewn with a fine thread and the couch-

Fig.
225

ing worked over the edges and across the material at any point where the interlaced effect is necessary.

SOUTACHE " EMBROIDERY "

The particular type of narrow braid known as " soutache " (obtainable in white or colours) can be used with good effect for working out an interlaced letter of Celtic design such as the " N " shown in *Fig.* 226 A. This produces a letter (or a design) in bold relief, effective on blotters, handbags, etc. First

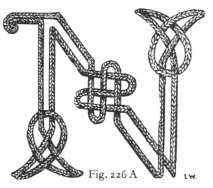

Fig. 226 A   ɪ.w.

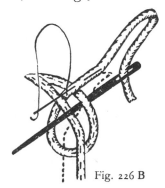

Fig. 226 B

plan out the letter in single outline and offset it to the material. The braid is attached with small invisible running stitches in a matching thread and the work commenced △ at a spot where the join will be least noticeable, and from whence the braid can conveniently travel round the whole letter (or design as the case may be) and return to the same spot without a break. The extreme bottom right-hand corner of the " N " in *Fig.* 226 A suggests the best spot.   Leave a gap in the running stitches where the braid must interlace and for this thread the braid into a large-eyed needle and draw it through, following along behind with the running stitches as shown in *Fig.* 226 B. Any design in Soutache Embroidery is worked on this principle, and should be completed if possible without a join in the braid.   Should this be unavoidable in large patterns then it must be arranged beneath the interlacing, carrying the joining ends through to the back of the material.   All designs must be planned with long unbroken lines, for which purpose the interlaced Celtic patterns are particularly suitable.

Cut Work.   A Cipher in Cut Work producing a rich lacy effect is shown in *Fig.* 227.   The embroidery is comparatively easy, but the design needs to be carefully planned △ as no portion of either letter must hang loose when the background is cut away.   A clever " interlaced effect " is shown in *Fig.* 227, with the letters " E. B. S." " tied up " at each point with a few extra bars for strengthening purposes.   First offset on the material and then outline with running stitch, working in any necessary bars at the same time.   The letters are then padded in the usual way and covered with satin stitches.   When all the embroidery is finished, cut away the background.   The work is rather fragile and better used on articles not frequently washed.   On delicate fabrics and silk stockingette scarves, first back with organdie and trim away afterwards.

Drawn Fabric Work.   *Fig.* 228 shows the initial " P " on a background of punch stitch, a favourite treatment for modern lettering.   △ The Punch Stitch background is worked first, after which pad and complete with satin stitch as before.   Any other drawn fabric stitch can be substituted and on broad thick letters an attractive effect is obtained by filling the letter itself, and leaving the background plain.

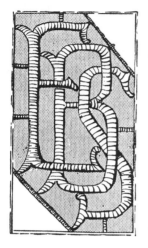

Fig. 227

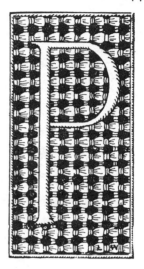

Fig. 228

Fig. 229

Initials and monograms in oriental letters are always popular for dress decoration and a complete alphabet, based on Chinese characters, is given in *Fig.* 229, which can be copied and worked in almost any of the methods previously described.

This also applies to the popular " sans serif " alphabet given in *Fig.* 230, which is employed to build up most of the ultra-modern ciphers and monograms now in use.

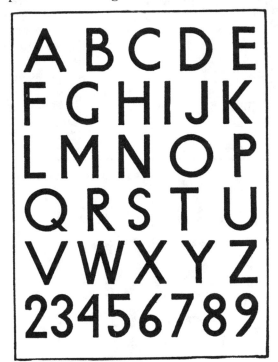

Fig. 230

JACOBEAN EMBROIDERY

J ACOBEAN EMBROIDERY is a rhapsody of the Restoration characterised more by its designs than by any particular working method or stitchery. The glorious colours were strongly influenced by the embroideries and printed fabrics of the Orient brought to England during this period, and the dominant motif—that of the Tree of Life—was enthusiastically adopted by the English embroiderers. This Eastern influence, coupled with Tudor tradition of delicate traceries and floral forms, produced what is popularly known as Jacobean work, although the name Stuart embroidery would perhaps be more correct.

The designs invariably displayed the central tree motif springing from a base of semi-circular hillocks known as " terra firma." The main stem, branching in all directions, bears leaf, flower and fruit of every conceivable kind. Very elaborate in conception, sometimes florid and utterly without counterpart in nature. That is its charm, captured without doubt from the riotous gaiety of the Restoration days.

The design shown at *Fig.* 231 (p. 180), based on the original pieces which abound in museums and private collections, is typical of its kind. No tree such as this ever grew on earth, yet of what irresistible charm and appeal. The characteristic acanthus-like leaf, extravagantly curled and quite out of proportion to the rest of the design grows beside the English rose (a national emblem), the carnation (a symbol of the Stuart family) the iris and the potato flower. Potatoes were news! not so long before imported by Raleigh, and still a rarity in the land. Strawberries, too, were new, and with these, bunches of grapes, pomegranates, vine-like tendrils, seed pods, interlacing stems, etc., found their place in this pleasing extravaganza. Birds, beasts and insects, each portraying some symbolic meaning, harts, rabbits, squirrels, snails, caterpillars, butterflies, birds and so on, reposed snugly in most Jacobean designs.

Fig. 231

The embroidery was worked in wools of rather soft but
dark shades on a stout twilled fabric and used for bed hangings, window curtains or wall panels. Some of the pieces
being planned on a very large scale. From then until now
the embroidery has remained a favourite type for reproduction,
its fascinating colour schemes and multitude of stitches being
an irresistible bait to every successive generation. A study
of the beautiful existing specimens in museums and collections
will give all the inspiration necessary for working out the

colour schemes and stitches, but since it is not given to every-
one to live within easy reach of a museum, the following
pages *attempt* to give a few brief suggestions as a guide for
the beginner.

Materials. Original Jacobean work was done on strong
natural coloured twilled cloth and twilled linens still make
the best choice, though other good quality linen may be used,
providing the weave is firm and close and the colour natural
or unbleached. Fine embroidery or tapestry wool is now
generally used, though some of the modern pieces are in
silks and mercerised cottons.

Colours. The predominant colour in most traditional pieces
is green, with blue and brown important secondaries. Several
shades of green were used, but softer tones, such as grey-green,
leaf-green were preferred. Blues of indigo variety, shading
to blue-grey were favoured with browns of warm chestnut
ranging to yellow. The soft dull reds were used sparingly,
likewise black and grey. These colours were not applied in
any naturalistic way, such as red and yellow for the fruit and
flowers, or green for leaves and stems, but mixed willy-nilly
throughout, using colour for colour's sake. A flower could
be brown with a blue centre, a leaf green with a blue or red
filling and so on, this mattered not since throughout the
leit-motif, green was maintained.

Green, shading from dark on the outer edge to yellow in
the centre, or vice versa, with darker colour inside was used
for the " terra firma." The animals were generally brown, and
insects worked in more or less natural colours. Stems shaded
from green to brown, green to yellow, or brown to yellow,
but the leaves and flowers obeyed no rules beyond keeping
green predominant. A few of the original designs maintain
deep indigo blue as the leit-motif throughout, but instances
of this are rare, though there is no law governing the leit-
motif and any colour could be used with proper attention
to the other shades. Modern workers with a sense of colour
should wave tradition aside and please themselves. △ After
all the old workers only selected green because it blended so
well with their furniture, but had pink been more suitable
it would most probably have been chosen!

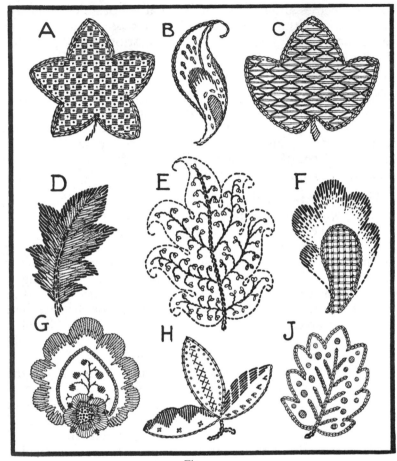

Fig. 232

Stitches.   These in common with design and colour obeyed no rule, but those most frequently found are long-and-short, satin, stem and outline, buttonhole, chain, split, coral and a variety of couched fillings, employing cross, fly, cretan, herringbone and French knots.*

The best explanatory method is to take a few typical examples of leaves, flowers, fruits, etc., with suggestions for stitches.   But these are by no means dogmatic, merely a guide to study and further experiment, with possibly a closer comprehensive understanding of this most fascinating subject.

LEAVES

Fig. 232. A. Outlined with chain stitch and filled with four block satin stitches arranged in chessboard fashion with French knot between each.

B. Outlined left with chain stitch, right stem stitch. Filling: Long-tailed daisy stitch, long-and-short, satin and running stitches.

C. Outlined with chain stitch, filled with couched lines arranged horizontally and diagonally.

D. Entirely long-and-short stitch with running stitch for the veining.

E. Outlined in running stitch, centre vein in chain stitch, and branches in stem stitch ending in daisy stitch.

F. Outlined in long-and-short stitch, centre outlined in chain stitch, couched with chessboard filling.

G. Outlined in long-and-short with centre in chain, satin and stem stitch. Floweret in satin stitch centred with French knots.

H. Outlined with couching, buttonhole, satin and stem stitch. Herringbone stitch and French knots fill the centre leaf, cross stitches the left and fly stitches the right leaf.

J. Outlined with chain stitch, veining in chain stitch, and spots in satin stitch.

FLOWERS

Fig. 233. A. Rose in long and short stitch, couched filling for centre outlined with chain stitch.

B. Potato flower worked in chain stitch with satin stitch and French knot for centre.

C. Geum outlined in stem stitch and darning with French knots for centre.

D. Carnation outlined with long and short and back stitch, with chain stitch and daisy stitch on the calyx.

E. Passion flower in buttonhole, stem and satin stitch. Fly stitch on the petals, central stamens of fishbone and others of stem stitch with French knots.

F. Fuchsia outlined with satin and stem stitch, darning stitch on the petals, stem and satin stitch for the stamens.

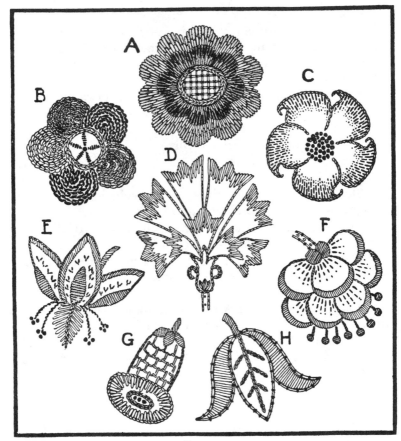

Fig. 233

G. Canterbury Bell outlined in stem and buttonhole stitch, filled with blanket, chain stitch and French knots.

H. Iris outlined with couching, filled with solid satin stitch, veining in chain stitch.

FRUIT AND ANIMALS

Fig. 234. A. Berries worked in satin and daisy stitch. Stems in stem stitch.

B. Grapes filled entirely with concentric rows of chain stitch.

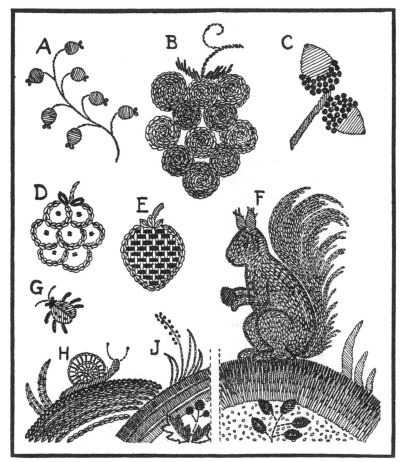

Fig. 234

C. Acorns in satin stitch and French knots.

D. Berries outlined in chain stitch, details in satin stitch and daisy stitch.

E. Strawberry outlined in chain stitch, filling of surface darning, leaves in daisy stitch.

F. Squirrel outlined with chain stitch and filled with split stitch, tail in stem stitch, ears satin stitch and " terra firma " in brick stitch with seed stitch. Leaf spray in cretan stitch.

G. Beetle in satin stitch with chain stitch legs. Antennæ in stem stitch.

H. Snail in satin, stem and straight stitch, antennæ in running stitch. " Terra firma " in chain stitch.

J. Flower spray and leaves in stem stitch and French knots. " Terra firma " in buttonhole stitch.

STEMS

Fig. 235. A. Wide stem outlined in heavy chain stitch filled with rows of blanket stitch.

B. Wide stem in brick stitch.

C. Wide stem outlined in Vandyke buttonhole stitch with satin stitch spots down the centre.

D. Stem left outlined with blanket stitch, right chain stitch and darning filling.

E. Narrow stem three rows of stem stitch, flanked with two straight stitches either side.

F. Stem in chevron satin stitch.

G. Stem in stem stitch with daisy stitches on either side.

H. Stem outlined in chain stitch with running stitch centre.

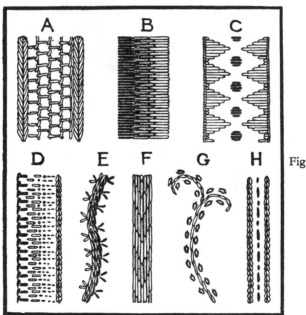

Fig. 235

MOUNTMELLICK EMBROIDERY

CONTRARY to most other forms of white work, there are no open or drawn spaces in Mountmellick Embroidery. The stitches are planned to lie on the surface of the material with as little thread as possible beneath, and to provide the sense of "stitchery in relief." The embroidery is of a bold, coarse nature, producing the maximum effect with the minimum number of stitches. It covers the ground quickly, and yet withal has a quality of great charm and achievement, since each stitch is intelligently chosen, both with regard to its æsthetic and practical interpretation. A typical example is shown in *Fig*. 236, which reveals how this art of stitchery and variety in grouping quite compensates the loss of any variety in colour. The aim is realism.

The bramble berries are bold, even semi-spherical as the Bullion Knots, are hooped to give the effect of high relief, gradually decreasing in size from the centre, while the main stem effects the rough prickly character of the bush in Braid Stitch. The leaves obey no law of nature, except in outline, each filling being different, and one half rarely a repeat of the other. The frequent and profuse use of bullion knots is a characteristic of the work, and here they are seen grouped singly and in pairs to form spike-like leaves, while a massive border in fancy buttonhole stitch carries the weight of the heavy embroidery to the edge with a feeling of balance and proportion. The original work was generally finished with a heavy knitted fringe.

This embroidery is a peasant work of Ireland and takes its name from the town of Mountmellick in Leinster, where it was originated by a lady member of the Society of Friends, who taught it to the poor folk as a means of livelihood. It is used for mats, table cloths, cushions, bedspreads, curtains and other household articles.

Designs. Realism being the aim, the designs are realistic and no conventionalised forms are used. Almost any flower or fruit can be reproduced, but the favourite subjects are those which nature intended to be rough and nobbly in character, such as the bramble, thistle, wild rose, wheat, barley, poppy, pomegranate and so forth. Should the more delicate plants be chosen, the flowers are generally padded and all stitch variety left to the leaves and stems, such as *Figs.* 239 and 241. △ Considerable attention is necessary in designing the border, which must be bold and strong in character, otherwise the work peters out unsatisfactorily at the edge. The old method of using a bold knitted fringe does not appeal to modern taste and to offset the important loss of this, a broad border of scallops should be formed, worked in irregular stitchery, as in *Fig.* 236. If plain scalloping is used, then one, two or three rows of stitching are added within the scallops to give greater weight and importance. A favourite way of linking up the embroidery with the edge is to use a powdering of French knots.

THREADS AND MATERIALS

Both threads and materials are of a coarse variety. A soft strong cotton with a coarser for the padding stitches and a finer for the details is needed, but not so fine that it merges into the material, or the effect is poor. Any strong heavy material can be used, a closely woven linen or even a drill, since the weave does not matter as the work is not done on counted threads. Modern materials suggest great adventures for the ambitious worker, and in this age of fast dyes, there is every reason to use coloured fabrics with a matching embroidery thread.

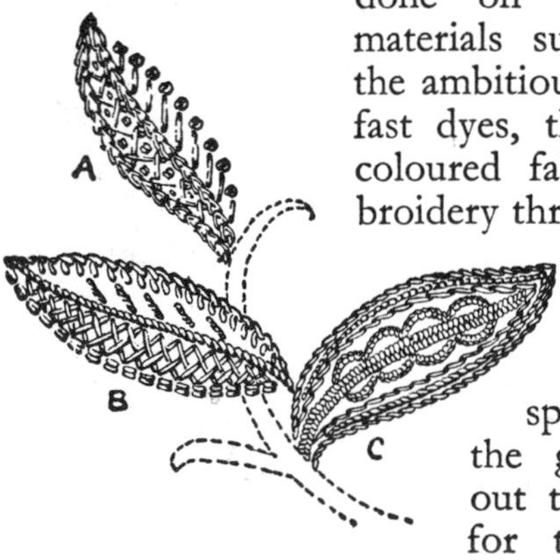

Fig. 237

STITCHES

Variety of stitchery is the spice and joy of the work, and the great diversity of working out the leaves affords vast scope for the imagination. *Fig.* 237 gives an interesting group of three.

Fig. 236

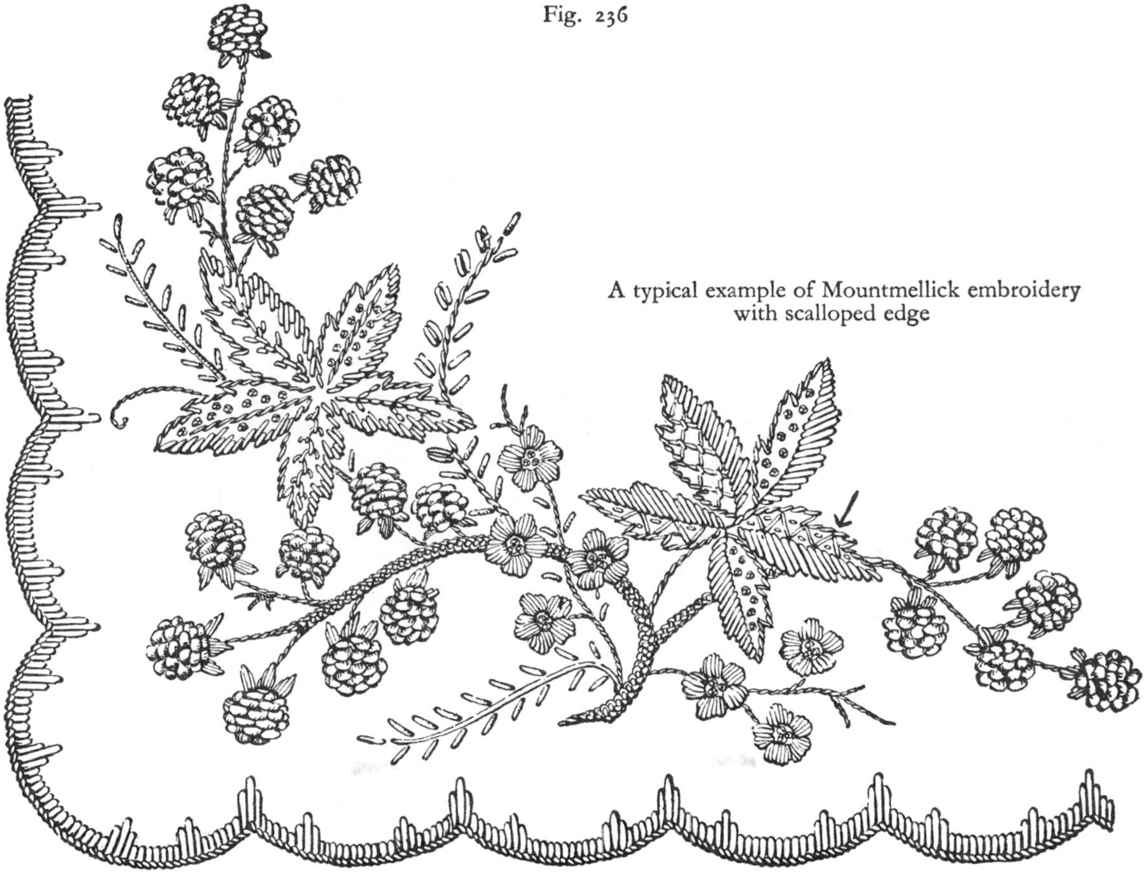

A typical example of Mountmellick embroidery with scalloped edge

That at A shows a vein and one half of the leaf outlined in chain stitch filled with herringbone and dot stitch. The other half is in "porcupine stitch." This consists of a long straight stitch taken from the base to the top where a small stitch is made in the direction of the slant, after which the long stitch is overcast two or three times without entering the material to the base. Here the needle is inserted into the same hole and carried along beneath to the next long stitch. When all are completed the points are decorated with French knots. LEAF B. Vein is whipped running stitch, lower edge in dot stitch filled with close herringbone stitch, upper half outlined with buttonhole stitch, with veins of bullion knots. LEAF C. Centre vein is a detached woven bar. Four long threads are thrown from the base to the tip of leaf and the thread woven under two and over two until a solid detached bar is formed. This is kept in position with the buttonhole loops either side. There are four of these loops, made with five large blanket stitches, the looped edge being placed away from the centre vein and the stitch just piercing the edge of the bar to hold it in position. These

Fig. 238

loops are then covered with button stitch, passing from loop to loop without a break and without taking the needle through the material as they are all quite detached. The outline of the leaf is then completed with two rows of stem stitching centred with a row of whipped running stitches.

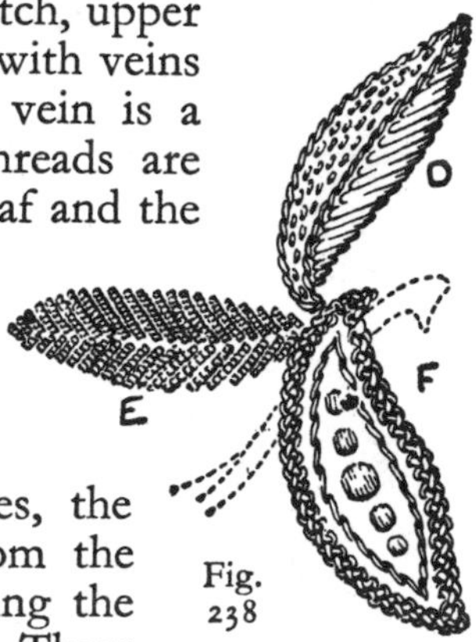

Fig. 238. LEAF D. Outline of stem stitch. Left side filled with darning stitches. Right, padded satin stitch.

LEAF E is composed entirely of bullion knots.

LEAF F. Outline of braid stitch, inner outline in stem stitch and vein in satin stitch spots.

Other leaf fillings in French knots, feather stitch, back stitch and couched diamond lattice will be seen in *Fig.* 236. The leaf marked with an arrow is filled with reverse herringbone stitch, worked from right to left. Bring the thread through at the arrow and make the next stitch on the lower line and to the right of the first, and bring the needle out still

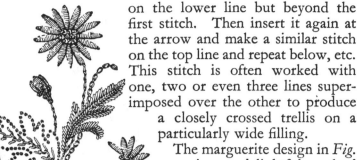

Fig. 239

on the lower line but beyond the first stitch. Then insert it again at the arrow and make a similar stitch on the top line and repeat below, etc. This stitch is often worked with one, two or even three lines superimposed over the other to produce a closely crossed trellis on a particularly wide filling.

The marguerite design in *Fig.* 239 gives a delightful method of producing high relief on a simple flower not naturally rough in character. The petals and buds are in padded satin stitch worked across the width of the petal, centred with French knots, larger in the centre to impart a spherical effect. The calyx of each bud is also of French knots. The solid leaf is in Cretan stitch with the turn over at the bottom right and that at

Fig. 240

the extreme base in single blanket stitch. The two larger leaves are outlined in French knots, one having a vein of feather stitch and the other below a vein and offshoots in braid stitch and bullion knots. Stalks of braid stitch, French knots and cable stitch.

The method of working braid stitch is shown in *Fig.* 240. Here it will be seen how very different this stitch appears used as a line stitch spaced wide apart from that when worked in close formation with wider and closer stitches (*see* Leaf F, *Fig.* 238). Always pull the loop up tightly round the needle before drawing it through as shown in the diagram.

Fig. 241

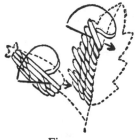

Fig. 242

The wild rose in *Fig.* 241 is characteristic. The flower petals are bordered in padded satin stitch with centre of satin and porcupine stitch. The berries are in Bokhara Couching with tips of satin. The leaves on one half are all outlined with stem or blanket stitch, filled with darning stitches or bullion and French knots, while the solid parts are filled with Roumanian Couching, or Indian Stitch as it is often known when associated with this embroidery. The working methods of Bokhara Couching and Indian Stitch are shown in *Fig.* 242. For the first, on the berry, a long thread is carried across the space (not too tightly) and tied down with small slanting stitches made on the return journey. △ The stitches are quite small on the surface and placed at regular intervals to form pattern lines across the work. A space of any size can be filled. For Indian stitch, the needle emerges on the leaf vein and is carried over to the edge and emerges to the right of the stitch, almost in the centre. The next stitch is made as shown by the arrow.

Fig. 243 shows the pomegranate design on a slipper front with various different leaf fillings and an edging of Mountmellick knitted fringe. The pomegranate is outlined in stem stitch with couched diamond filling and head of porcupine stitches and French knots. *Fig.* 244 gives two other ways of filling pomegranates. That at A is outlined in plaited edge stitch filled with French knots, with stem and detached buttonhole loops*

Fig. 243

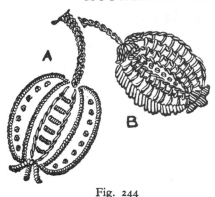

Fig. 244

down the centre.   Stalk of braid stitch.   That at **B** has a filling of spaced button-hole stitch worked from left to right with the next row from right to left, and so on.   The stitches of the second row are fitted between those of the first and the needle pierces the material with each stitch, though if preferred this filling can be worked detached.

KNITTED FRINGE

Use knitting or crochet cotton and knit with four threads simultaneously, four separate balls of cotton being kept in action at the same time.   The fringe works out surprisingly wide and a small length of four inches should be made and frayed out as an experiment.   Twelve stitches in a coarse crochet cotton will produce a fringe 6″ wide; only six stitches were used for the slipper fringe.   There are two methods of working.   Method 1 produces long horizontal lines of solid knitting and fringe as on the slipper, Method 2, diagonal lines and fringe.

Method 1. Work with four threads and cast on a number divisible by three, six for slipper.   1st Row. K. 1 (passing all four threads over the needle together), Make 1, K. 2 together, and repeat to end of row.   2nd Row. Same as first and repeat until sufficient length for article is knitted and cast off as follows: With six stitches on the needle cast off three only in the usual way and here cut thread and draw through last stitch to finish.   Slip the three last stitches off the needle and unravel to form the fringe.

Method 2. Cast on a number of stitches, divisible by three, say 12, using from four balls as before.   To commence: Make 1, K. 1. K. 2 together.   Repeat.   2nd Row. Same as first.   Cast off seven stitches and unravel the remaining five to form the fringe.

△ Crochet does not make a good substitute for this fringe,

it has quite a different character and a scalloped edge is preferable.

The following is a list of stitches, suitable for Mountmellick Embroidery, the working instructions for each being given in the Dictionary:

Single, Double, Closed and Spanish Knotted Feather Stitches. Zigzag Coral Stitch. Cloud Filling. Twisted Chain, Threaded Chain, Rosette Chain, Knotted Chain and Feathered Chain Stitches. Knotted Buttonhole and Crossed Buttonhole Stitch. Fern Stitch. Detached Overcast Stitch. Double Knot Stitch. Petal Stitch. Scroll Stitch. Whipped Satin Stitch. Whipped Stem and Portuguese Knotted Stem Stitch. Vandyke Stitch. Closed and Open Wave Stitch. Loop Stitch. Raised Honeycomb Filling and Fly Stitch Filling.

NEEDLEWEAVING

NEEDLEWEAVING is a decoration woven upon the warp or weft of the material after certain threads have been withdrawn. It is a form of drawn thread work and is often known as woven hemstitching when done in narrow borders on linen. Needlewoven borders are far stronger than most forms of hemstitching, as the withdrawn threads are replaced again by the woven decoration. It is a very ancient craft, and early examples have been found in Egyptian tombs dating back over 3,000 years, while many of the lovely Coptic fabrics treasured in our museums bear this form of decoration, often, it is supposed, woven in by hand upon the loom during the actual process of weaving.

Designs can be worked out on graph paper and usually consist of geometrical patterns based on the square or diamond, arranged in diagonal or zigzag lines to form border decoration for chair backs, towel ends, runners and so on. The pattern can be (1) repeating motifs or (2) arranged symmetrically to fill a certain space. △ Long vertical lines should be avoided, as they cause gaps which are difficult to negotiate on a design worked out in several colours. But there is an exception to this rule as when weaving in *one* colour only, the thread can be kept much tighter and then these gaps and long lines actually contribute to the charm of the pattern (*see Fig. 256*). The simplest pattern for Needleweaving is shown in *Fig. 245*, comprising two blocks in two different colours.

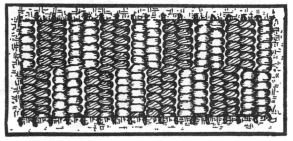

Fig. 245

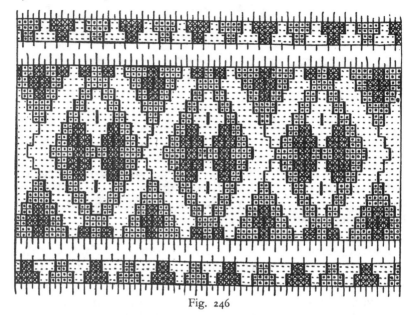

Fig. 246

Fig. 246 shows an elaborate repeating design with small subsidiary borders above and below, prepared as a chart to be worked out in three or more colours.

The nature of the work must be considered in planning wide borders which necessitate the withdrawal of many threads, and which make the work difficult and unwieldy to handle. Plan the border in strips or sections, as in *Fig.* 247, leaving between each a few weft threads of the material for strengthening purposes. These scarcely disturb the symmetry of the design

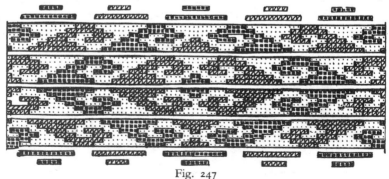

Fig. 247

at all, and the weaving is more easily worked in narrow sections, one at a time.

Materials. Choose loosely woven materials such as linen, crash, or huckaback. Most furnishing fabrics are excellent. The thread, wool or silk chosen for the weaving should be a little thicker than the withdrawn threads. Use a blunt-pointed needle.

Colours. Bright basic colours similar to peasant embroideries are better for this work as the paler half-tones are rather lacking in character. A simple pattern can be strikingly worked out in one colour only and is often preferred on household articles.

WORKING METHODS

The beginner should commence with a simple design such as *Fig.* 245, as the technique of the work needs a little practice to acquire, but once the method of " passing " from group to group and colour to colour has been mastered, the more elaborate patterns may be confidently tackled. *Fig.* 245 is used as an explanatory model.

First withdraw the necessary threads (the number will vary with the width of border required), but an inch will be sufficient as a model. △ These are not removed across the full width of the material but a narrow margin of about an inch is left either side. *Figs*. 248 and 249 show the respective methods of withdrawing threads on (1) fine and (2) coarse materials, and how to dispose of the ends. In *Fig.* 248 the fine threads are cut across in short lengths

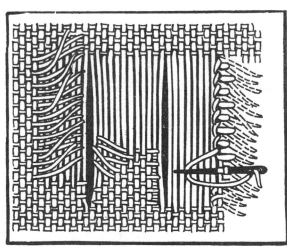

Fig. 248

Fig. 249

and quickly withdrawn. The side ends are then turned back and first buttonholed and then trimmed. On coarse materials (*Fig.* 249) the process differs as the weft threads are cut once only across the △ centre of the border and unravelled to the left and then to the right without breaking. Upon reaching the limit of the border each is threaded into a needle and woven back into the material either end to neaten the sides. This weaving must be done accurately, over and under each material thread, as in the diagrams.

The next step, that of hemstitching the top and bottom of the border (*Fig.* 250) is optional, but very helpful to the beginner

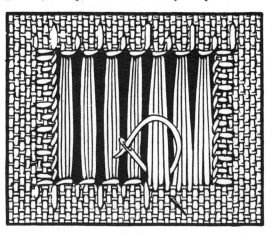

Fig. 250

as it makes a regular unit of four threads to the bundle and obviates the necessity of constantly counting, but it is better to omit the hemstitching altogether on fine materials. At this point the border is ready for decorating.

THE WEAVING PROCESS

The weaving must be as neat on the back of the work as the front and all thread ends are disposed of after the weaving process is finished. Commence by running the thread (unknotted) into the material an inch or two above the first block of weaving (*see* A in *Fig.* 251), leaving sufficient length to be pulled out later and threaded for finishing. The needle is now brought through at the arrow between the material and

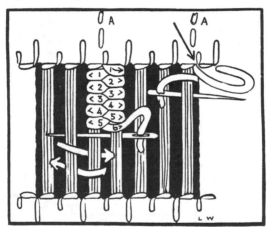

Fig. 251

the first bundle of threads and a stitch made to the right over three threads of the material, then out and over the bar, and back again under the bar and into the material, and so on until a block half the width of the border has been worked. The method of passing to the next block, which this time is worked over the first and second bars, is shown by the second needle. After this the weaving continues as before, alternately over and under the two bars, until the bottom of the border is reached. The numbers and arrowheads show the journey of the thread, △ and the needle must always come up in between the two bars, and down on the left and right alternately. Upon reaching the bottom of the border, run the thread loosely into

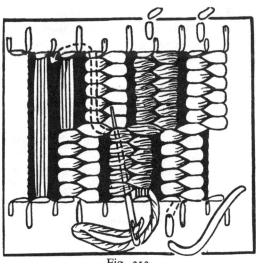

Fig. 252

the material for an inch or two and leave it until next required. The weaving is now commenced again at the top in the second colour and proceeds exactly as before. (The first block of a border is of necessity different as part is taken through the material.) *Fig.* 252 shows the border in progress, also the method of " passing " a thread of one colour over another to its next position by slipping it invisibly between the woven blocks. By this means two different coloured threads in two needles can be used along the border with the minimum amount of starting and finishing off.

△ A completed block of weaving is shown in *Fig.* 253, and this " key " should be studied with care as it shows with arrows and numbers the entire journey of each thread in composing a block, and once this principle is understood the technique of needleweaving is mastered. Each bar must be packed quite firm and tight by pushing the weaving well up together as the needle comes up between the two bundles, and notice with care how the passing is made from one block to another, the right thread always above

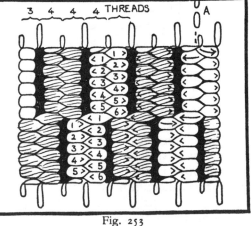

Fig. 253

the left in order to keep the correct " pull " throughout the pattern.

FINISHING OFF

When all the needleweaving is completed there will remain a small portion of the material still uncovered at the beginning and end of the border, which is covered with overcasting stitches (*Fig.* 254) in the appropriate colours. It should be noticed that while the weaving is done over four loose threads, the overcasting is only taken over three threads, as the material does not " close up " so readily as the loose bars.

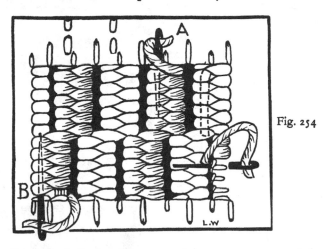

Fig. 254

The thread ends left in the material are now unpicked, threaded into a needle and slipped invisibly inside the blocks as shown at A and B, and the border as shown at *Fig.* 245 is then completed.

In complicated patterns the weaving will frequently cover several bars instead of two, as in the counterchange pattern along the extreme top and bottom of *Fig.* 246. This is woven over four bars, but the method is exactly the same, and providing the weaving and passing is done in the correct order, there should be no difficulty.

△ When weaving a complicated design, it is better to commence in the centre of the border and from here work outwards to the left and then to the right to ensure the pattern being centrally placed.   In multi-coloured designs the weaving should not be pulled to form noticeable gaps, but quite the contrary when weaving in one colour only.

Needlewoven borders are usually finished with some simple embroidery stitches as suggested in *Fig.* 255, arranged in broken lines to soften the hard decisive line of the weaving.   At A, Blanket and Holbein stitches are used, and at B satin stitches are arranged in vandyke form to give a pleasing finish whilst at C a more elaborate effect is obtained by placing a wide line of ladder hemstitching* above and below the woven border, secured with herringbone stitches.   Any number of these simple little borders can be evolved with a little experiment and patience.

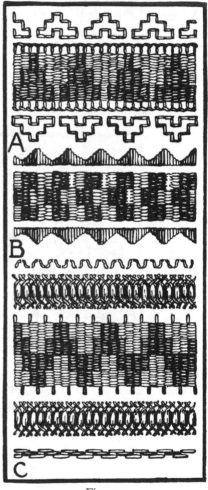

Fig. 255

WOVEN HEMSTITCH

Needleweaving in self colours or in white on white material is rather more openwork in design, and overcast bars as shown in *Fig.* 256 are often introduced. The work as mentioned before is drawn more firmly to produce a pronounced open effect, so while lacking in colour it makes up with a peculiar lace-like charm of its own induced by this tightening up process.   This form of needleweaving is often referred to as Woven Hemstitching.   The method is a little different and requires some manipulation in order to avoid breaking the thread too often. The block at A is first woven over four bars, merging into two bars. Beneath this the single bar to the right is then overcast and the needle slipped up through the overcasting as directed by the arrow, and taken invisibly through the woven block above in order to overcast the left bar. After this the weaving is continued below. Each shaded block in the diagram is worked in a similar way, leaving the long single bars until later. These are then commenced at B. Overcast downwards to the middle portion which is woven, and then proceed with the over-casting to C. Here the needle is taken down through the weaving and up through the next block as invisibly as possible to D, when the overcasting is continued up the left side to the top. This process is repeated all along the border until it is completed.

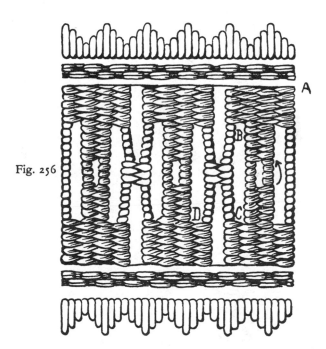

Fig. 256

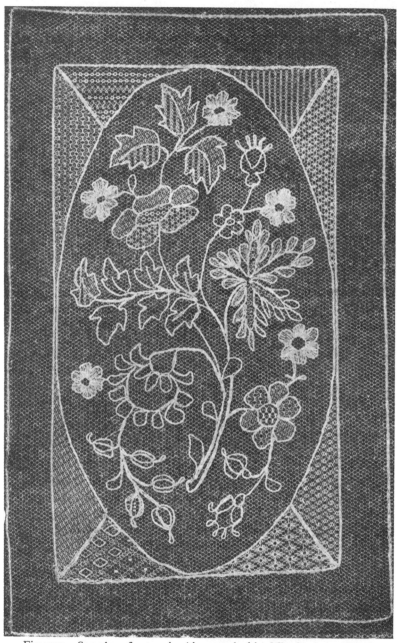

Fig. 257. Sampler of net embroidery worked by Miss H. Lyon Wood, unfinished to show working methods

NET EMBROIDERY

NET EMBROIDERY is an elementary form of lace perfected in Limerick and Imitation Brussels Lace. It is delicate and dainty in appearance and can be used for edgings on lingerie, modesty vests, scarves, covers, or wedding veils, etc.

Designs. There are two forms of design. The first, free and realistic, is illustrated in the " Sampler of Net Embroidery " opposite, *Fig.* 257 (the reproduction is about two-thirds the size of the original). Here the delicate simple lines of the floral motif are all connected up to the central branch and the design void of any isolated spots. △ This is typical, as the work permits of few breaks, and demands simplicity of outline, as the detail is rich, each flower petal and leaf being filled with a different stitch to enhance the lacy effect. The leaf and flower on the left are purposely left unfilled to show the progress of the work. Eight different filling stitches are used, and these are all recorded at the four corners in sampler fashion and described later in detail. This first type of design is worked out on paper, and then traced in bold lines upon a blue wax paper. For any repeating pattern or corner motif it is only necessary to draw out one unit and move as desired.

The second form of design is geometric and shown in diagram form in *Fig.* 258. Here it will be seen how the pattern is strictly governed by the diagonal direction of the net. (This is shown here and in all other diagrams in diamond formation, instead of hexagonal, to avoid confusion, but it does not affect the working method at all.) The embroidery is worked in darning stitch and the pattern evolved by counting the mesh of the net. Any number of repeating borders and motifs can be evolved after this style with a little practice. △ It will be found that the net is not made with the same number of holes to the inch in both directions and this should be taken into consideration when planning a design.

Materials and Colours. Only the best quality hexagonal net

Fig. 258

or tulle, such as Brussels, should be used as the cheaper nets
shrink and tear so easily in the wash. To test a good net
insert a stiletto into one of the meshes, which should stretch
but not break.

Use a fine linen floss for all the outlines, with a much finer
lace thread of " cobwebby " texture, similar to that of the
net itself for the filling stitches. Net embroidery is usually
worked on white or parchment net with a matching thread, but
a net of blue, brown, black or any other colour can be used and
the floral type of design worked in naturalistic colours, or the
geometric in bright jazz effects.

WORKING METHODS

The design must be traced in bold outline on waxed tracing
paper (preferably blue, as this shows up better and does not
try the eyes), and laid on the table and over this the net △
which is tacked down on each of the four sides (*see Fig.* 259).
This shows the net covering one half of the pattern only to

demonstrate how clearly the design shows through for the outlining; which is run in with a blunt-pointed needle, taking each stitch in and out of the mesh in a darning movement. △ The outlining should be as continuous and unbroken as possible, and a new thread run in alongside the end of the other, as no knots are used. The stems or stalks are usually formed of double thread and this is a convenient place to make a join. Continuity of outline is illustrated in *Fig.* 259, where

Fig. 259

the thread travels from the petal of the centre flower, enclosing the two leaf sprays in the journey, and back again to the starting point without a break. Keep the thread pulled just tight enough to form a clear and defined outline, without puckering.

If the pattern is a repeating one, the tracing is removed after the outlining is complete and placed further along with the △ pattern joining up accurately. The net is again tacked in position and the outlining continued. This process is repeated until the border or outline is complete, when the tracing is removed and the work is ready for the filling stitches.

THE FILLING STITCHES

The number of filling stitches and the various different combinations of these stitches is legion, and it is only possible to give here in diagram form the eight filling stitches arranged at the four corners of the sampler in *Fig.* 257. These eight are the most popular and widely used and will form a good basis for study.

The diagrams themselves are practically self-explanatory and a brief word concerning each with a reference to their position on the sampler for comparison is all that is required. The description begins with the filling in the top left-hand corner (lower half), and from here each stitch is described separately in clock rotation round the sampler.

Eyelet Pattern (Fig. 260). A simple all-over filling of tiny

Fig. 260

holes (top left-hand corner, lower half), also on petals of flower.

Herringbone and Ring Pattern (Fig. 261). Work a row of ordinary herringbone stitch alternating with a row of tiny rings made by carrying the thread twice round the outside of a mesh.

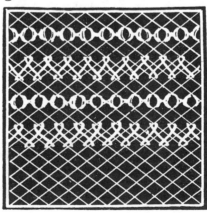

Fig. 261

To pass from ring to ring make an overcasting stitch round the intervening mesh. (Top left-hand corner, upper half.)

Ridge Pattern (Fig. 262). Made by working rows of cross stitches in two journeys. The first journey upwards is shown to the right of the diagram with the return journey half com-

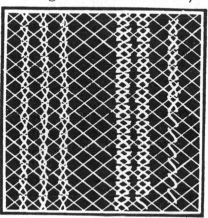

Fig. 262

pleted. Two loosely worked rows appear in the middle of the diagram, but in order to achieve the " ridge " effect, the stitches must be pulled up so that the crosses take the elongated form shown to the left. (Top right-hand corner), also on the leaves, and looks like stripes.

Chequer Pattern (Fig. 263). This delightful filling appears

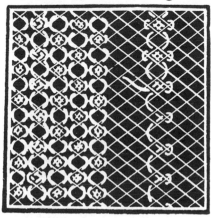

Fig. 263

almost solid in effect.   Each row is worked in two journeys, the method being shown in the isolated and unfinished row to the right of the diagram (Top right corner, lower half), and on the largest flower, and looks like elongated spots.

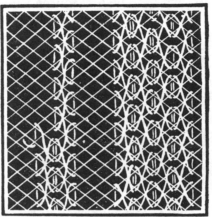

Fig. 264

Herringbone Pattern (*Fig.* 264).   Herringbone stitch is again used to make the filling but instead of taking the stitches behind the intersection of each mesh as for *Fig.* 261, they are taken behind one complete mesh to get a broader effect.   A single row and part of the second row are shown for construction (Lower right-hand corner, top half), and builds up small circles.

Diamond Pattern (*Fig.* 265) is a great favourite, but since each

Fig. 265

unit is rather larger than most fillings, it shows to better advantage on larger shapes. The diamonds are worked in two journeys, the first journey completing one half of a diamond and the second the opposite half, as clearly seen in the diagram. It should be noticed how the long vertical stitch in the centre is carried across from the centre of one diamond to the centre of the next. This stitch is repeated on the second journey, causing a double link-up stitch all along the row (Bottom right corner, lower half).

Lattice Pattern (*Fig.* 266). This filling, like Diamond Pattern,

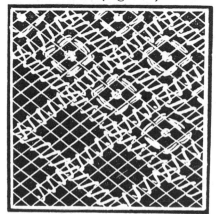

Fig. 266

is rather large and looks better set in larger shapes. The long diagonal lines are overcast first in one direction and then in the other to form a lattice. Each diamond is then filled with a smaller diamond of darning stitches centred with a spot which is reached by twisting round the intervening lines of the mesh (Bottom left corner, lower half), which also gives an alternate method of using this filling.

Diagonal Pattern (*Fig.* 267) produces an effect of faint diagonal lines over the surface and is surprisingly effective yet easy to work. The stitch is made in a wide overcast movement in vertical rows as shown in the isolated row which gives the construction quite clearly (Bottom left corner, top half), and on the petals and leaves of the top spray.

Fig. 267

All fillings used in net embroidery should be worked with as few joins as possible and no break or join must ever occur in the middle of a row. Commence by securing the thread invisibly to the outline and fasten off in the same way. Any of the fillings described here may be arranged vertically or horizontally and in a shape of any size.

The five solid looking little flowers shown in the sampler (*Fig.* 257) are obtained by darning the thread backwards and forwards from the centre to the edge of the petals until each is filled. The method is only suitable for quite small shapes but provides a pleasant contrast to the delicacy of the other fillings.

GEOMETRICAL BORDERS

The geometric border shown in *Fig.* 258 is worked entirely in darning stitch with the exception of the broad vandyke line near the bottom which is satin stitch. The darning should be done with as few breaks as possible, and in order to do this it may be necessary to take an occasional extra stitch or re-trace a mesh or two, but this is quite permissible and will not be noticeable (*see* Filet Darning, *page* 133). All double outlines such as those just above and below the broad vandyke line are better worked in two journeys (*Fig.* 258). Here the upper line with its offshoots are worked in the first journey, and the lower row on the second journey. This can be followed quite clearly in the diagram, and the principle should be applied to all designs of this nature.

Should the border be finished with a straight edge, then the net could be used double as a hem with the fold falling along the edge of the pattern and secured in working the design. Finished with a vandyke edge, the net must be cut a mesh or two beyond the edge of the design, and then turned under and caught down as invisibly as possible to the back of the stitching.

PATCHWORK

PATCHWORK is the art of joining small pieces of material together in patterns of geometric formation. The work is most fascinating and wholly creative as the scraps which otherwise would find their way into the rubbish basket are assembled into articles of great beauty and utility. A triumphant example is shown in *Fig.* 268 (*page* 214), part of a large curtain made in the 19th century. The motifs are all cut from the scale template and assembled into large diamonds and finally applied to a background of plain material. Each patch, colour and print is cleverly placed with thought, care and ability. Contrast this with crazy work, which so often passes as patchwork! Even so, out of that jumbled mass of fabrics once wedded without thought or reason, the modern worker is evolving something original and symbolic of our age as shown in *Fig.* 269. The design is restless, each piece a

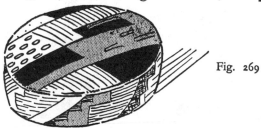

Fig. 269

different shape, yet withal pleasingly united. Such work is individual in expression, and without method, but the older and more scientific forms can be brought to rule and note, and once mastered will pave the way to any modern interpretations.

Patchwork can be used to make almost any article. In the days of our great-grandmothers it served for quilts, curtains, rugs, chair upholsteries, cushions and coverlets, etc., as it offered this practical and economical purpose of using up odd bits; while the luxurious finish of wadding and quilting instead of just lining was often used, especially for bed covers.

Fig. 268.   A glorious example of early 19th century English Patchwork
forming part of a curtain

Materials. To-day, materials are often bought for patchwork, as we have grown more fastidious about colour schemes, yet the old method of using up scraps has much in its favour, and the charm of this work can be lost by over-cultivation and too close an imitation of printed fabrics. In choosing odd scraps, as a basis of work, the practical proviso of not mixing washable materials with those of an unwashable nature should be remembered. △ Also, a more regular effect is produced by keeping the same kinds of fabric together on any one article— that is, linens and cottons together, silks and satins together, and so on.

The colours need to be skilfully balanced, especially when working out patterns such as shown in *Figs.* 272 and 273, as a bright patch in the wrong position could upset the whole mosaic. An effort to balance the various printed or plain-coloured pieces over the whole surface must also be made in order to produce a harmonious whole. Any decorative stitching is better in neutral shades chosen to blend with the background colours. Bold modern geometric designs are often composed of plain linens either in contrasting colours or in several tones of the same colour with very beautiful results. *See Fig.* 270, a linen quilt in three colours only.

Fig. 270

DESIGNS

Patchwork designs are " built " by the aid of a template,

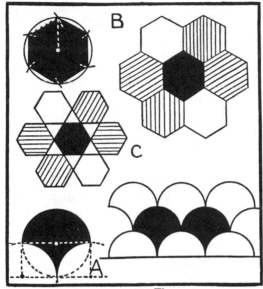

Fig. 271

and the old patch-work of the 18th and 19th centuries was usually based on the units shown in *Fig.* 271 A, the " Scale," and B, the " Hexagon." In each case the method of con-structing the tem-plate and the pattern it builds, is shown. The hexagon pro-duces the famous " Honeycomb de-sign " (B), and the " Scale " is that used for the magnifi-cent curtain in *Fig.* 268. (Both units are based on the circle, and for a hexagon the radius is marked off six times round the circumference to obtain the shape.) A variation of the honeycomb pattern is shown at C. This includes small tri-angles the shape and size of which form a one-sixth section of the hexagon unit, and a template can be made in this way.

Designs based on a square are given in *Fig.* 272. At A the

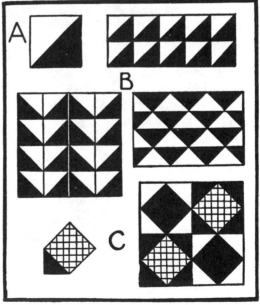

Fig. 272

interesting suggestion of splitting a square diagonally is shown, together with the resulting pattern.   At B two clever variations of this same unit are arranged in different formations. The unit at C comprises a square and a quarter square, and together build up the delightful mosaic-like design shown to the right.

All the designs shown in *Fig.* 273 are evolved from the diamond unit shown in the top left-hand corner.   In each case

Fig. 273

the diamonds are set at different angles and this, together with the judicious placing of different colours, produces the illusion of solid blocks.

In seeking new ideas for patchwork designs, study those made for mosaic, tiling and parquet flooring.   Different templates could then be constructed in cardboard and the mosaic reproduced in patchwork.

WORKING METHODS

The progressive diagrams shown in *Fig.* 274 give the entire working process for geometrical patchwork.   The first

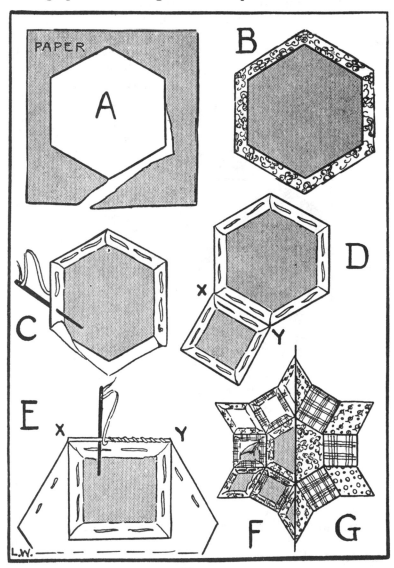

Fig. 274

requisite is plenty of thick paper, either brown or white. The selected template from which the pattern will be built is then placed upon the paper and cut to shape as at A. Quite a number of similar shapes are then cut, each being an accurate reproduction of the original template. △ Next cut the pieces of material, using the same template but allowing ¼″ turnings all round as at B, laying the patch right side down and over it the paper shape. The material is then turned back over the edges of the paper and tacked, taking the stitches through the paper and material as shown at C. Having prepared several patches in this way, they may be joined together in the following way.

Fit two patches together as at D, with the edges X Y touching, wrong sides uppermost. Then overcast, using a fine needle and thread as at E, taking care that the needle does not pierce the paper backing △. Each patch is joined to the next in this way, and the size of the article gradually increases. When a single patch is entirely surrounded by others, it is sometimes convenient to pull out the tacking threads and remove the paper backing, as this can then be used again. The back of the work in progress is shown at F, and the reverse or front at G in *Fig.* 274. When the whole article is complete, the final tacking threads and papers are removed and the patchwork pressed on the wrong side.

The addition of any decorative stitching on the front of the work is quite optional, but feather stitch is the most popular (*Fig.* 275), and herringbone stitch a good second (*Fig.* 276), though any narrow line stitch* will serve for this purpose.

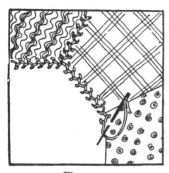

Fig. 275

Fig. 276

All patchwork articles must be finished with a lining, and this is slip-stitched all round the outer edge of the work on the wrong side. Bed covers are often interlined and quilted, working run stitch round the outline of each patch.

DECORATIVE JOINS

A less solid effect is given to patchwork by joining the patches with open seams (*see page* 243). The most usual method is to work buttonhole or blanket stitch over the turned-in edge of each patch and join by whipping together the looped edges of the stitching. Another suggestion is to blanket stitch all the edges and then work into the blanket stitching a single row of double crochet, and afterwards whip the edges of the crochet together. This produces an openwork effect rather like an insertion. The methods demand fairly large patches to build up the design.

CANADIAN PATCHWORK

Fig. 277 shows what is known as Canadian Patchwork or Loghouse Quilting. The material is folded double and arranged in a series of overlapping strips round a central square (shown black in the diagram), the idea being to simulate the arrangement of wooden logs. Plain fabrics only are shown in the diagram, but printed and different coloured materials are used just as in ordinary patchwork. The strips should but cut 1½" wide and then folded to measure ¾" wide, and to get the best effect a dark and light shade of the △ same colour should be used, grouping the darker shades on two sides of the square, and the lighter colours on the opposite two sides.

Cut a foundation square of any linen measuring 12" by 12", and in the centre of this run-stitch a small square of plain material 1½" in size (*see Fig.* 277). Down the right side and along the bottom stitch two light folded strips and at the top and left side two dark folded strips. The work is continued in this way until the square is completely covered. The colours should be carefully graded beforehand, and the two shades of any same colour should be used to form a complete square.

△ It is important that all strips are cut long enough to overlap a distance of ¾″ either end. These are then secured by the stitches of the next overlapping row to keep them taut and in position. Several 12″ squares covered in this way are needed to make a bed cover, these are then joined together in overcast stitch, arranging the dark side of one square to the dark side of another, and the light sides to meet in the same way. This produces an effect of light and dark diamonds all over the article.

For cushions, the foundation square should be about 5″ and the folded material proportionately narrower. Single mats are often composed of ribbon used single, instead of folded material.

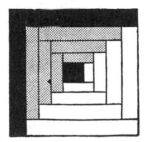

Fig. 277

QUILTING

QUILTING is a decorative means of stitching together two or three different layers of material, and long before it developed into a work of art, the method was used as a means to produce crude warm clothing and bed covers. The word " quilt " comes from the Latin " culcita " —a stuffed sack, mattress or cushion.

Like most very old works, its beginning is lost in the mists of antiquity, but 13th century specimens have been found in Europe, India, Persia and the Mohammedan countries of Northern Africa, while Babylonian sculpture and early Egyptian friezes reveal garments suggestive of primitive quilting. In England and Wales quilting has been and still remains a national art boasting centuries of glorious and unbroken tradition. During the Middle Ages, soldiers wore quilted garments beneath their armour to prevent the metal chafing their skin, and the quilted surcoat of Edward the Black Prince may still be seen as one of the treasures of Canterbury Cathedral. In Tudor days, quilted doublets and petticoats were an essential part of both masculine and feminine dress, but it was in the reign of Queen Anne that the work reached the pinnacle of its glory, gradually declining and almost vanishing during the 19th century. To-day, the work springs to life through such centres as Durham and Wales, where traditional designs have been handed down from mother to daughter for hundreds of years. During the 17th century quilting was carried by the old settlers to Virginia and Carolina, where from then to now it has enjoyed an almost unbroken reign of popularity.

There are two forms of quilting—English and Corded, the latter known as Italian quilting. In the former the whole article is padded, and the design outlined in stitchery taken through three layers of material. For the latter, no interlining is used, as the design is stitched in double outline through two layers of material only, and a cord inserted to produce a pattern in relief. This form of quilting is by no means peculiar to Italy, but the name has crept into popular

Fig. 278.   A very fine Durham Quilt in traditional design

use for which reason it will be used throughout this book.

Quilting is used for bed covers, dressing-gowns and jackets, babies' coats and bonnets, cushions, tea-cosies, handbags, etc., or on any article where padding is introduced either as a decoration, or means of warmth.

ENGLISH QUILTING

Designs.   Designs are all-important as the actual stitching is simple; and since the object of quilting is to hold three different

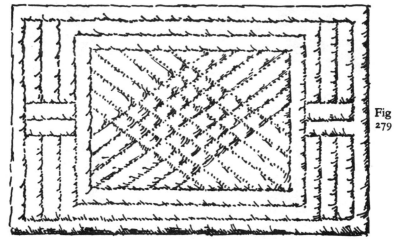

Fig
279

layers of material firmly in position the design must be
planned to cover the entire surface of the article, as in *Fig.* 278,
page 223.   This is an elaborate example, but simpler designs
are shown in *Figs.* 279 and 289, while in *Fig.* 280 the quilting
forms a subsidiary background often worked in a thread to
match the material.   The flowers are bright and in naturalistic
colours.   Another subsidiary background or " filling " is
shown in *Fig.* 278, where the spaces between the main lines of

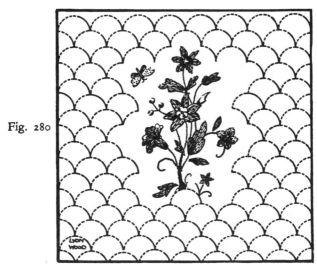

Fig. 280

the design are " filled " with a close diamond pattern.   This
tends to flatten the background and throw the design into
pronounced relief with excellent effect.   For other " fillings "
see Figs. 282 and 288.

Quilting designs are planned straight on to the material by

Fig. 281

drawing round a " template " with the needlepoint.   The
old workers divided their material in halves and quarters,
manipulating the template into patterns as habit and tradition
had taught them.   The amateur will find it useful to plan out
some comprehensive outline on paper.   The old templates
were made of wood or metal, but cardboard or stiff paper

Fig. 282

will serve, and some idea of the various shapes and the
methods of use are shown in *Figs.* 281, 282 and 283.   The
actual " templates " are shown on the left of each diagram.

Fig. 281 is the " ellipse " from which a simple but
attractive border has been evolved; in *Fig.* 282, the " Heart "
template has been manipulated to form large and small
motifs, finished with a filling of squares as a background.

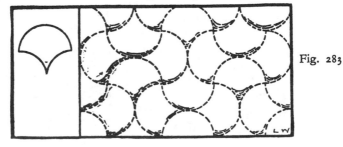

Fig. 283

A few additional lines added within the heart-shaped motifs has a good effect. *Fig.* 283 is the famous " Scale " template from which an unusual all-over design has been created. This same scale template was used to form the background in *Fig.* 280 and can also be used to form any number of isolated motifs, as a study of museum works will show. A clever method of using the " Scale " as an all-over pattern

Fig. 284

is shown at *Fig.* 284. The same template is used throughout, but an ever increasing width is left between each row towards

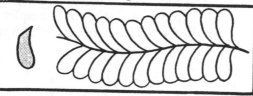

Fig. 285

the bottom of the design. These lengthening shapes are then converted into lovely little feather patterns, using the template shown in *Fig.* 285.

Two famous traditional patterns, known respectively as the Feather and the Cable Pattern, are shown in *Figs.* 285 and 286, to-

Fig. 286

gether with the templates from which they are built. The tiny notches on the Cable template serve as a guide for placing the inner coiled lines. This beautiful Cable pattern is often used as a border on large pieces of work. Finally, the Shell pattern, a more elaborate unit, is given at *Fig.* 287, from which any number of beautiful and intricate designs can be built.

Fig. 287

After a little practice and experiment it will become surprisingly easy and extraordinarily fascinating to evolve quilted patterns in this way.

Fig. 288 gives nine different background "fillings" all built from straight lines or circles. For the latter, a template can be made, though a cup or plate served the old workers. The centre square gives what is sometimes known as the Wineglass pattern, a name which tells its own story. Ultra-modern designs favour "fillings" of geometrical shapes and patterns somewhat after the fashion of the three upper squares in *Fig.* 288.

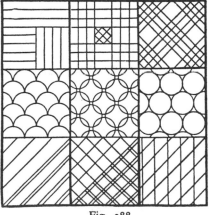

Fig. 288

Colours. Almost any coloured material can be used, but the lighter shades respond better to the play of light and shade over the undulating surface. A contrasting colour is often used for the underside of bed covers, and since all good quilting should be reversible, this is a useful idea. The working thread generally matches the upper layer of material, particularly in the traditional designs, but in modern and more unconventional forms a contrasting shade is often used.

Materials. Silks and satins are favoured for rich effects, though the workers in the quilting industries invariably choose cotton, printed or plain, and sateen. Always use materials of good quality (not likely to fray and not transparent), both for the top and underside of the article. For padding use cotton wool or wadding, and remove the skin before beginning the work. Professional quilters prefer lamb or sheep's wool which should be bought already scoured and carded from a woollen mill, otherwise the grease contained in the raw wool will spoil the work. This is quite inexpensive and by far the best padding. Domette, flannel, blankets and other soft woollen materials are also used, but these being flat do not produce a nice

" blistered " effect. For bed covers and other reversible articles the under side should be of the same quality material as the top, but for cushions, bed jackets, etc., ordinary butter muslin may be used as all garments are lined in the ordinary way, and the back of the work will not show. Threads should correspond with the material, silk or mercerised with silks and satins, cotton or mercerised with cotton fabrics.

WORKING METHODS

Large articles, such as bed covers, are better worked in a frame. This may be constructed of four strong strips of wood dressed with some firm material to which the quilt is tackled or pinned. Small articles may be worked in an ordinary em-

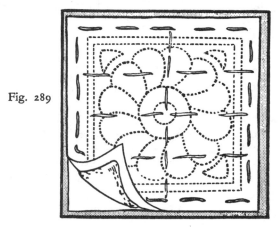

Fig. 289

broidery frame, but many of these are quite easily done in the hand. Arrange the three layers of material—(1) the bottom, (2) the padding, and (3) the upper, one above each other flat on a table and then tack all three together (see Fig. 289). △ Plenty of tacking is the secret of all good quilting, especially that done in the hand, as it prevents the different material from shifting. Start the tacking from the centre, and constantly smooth out the material, tacking horizontally, diagonally and vertically all over the surface. At this stage the work is ready for the design when the template method is being used.

Mark the centre of the material, and from here use a pin and long string as a compass to mark off regular distances. The design is then evolved with templates as described and marked out direct on the material, using tailor's chalk which easily brushes off, or scratching lightly round the template with the needle point, marking in a small portion of the design as the work progresses. This needle-made outline remains long enough for the pattern to be worked and is afterwards quite invisible.

Should a transfer be used instead of the template method, it is better to offset this on the *back* fabric *before* tacking the three layers together, △ especially if working in running stitch,

Fig. 290

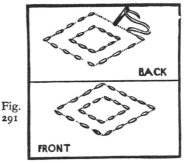

Fig. 291

which leaves spaces and allows the transfer lines to show. (It is possible to offset on the front when working in back stitch or chain stitch, but see that the transfer has a fine outline.)

There is a choice of three different stitches—back stitch, running stitch or chain stitch, but the same should be used throughout on any one piece of work, and of these back stitch is the best, being more durable and unbroken in outline.

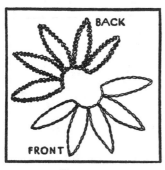

Fig. 292

Commercial work is usually done in running stitch as it is quicker and easier to keep neat on the reverse side. Back stitching is illustrated in *Fig.* 290, showing the front and back alike on both sides, while running stitch is shown in *Fig.* 291. Chain stitch (*Fig.* 292), though seldom used, is quite a good method, as it is usually worked on the back and produces a neat unbroken line of back stitching on the front.

The choice is purely personal but △ one golden rule applies to all.   Each stitch must be made in *two* separate movements, *downwards* and *upwards* and through all three layers of material, and not in one movement, as in other work.   *See Fig.* 293, which shows at A the correct method with the needle taken vertically down and vertically up (a machine movement) through all three materials.   The sectional view of the stitching below shows how this method produces a direct "pull" and keeps the materials in position, and the stitches of equal space on both sides of the work.   The wrong way △△ is shown at B.   Here the stitch is made in one movement, with the result that it fails to penetrate the padding or is so small that it has no grip, and the

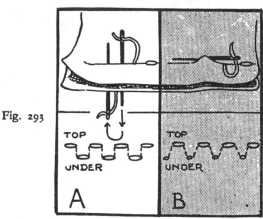

Fig. 293

material shifts, each thread pulls at an angle and the top of the work appears wavy and puckered.   A conscientious quilter should prick her finger at every stitch as she feels for the needle point under the work with her left forefinger!   The length of the stitches must be governed by the thickness of the padding.

To commence, make a knot at the end of the thread and bring the needle through to the surface, then pull gently but firmly and the knot will slip through the lower layer into the padding where it will be quite secure.   To finish off, make a single back stitch and run in through the padding.   Cut, and the end will be lost.

When the quilting is complete, remove all the tacking threads and neaten the edges.   The two outer layers of

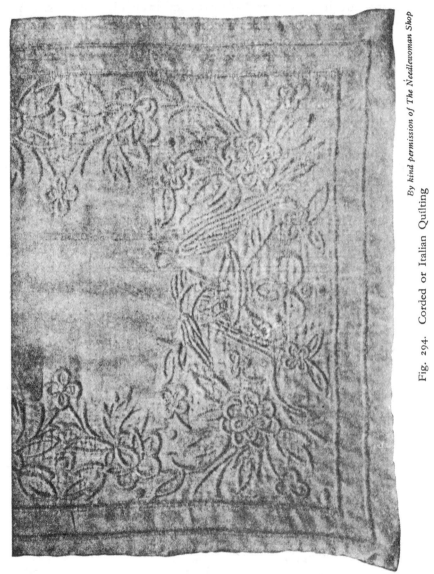

Fig. 294. Corded or Italian Quilting

material are turned in and slip-stitched invisibly together. A bed or cot cover is often finished with a cord encased in the same material. For articles needing an additional lining such as a dressing-gown or sachet, both the under layer of material and the padding are trimmed away, and the upper material turned in to a separate lining and slip-stitched.

ITALIAN QUILTING

Only two layers of material are necessary for Italian Quilting, and the design is outlined with a double row of stitching taken through both layers. This forms a narrow channel into which cord or thick wool is threaded from the back, throwing the outline of the design into pronounced relief on the front (*see Fig.* 294, *page* 231).

Designs. This form of quilting is purely decorative, and not like the English which is designed for warmth. The designs

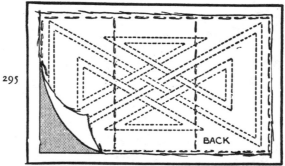

Fig. 295

are constructed in double outline and offset in the usual way and without the use of a template. Simple floral motifs, with occasional birds and butterflies, are the most popular. Celtic patterns are excellent, and *Fig.* 295 shows how well the interlaced lines lend themselves to this work. Quite a number of simple designs can be adapted by merely doubling the outlines, and Cut Work designs, which are always double in outline, are particularly adaptable.

The work is used on cushions, cosies, handbags, bed-jackets, cot covers, etc., but any lining or padding is added separately after the quilting is finished. Bed and cot covers are backed and sewn up the sides like cushions and a separate pad inserted. This is fastened at the four corners and with an occasional stitch or eyelet in the middle to keep its position.

Materials suitable for English quilting are also suitable for Italian, except that the richer kinds are more frequently preferred. Butter muslin only is required for the under layer, as the back of the work is always covered, and soft cotton cord, wick or thick wool is used for the padding.

WORKING METHODS

The design is pounced or stamped on to the muslin lining which is then laid over the surface material and the two securely tacked together as in *Fig.* 295 with the traced pattern uppermost. The work is now ready for quilting which is

Fig. 296

done △ on the *wrong* side and in neat small running stitches made over all the double outlines as shown in *Fig.* 295.

The PADDING is also done from the wrong side. Use a blunt needle with large eye and thread with soft cord or wool of sufficient thickness to well pad the double outline so that it stands out in relief on the front. △ (If the padding is too thin, the effect is completely lost.) The needle is first slipped in between the two layers of material from the back and threaded between the double outline all round the pattern. At any pronounced curve or angle bring the needle out and insert again through the same hole or a little further along and continue with the threading, but leave the cord loose at

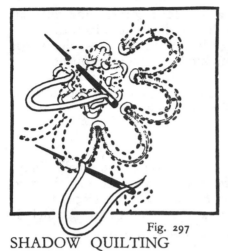

Fig. 297

the angle to form a small loop (*see Fig.* 297). This prevents the padding from pulling round the " corners " or shrinking when washed. In filling a wider space, such as the flower centres in *Fig.* 298, several stitches are made in and out until the space is well padded. These stitches never show on the right side as will be seen on the completed motif shown in *Fig.* 296.

SHADOW QUILTING

What is known as Shadow Quilting is in effect like Shadow Work. The working methods are similar to Italian Quilting, but a thin transparent material, such as organdie or jap silk, is used for the top, and the padding wools are of brilliant colours and show through as " shadow " effects in soft colours on the front.

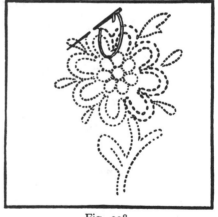

Fig. 298

TRAPUNTO

This form of quilting is also stitched from the back and through two materials, a muslin and silk (or taffeta), but the design is in single outline only. The padding consists of cotton wadding drawn through the muslin from the back with a steel crochet hook to fill each flower petal or leaf and not just the outline as in Italian Quilting. The result is a motif in high relief, similar in effect to that shown in *Fig.* 81. Each flower petal and leaf is padded separately, and designs such as *Fig.* 289 could be treated in this method. Very large shapes should be avoided, as they are difficult to pad evenly.

By courtesy of the Victoria and Albert Museum

Fig. 299.   Early 17th century Sampler showing a unique collection of
different stitches and patterns

SAMPLERS

"SAMPLER," derived from the Latin "exemplar," is defined in the dictionary as "a pattern of work—an example." According to this definition, a needle-worked sampler should be an "example of stitches and patterns" recorded as "samples" for future work, in much the same way as notes are collected in a notebook. The old samplers actually fulfilled this purpose, but the word is perhaps better known as applied to small cross-stitch pictures into which, alas! the old samplers developed, and which depicted by no means a record of stitches or patterns, but merely an example of proficiency.

Specimens of the genuine type are somewhat rare, but a few dating back to Elizabethan days, and possibly earlier, are to be found in museums and private collections. In the heyday of samplers during the late 16th and early 17th centuries, it was the aim of every woman worthy of the name to be skilled in needlecraft; and it was at this period that the rare and precious Italian pattern books were being published which gave zest to the stitch collector. Should these expensive treasures ever fall into her hands as a loan, the first thought was to record some of the most fascinating patterns and stitches which most pleased her, upon a sampler. In this way many interesting and excellent "samplers" were evolved such as that shown in *Fig.* 299 (*page* 235). Here it will be seen how these stitches and patterns were "jotted" down, each with some particular meaning and future purpose. Alas! no signature was added, though perhaps the letters M. J. give some clue to the worker's initials.

This particular specimen is about 20" deep, but there are many in existence which measure anything up to three feet! These longer samplers were generally about seven or eight inches wide, and the patterns and stitches arranged in borders across the width, and quite a number were devoted exclusively to lace stitches as needlepoint lace was a vogue of the day.

Fig. 300. A 19th century Sampler. Development of pictorial effect in
cross stitch

Fig. 301.   A modern Sampler worked by Miss N. Stanley depicting
over sixty different stitches

Samplers were not only worked by the skilled and proficient needlewoman as part of her stock-in-trade, but each mother handed down to her daughters the stitches and patterns she had collected, and soon it became part of a young worker's training to make her own " sampler." This often took a considerable time to accomplish, as we discover from the later habit of signing and dating samplers, which reveal that anything from several months to several years might be spent on the work! With this addition of name and date, other lettering was gradually added as an " example " for marking garments or household linen and ultimately the whole alphabet was included. It is about this time—the beginning of the 19th century—that the " sampler " began to deteriorate, and instead of remaining the valuable record of patterns and stitches as of yore, gradually developed into pictorial design worked at an incredibly early age to exhibit the extraordinary proficiency of the little needlewoman.

The old method of arranging the motifs in isolated fashion over the material was retained, but these, instead of recording different patterns and stitches, were little figures, animals, trees in pots, flowers and formal shapes, etc., worked entirely in cross stitch or petit point. Later on borders, landscapes, little houses, probably the worker's own home, were added, together with texts, proverbs and precepts, presumably included with the intention of impressing their sentiments upon the child as she diligently and laboriously stitched. Thus the sampler passed from an interesting and most valuable record of patterns and stitches, to an equally interesting but purely decorative form of needlework, which survives to astound us with the minuteness and regularity of the stitches worked at an age when the modern child is still playing with toys in the nursery! A sampler of this description is shown in *Fig.* 300, signed Sophie Stephens and dated June 30th, 183–, the final figure being omitted. The design includes the little worker's home labelled " Horse Hill House Near London," the usual verse, this time of a religious nature, and a great variety of motifs, all in fine cross stitch.

(It is of interest to note that samplers bearing a name and date are often accepted in lieu of birth certificates, and in cases where church records and family Bible have failed to supply evidence of birth, a tiny sampler signed, dated and treasured through the years, has been of sufficient importance to obtain a person the legal right to the Old Age Pension!)

About 1880 the making of samplers faded from fashion, but happily with the present-day revival of interest in embroidery, the practical use of the old sampler is being more and more appreciated. The modern embroideress, surrounded though she is with embroidery and pattern books of all kinds, still finds, like her Elizabethan predecessor, that a little " worked sample " of a stitch or pattern is more valuable and informative than all the books in the world, as well as an excellent means of practising the many stitches collected in book form from the old and new embroideries of all countries. Many of the modern samplers aim to combine both types described, being practical and decorative at the same time, as shown in *Fig.* 301, where over sixty stitches have been worked into a design for a cushion cover, a student's work of the Royal School of Needlework, which will serve as a permanent reminder for many years.

Every would-be embroideress is strongly advised to commence her apprenticeship by making herself a sampler. The first effort may be a crude attempt at reproducing a few favourite stitches, but with practice, the ability to blend and weld these stitches into patterns of original charm and beauty will grow, and not only serve her as an embroidery " notebook " for all time, but remain as an heirloom of great interest to her descendants. Such a work should bear the name, date of commencement and completion.

SEAMS AND HEMS

EVERYTHING made by the enthusiastic needlewoman, be it a garment, bedspread, tray-mat or handkerchief, must be finished with a hem or a seam, both of which may serve a decorative as well as a practical purpose. Seams may be " open " or " closed " and hems deep or just rolled. A " closed " seam is better for heavy materials, and an " open " seam for finer, lingerie silks, satins, cambrics and so forth. The working thread should be chosen in proportion to the material and the colour repeat any of those used in the embroidery, or to match the background.

CLOSED SEAMS

Blanket Stitch, as shown at A in *Fig.* 302, is the simplest decoration to a run-and-fell or " closed " seam. This may be first run and felled or just tacked together, and blanket stitches of even length worked along the edge or arranged to alternate one long one short, as in the diagram. If desired a second row may be added, worked in the opposite direction with the loops arranged to the outside and the tails of the two stitches interlocking as in Double Button Stitch.*

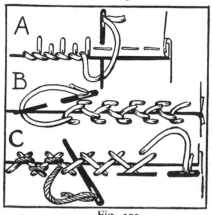

Fig. 302

Other stitches used on closed seams are Feather Stitch (*see* B, *Fig.* 302), Closed Feather Stitch*, Feathered Chain Stitch*, Cretan Stitch*, Zigzag Chain Stitch*, Double Chain Stitch*, Herringbone Stitch* and Zigzag Stitch*.

Fig. 302 C shows how Laced Herringbone Stitch comes into use as a seam decoration, and several others such as Tied

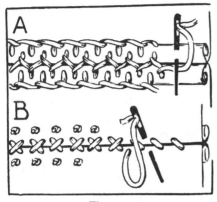

Fig. 303

Herringbone Stitch*, Sham Hemstitch*, Chevron Stitch*, Raised Chevron Stitch*, etc., can likewise be used in similar manner.

Two simple stitches used together on a " closed " seam provide a more elaborate effect as in *Fig.* 303 (a method often used to join the wide side panels on a bedspread). At A the hems are turned up on the right side of the article, tacked, and then joined with Open Cretan Stitch, while the turned-in edges top and bottom are secured with Blanket Stitch worked with the tails fitting into the open spaces of the Cretan Stitches. Cross Stitch is worked along the seam line at B (*Fig.* 303), and finished with a row of French Knots above and below.

Fig. 304 shows a fancy overcast stitch, often used to secure the edges of a tea-cosy or the sides of a cushion cover. This is completed in two journeys, the two movements of the stitch used for the first being shown at A and B. At A an upright stitch is overcast into the same spot with the next a short dis-tance to the right as at B, carrying the thread over and behind the edges of the material as shown by the dotted lines. The return journey of overcasting is shown at C, where the needle is inserted each time at the base of the upright stitches made on the first journey, thus slanting the long stitches in the oppo-site direction to those made on the first, to form a cross.

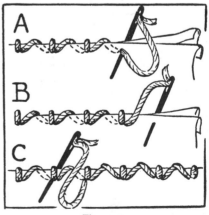

Fig. 304

OPEN SEAMS OR FAGGOTING

An open seam must be prepared in the following manner before any decorative stitches can be added. Turn the raw edges of the material under as for ordinary hemming and

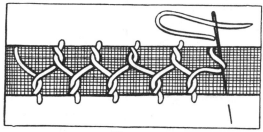

Fig. 305

tack. Some workers prefer to slipstitch these in position though this is not necessary on a narrow hem, as the decorative stitches serve this purpose. Both hems are then tacked to a strip of stout brown paper, leaving a space between varying in width from $\frac{1}{4}''$ to $1\frac{1}{4}''$, according to the stitch chosen for joining.

FAGGOTING

Faggoting is the method of joining together any open seam, and the work includes a great variety of different stitches. The most popular is Twisted Insertion Stitch, shown in *Fig. 305.*

The working method is easily followed from the diagram, △ but it should be noticed how the needle enters the material from beneath the hem in making each stitch. △ Regularity of spacing and the same tension throughout is essential when working any stitch used in Faggoting.

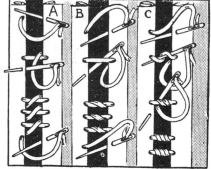

Fig. 306

Other popular stitches are shown in *Fig.* 306. That at A, Half Cretan Stitch, comprises one straight stitch crossed with another in a slanting direction as shown in the diagram. That at B is a reverse

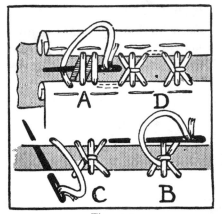

Fig. 307

Roumanian Stitch. The needle is brought out beneath the thread in making the first stitch and taken over and beneath for the second. A " Bullion " bar is shown at C, where the needle is twisted as shown to produce a firm solid bar. For both B and C the working thread must be pulled quite firmly after each stitch so that the twists are neat and tight.

A more elaborate form of Faggoting is shown at *Fig.* 307, consisting of three stitches tied together in " Faggot Bundles," an effect which justifies the name. The decoration is worked from right to left and the first two and a half stitches are given at A, which also shows the needle making a kind of back stitch as a binding. After this, the last half of the stitch is completed as the needle passes to the commencement of the next three stitches (*see* B). On each alternate faggot the working direction of this last half stitch is inverted (as at C), so that it falls first on the lower and then on the upper edges (*see* D).

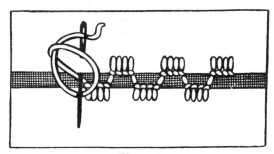

Fig. 308

In addition to these more popular stitches there are a number of different embroidery stitches often used in Faggoting. Three examples are illustrated, and these will be found more fully described in the Dictionary. Buttonhole Insertion Stitch (*Fig.* 308) can also be worked with ordinary buttonhole stitch or with tailor's buttonhole stitch, as shown in the diagram, and grouped in two, three or four stitches. Knotted Insertion Stitch* (*Fig.* 309) suggests a particularly

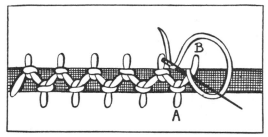

Fig. 309

attractive decoration, and is worked like ordinary Knot Stitch*. Laced Insertion Stitch* (*Fig.* 310) comprises two

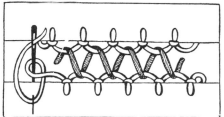

Fig. 310

rows of Braid Edging Stitch* laced together with a matching or contrasting thread. This is a favourite Mexican border. Other and still more elaborate stitches are Diamond Stitch,* Italian Buttonhole Insertion Stitch*, Interlacing Insertion Stitch* and Plaited Insertion Stitch*, all three of which make very handsome decorations especially when a wide filling is necessary.

HEMS

Three simple methods of finishing a hem in lieu of hemstitching or scalloping are given in *Fig.* 311. The hem in each case is turned up on to the right side. At A, Blanket Stitches are prettily arranged in groups

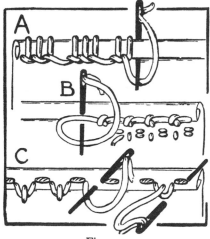

Fig. 311

of three, with the looped edge of the stitch to the inner side of the hem.   At B, Coral Stitch is worked along the edge of the hem, and a further decoration of tiny straight stitches arranged in pairs (Dot Stitch), intersected by a single vertical stitch.   At C, the hem is first secured with even running stitches of one colour and these are then linked with a festoon of fly stitches worked in another colour.   Any number of other stitches can be used to build up little borders of this description with the help of the Dictionary.

Several of the edging stitches, such as Armenian Edge*, Braid Edging*, Plaited Edge Stitch*, Knot Stitch*, etc., will be found to make effective lace-like edgings.   For these, small rolled hems lightly stitched are sufficient.

SHADOW WORK

Amongst the many forms of embroidery popular in the 18th century was that now known as "Shadow Work." This consists of stitching worked on the back of transparent materials to produce a "shadowy" effect on the right side, as in *Fig. 312*. The work is probably of Indian origin, and until the present century was worked in

Fig. 312. Shadow Work on Organdie embroidered by
Mrs. Campbell Preston

white on white material.   The recent introduction of coloured working thread into the embroidery has somewhat changed its character, since bright colours used on the back of pale transparent materials, produce an elusive, opalescent effect on the front quite distinct from the more opaque effect of white stitching on white materials.

The delicate appearance of Shadow Work renders it particularly suitable for lingerie decoration, or for duchesse sets, sachets, children's party frocks, dressing-gowns (interlined), and other articles made of light coloured or white transparent material.

Designs are mainly floral and simple in outline as shown in *Fig.* 313 with few, if any, interior markings on the flowers, leaves,

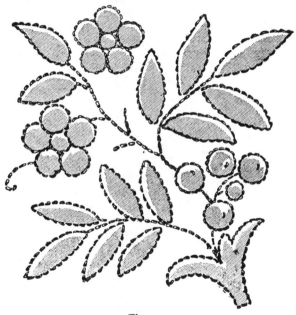

Fig. 313

fruit, berries, etc., and with the minimum number of stalks or branches.   See also the iris flowers and leaves in *Fig.* 312. The transparent material can be placed over any drawing and marked in with pencil.

Materials. A transparent or semi-transparent material such as organdie, muslin, fine silk, thin crêpe-de-chine, or georgette is used, organdie being that most favoured. The material should be pale and delicate in colour so that the embroidery can show through from the back in elusive shades. A fine thread, either stranded cotton, mercerised or silk, should be used, and in a colour twice as bright as the desired finished effect, since the covering material softens down the tones very considerably. Bright coloured wools are often used on objects not frequently laundered, such as a kimono worked in large sprawling flowers, though on the whole cotton threads are better.

WORKING METHODS

The embroidery can be worked in naturalistic shades or treated conventionally. The design is traced on the *wrong* side of the material, and all the principal parts of the design are worked in Close Herringbone Stitch also on the *wrong* side of the material. Close Herringbone Stitch builds up two lines of back stitching on the front as shown in *Fig.* 314, and is worked from left to right as for ordinary herringbone but with

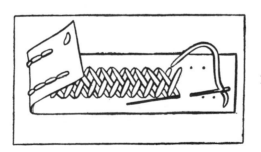

Fig. 314

this difference, each stitch touches its neighbour in " close " formation. The working method can be followed from *Fig.* 314 and the method of using it on a leaf in *Fig.* 315 A.

The stitch follows the outline of the shape exactly (*Fig.* 315) and must commence and finish right up to the point of a leaf or flower, otherwise the outline will not be complete on the right side. An occasional extra stitch or two on the back is sometimes necessary to achieve this. Extra wide leaves or shapes

are filled with two rows of Close Herringbone Stitch as at B
(*Fig.* 315).   This divides the shape down the middle and on the
right side of the work will produce the effect of a double vein.
The Close Herringbone Stitch can be divided at any point to
suggest the interior marking of a flower or berry as at C
(*Fig.* 315).   The appearance on the right side of the work is
shown at D (*Fig.* 315).   After filling all the shapes in this
manner it may be expedient to emphasise the colours of the
smaller shapes such as the berries in *Fig.* 313.   For this purpose the criss-cross stitches on the back may be darned in a
matching thread over and under without taking the stitches

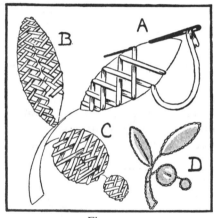

Fig. 315

through to the front.   This completes the embroidery on the
back of the material and any single lines in the design are
worked in with back stitch (*see Fig.* 313) on the *right* side of the
material.   Stem stitch may be used for this purpose on the
stalks of larger flowers (*see Fig.* 317).   Very wide branches are
filled in with the Close Herringbone Stitch as in *Fig.* 316.
This motif has been photographed against the light in order
to show the crossed stitches on the back of the work and their
shadowy effect on the front.

Fig. 316. Shadow Work photographed against the light to show the stitches

Fig. 317. Indian Shadow Work

INDIAN SHADOW WORK

The attractive little shadowy motif at *Fig.* 317 illustrates another method of working the stitching and is sometimes known as Indian Shadow Work. The effect is much the same but the stitches do not cross on the back, but zigzag from side to side as shown in *Fig.* 318. Only a very small portion of material must be picked up at each stitch, otherwise the threads will lie too openly on the back of the work and spoil the shadow effect from the front.

SHADOW QUILTING

What is known as shadow quilting is really Italian Quilting, padded with bright coloured threads beneath pastel coloured transparent material after the principle described on pages 232 and 234.

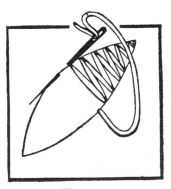

Fig. 318

SMOCKING

SMOCKING IS A work of peasant origin, being a decorative method of gathering together in regular folds a wide width of material. The word " Smock " comes from the Anglo-Saxon meaning a shift, chemise or shirt, and throughout the centuries from early Saxon days, the men who worked in the fields and villages have worn a loose tunic-like garment, known as a smock. As the years progressed these were gradually decorated or " smocked " in designs which incorporated the different emblems of their various occupations—trees and leaves for woodmen, and crooks, hurdles and hearts for shepherds, etc. A Berkshire smock of the early 19th century, probably worn by a carter, because of the wheel shapes, is shown in *Fig.* 319.

Fig. 319. An old English Smock. Berkshire, early 19th century

Fig. 320. Modern Smocking is light and dainty

The practical purpose of smocking, that of controlling the fullness on the upper part of a garment leaving the lower part free and loose fitting, is now appreciated for babies' and children's garments, where elasticity, freedom for expansion and growth are of primary importance. Such an example is shown in *Fig.* 320, and of late the work has been favoured on dresses and even tea-cosies and cushions.

Materials. Almost any material, plain or printed, in silk, cotton, linen or wool, can be smocked. The working thread should be of the same texture as the material, that is linen, cotton, mercerised or silk.

Colours are a matter of choice. The old country smocks were generally of white or natural colours, worked with a matching thread, though in some counties green, blue, grey and even black smocks were customary. Good smocking looks effective in contrasting colours, and on pattern materials the dominant colour in the print is a good choice for the working thread.

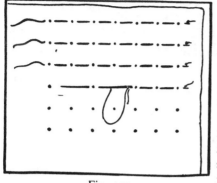

Fig. 321

WORKING METHODS

The width of material required for smocking is approximately three times the width of the finished piece of work. For thicker fabrics rather less is necessary and for very fine fabrics a little more, but the multiple of three is a good average. (A yoke of twelve inches wide will require a width of thirty-six inches for the gathering.) All smocking should be worked before the garment or article is made up.

First, cut out the garment and then pencil out the position for the gathering stitches on the *back* of the material as shown at the bottom of *Fig.* 321. These can be made with a ruler and sharp pencil, or a printed transfer, consisting of little dots evenly spaced in rows, may be used. The spacing varies from $\frac{1}{2}''$ on thick materials to $\frac{3}{8}''$ or $\frac{1}{4}''$ inch on fine, and it will be seen from *Fig.* 321 how equal spaces are left between both the horizontal and vertical rows of dots. (A fabric patterned with evenly spaced spots or regular repeating design affords a mechanical guide for the gathering stitches.)

The old workers disdained any such mechanical aids, merely counting the linen threads as they worked the running stitches, a task of comparative ease on the coarse hand-woven materials then used. Counting is still the best way, as it enables the gathering thread to progress along the grain of the material in a perfectly straight line, and when using linen or any fabric of which the threads can be easily counted, this method should be adopted.

The gathering is done along the spots on the *back* of the material with a long cotton of sufficient length to complete each row. Make a good-sized knot at the end, as should the tacking thread slip through when the material is gathered up, the work will need to be done over again.

Begin at the right-hand side as shown in *Fig.* 321, and △ pick up a small portion of material *beneath* each dot. As each line is completed unthread the needle and leave the thread lying loose; and when the required number of rows are worked draw the material up into gathers by holding the loose ends of thread in the hand and easing gently along until the required width for the smocking is attained. The long ends are then tied firmly together in pairs close up to the last gathering fold, as shown in *Fig.* 322, otherwise

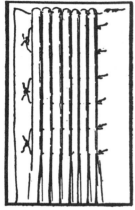

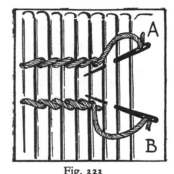

Fig. 323

Fig. 322

they slip out of position. The front of the material now presents a series of even folds, " tubes " or " reeds " ready for smocking.

SMOCKING PATTERNS

Three patterns only were used on the old country smocks: (1) Rope, (2) Basket or Cable and (3) Chevron, and all three are worked in stem stitch. Another pattern known as " Honeycombing " is so popular that the name is often used, and with some confusion, as an alternative for smocking. Most of the patterns are worked from left to right on the right side of the material, using the gathering threads as a guide to keep the stitches straight.

Rope Pattern (*Fig.* 323) simulates a twisted rope. Commence by making a knot at the end of the thread (in smocking a knot is permissible and necessary) and bring the needle up through the first " tube " on the left. From here a small piece of material is picked up on each successive tube, across the work as shown at A, keeping the thread *above* the needle and inserting it in a slanting direction. (The greater the slant, the shorter the stitch.) At B the same method is shown worked with the thread *below* the needle to produce a " rope " twisted in the opposite direction. Rope Pattern may be used in single lines or in groups. See the old smock in *Fig.* 319, also *Fig.* 327, where single lines in opposing directions are showr at the top and bottom of the smocking.

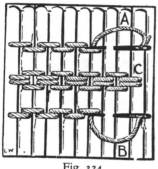

Fig. 324

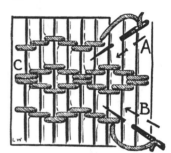

Fig. 325

Basket or Cable Pattern (*Fig.* 324) is also worked in stem stitch movement, but contrary to Rope Stitch, the needle is inserted horizontally and the stitches worked alternatively above and below. Both movements are shown at A and B, while at C two rows are stitched close together to give the effect of basket weaving. Single lines of this stitch were used for the major part of the smocking in *Fig.* 319. See also *Figs.* 327 and 328.

Chevron Pattern (*Fig.* 325) is a development of Rope and Basket Pattern and consists of stitches grouped first upwards and then downwards and worked with the thread above the needle in ascending and below in descending. Both movements are shown at A and B with two lines worked in contrary directions at C. Many other such patterns can be achieved by grouping the stitches and lines in different relationship to each other as in *Fig.* 328.

Other embroidery stitches used for smocking are Single Feather Stitch and Chevron Stitch*, which should not be confused with Chevron Pattern.

HONEYCOMBING

There are two methods of working this pattern, the most popular being shown in *Fig.* 326 A, where it will be seen that

Fig. 326 A

the little tubes of material are drawn aside and stitched to imitate the cell-like cavities from which the name is derived. This pattern gives more elasticity to the smocking than any other, and two rows of stitching are completed in one journey. The thread is brought through at the top of a tube, level with a gathering thread and the needle picks up a small piece of material from the second and first tubes as seen at A, after which a second stitch is made just above the first (drawn firm after each stitch). The needle is now inserted at B and slipped down through the *back* of the tube to the next gathering thread below and two similar stitches worked over the second and third tube, and then back again to the upper line at C, gathering the third and fourth tubes together. The work continues in this way first above and then below, using the lines of gathering threads as a guide and finishing the pattern to a point (if desired) as suggested in *Fig.* 328.

A study of *Fig.* 326 B will show that in this method of

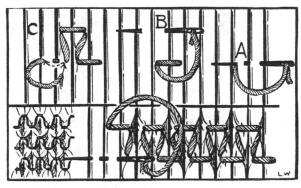

Fig. 326 B

honeycombing the working thread passes from stitch to stitch on the surface of the material, and is worked △ from right to left. The needle is brought through on the second tube, midway between two lines of gathering threads and here a back stitch is made over the first and second tubes as at A. The next back stitch is made above at B over the second and third tubes and from here the needle returns to the level of A and makes another back stitch over the third and fourth as at C.   A line in progress is shown at the bottom of the diagram and the finished effect, giving the position of the rows in relation to each other, in the bottom left-hand corner.

SMOCKING BORDERS

These four simple patterns as described represent the sum total of smocking patterns in general use.   These can be grouped in endless different ways to build up wider patterns of great interest by combining two or three patterns together or by using the same throughout but in different groupings. Two suggestions are given in *Figs.* 327 and 328, but numbers

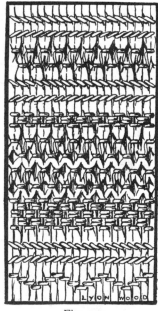

Fig. 327

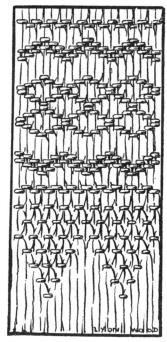

Fig. 328

of other variations can be easily evolved by just arranging these same patterns, in a different order.

FINISHING OFF

Smocking should be ironed before removing the gathering threads. Place the work right side down on the ironing blanket and above a damp cloth. Have the iron really hot and just pass it lightly over the surface of the damp cloth without pressing in order that the work is not flattened. The gathering threads are then removed and the work made up into a garment.

STUMP WORK

STUMP WORK, or embroidery on the stump or stamp, made its appearance during the reign of James I and had its origin in the raised ecclesiastical embroideries of Germany and Italy, prevalent during the 15th and 16th centuries. *See Fig. 329.*

The work enjoyed but a brief reign of popularity, disappearing completely about 1688, though odd relics are occasionally observed in the padded fruits and foliage used to decorate sachets and small boxes featured on stalls at various bazaars. *See Fig. 330.*

The salient feature of the work was its sense of relief produced by padding and stuffing the chief subjects of the design, and, exaggerated, this became grotesque. The embroidery was intricate, an endless amount of labour being expended on fine stitchery, but little or no attempt made to introduce proportion or any co-ordination into the design itself. Detail ran riot, seemingly the one desire being to crowd into an allotted space of a few square inches every possible figure, bird, beast or castle surrounded with trees, butterflies, tents, hangings and flowers, with the butterflies and birds possibly more than twice the size of a face or a tree! The figures and scenes chosen were usually Biblical or allegorical, although the two Kings Charles with their queens were popular. All figures and any portion of the design to be shown in relief, were stuffed with a pad of wool, horse-hair or even stumps of carved wood, especially the head and features, which were first carved and afterwards covered with fabric. The figures were then dressed and decorated with lace, brocade, pearls, beads, glass, talc and even human hair, some minute and intricate embroidery being added to the costumes in beautiful lace stitches. The costume drapery was made to project in folds, and to turn back and show elaborate petticoats, while tents and hangings, which often framed the design, were treated in the same way. The figures when finished were carefully stitched to the background,

which was invariably white satin on which the outlines of
the design had been previously drawn. The flowers, fruit
or birds, etc., were then added in beads, pearls, corals or glass,
and mounted on wire or padded, when the whole was finished
with touches of flat embroidery!

This work was used to decorate caskets, work-boxes, book-
bindings, mirror frames, and even small cushions, although
this would seem an uncomfortable form of embellishment!
The panels for each box would be worked and mounted and
finally sent to the cabinet-maker to complete. A work-box,
dating from about 1640, is shown in *Fig.* 329, and is typical
of this period. The box is covered with white satin and·the

By kind permission of the Victoria and Albert Museum

Fig. 329. A white satin work-box in Stump Work (about 1640)

stump work embroidery represents the visit of the Queen of Sheba to King Solomon, the story of Susannah and the Ten Elders, and the judgment of Solomon, the sacrifice of Isaac, and the Five Senses. Centuries of Biblical history crammed upon a very small box only 12″ high, and, with delightful disregard for history, since each figure is dressed in the costume of the 16th century!

Fig. 330

TAPESTRY

Tapestry is woven on a loom and cannot be classified under the heading of embroidery at all, but the name is so often wrongly applied and with such confusion to canvas work (*see page 36*), that it may probably be helpful to point out as briefly as possible the difference between the two.

Embroidery is an *additional* decoration to an *already woven fabric*, but in tapestry the weaver has no such foundation. He starts off on an empty loom and just makes ready the warp threads and upon these the patterns are woven. On the other hand, Canvas Work is purely and simply embroidery worked on a ready-made canvas foundation with needle, thread and embroidery stitches. The confusion between the two may have arisen because of the close imitation which canvas work bears to woven tapestry. Both are completely covered, seemingly alike, but the one woven and the other with close flat stitches, many of which have a woven appearance. Yet another link connects these two separate forms of work, that of design, as the typical tapestry designs were, and still are, constantly imitated in canvas embroidery.

Further perplexity may have been caused by that famous misnomer, the Bayeux Tapestry, which is not a tapestry at all, but an embroidery! But it is doubtful if anyone would consent to the name being changed to Bayeux Embroidery, which would, indeed, be correct.

Tapestry weaving is one of the most ancient arts in which the Greeks, Egyptians and Copts were all highly proficient many hundreds of years ago. The weaving differs from ordinary weaving as the warp threads are completely covered by the weft threads and the designs and colours are solid and distinct as in painting and embroidery. During the Middle Ages and Renaissance, tapestry weaving in Italy and France reached the height of its glory, and the " arras " which adorned the walls of castles and chateaux took its name from the great tapestry industry in the French town of that name.

In the 16th century the crown passed to the famous Flemish tapicers in Brussels, but was later regained by the French royal weavers of Gobelin and Aubusson. In England, James I instituted the tapestry factory of Mortlake which flourished until the end of the 17th century, contemporary with the Soho and Sheldon tapestry industries. William Morris again revived the art in this country at his tapestry factory at Merton, Surrey, towards the end of the 19th century. Tapestry is still being woven to-day, notably in the original Gobelin factories in France, but the art is becoming isolated and rare, as it is exceedingly costly and few modern rooms are suitable for the inclusion of the vast woven hangings which so nobly graced the castles of mediæval days. The subjects depicted were invariably pictorial (though some tapestry maps were produced in England during the 16th century). Historical, Biblical, legendary and mythical stories or incidents were all told in tapestry, with extraordinary beauty and minute attention to detail, while panels showing floral motifs, forest scenes, birds and animals, were also popular. Hundreds of pounds were spent on the original designs or cartoons, which perhaps explains why they were so eagerly copied by the hand workers on canvas, or more probably pirated by the commercial workers who found in canvas embroidery a cheaper method of reproduction, and had reason in naming these as tapestry.

The illustration shows a wonderful hanging which was woven at the tapestry factory at Mortlake, Surrey. It was produced in honour of the Prince of Wales, afterwards Charles II, and is one of a series of nine depicting the history of the god Vulcan. Coloured wools, silks and silver gilt threads were used in the weaving, and the tapestry measures about 18 by 14 feet. The extraordinary clearness of the detail is typical of the beautiful work created at that period, many more examples of which will be found in our museums.

Fig. 331.   16th century Tapestry woven at Mortlake, near London, in wool, silk and silver threads

TECHNICAL
AND MISCELLANEOUS HINTS

E MBROIDERY is the art of enriching a fabric with stitchery and only good fabrics are worth this trouble and pleasure.

Good needles and good threads (silks, wools and cottons), perfect-fitting thimbles, sharp scissors, tidy well-organised work-box or basket, and a thread case or cases, in which the various embroidery wools and threads can be arranged in their various colour groups, are all contributing factors to the joy and ease of working embroidery. Needles with worn eyes will fray the working threads and spoil the embroidery, and rough-edged thimbles are just as destructive. Use only the best of everything, best linens, best threads, and when a well-organised work-box is kept with all the various accessories in order as suggested, they will last twice as long and any extra initial expense be well worth while.

Should two distinct forms of embroidery be in hand at the same time, then keep them in separate work-bags, and certainly distinct from any dressmaking accoutrements, with separate thimbles and scissors, so that the work is always ready to pick up and lay aside without any inconvenience.

SIGNATURE

The old custom of signing and dating any elaborate piece of embroidery, with the idea that it should last, has now happily been revived. A signature may seem of no particular consequence to the worker, but it adds greatly to the personal charm and interest of the work, which later may be handed down with pride from generation to generation. It is for this reason that the little stitch samplers of the 18th century are so eagerly sought by collectors, as the name, age, date and sometimes even the address added in the corner brings these seemingly forgotten works to life. Work the signature and date in fine stitching quite unobtrusively in a corner, and if the work is a gift then the recipient's name worked in the opposite corner brings yet further joy in accepting.

Needles. A good needle makes embroidery work a joy, and an inferior cheaper kind exasperates, bends and quickly breaks. See that the eye is large enough to take the thread easily without rubbing or fraying it. Crewel needles are generally used, as they are long and sharp and easily threaded. Chenille needles are shorter with longer eyes. For canvas work, net embroidery and drawn fabric work, use blunt-pointed wool or tapestry needles. A bent needle is apt to make a crooked stitch and should be discarded.

Scissors. Special embroidery scissors are advisable as these are so fine and sharp, and for all forms of cut work sharp scissors are a necessity in order to obtain a clean-cut edge. Ball-pointed scissors are more convenient for cutting away the nets and finer fabrics in net appliqué.

Threads. The word " thread " has been used throughout this book as a generic term for wool, cotton, silk, or mercerised, but the appropriate kind is mentioned with each type of embroidery in each of the preceding chapters. In making an original choice, suitability of purpose is the chief consideration. Cotton, mercerised and linen threads are better suited to cotton, linen and dull silk fabrics, while pure silk demands the richer silks, satins and brocades, as do also gold, silver and other metal threads. A mercerised thread does not look at all out of place on dull silk fabrics, because of its silky appearance.

Embroidery wool, both for modern designs and reproductions, is generally used on the thicker twilled linens and, of course, for canvas work. The finest is a two-ply crewel or tapestry wool, suitable for Jacobean and fine canvas work, while the thicker variety, known as embroidery wool, is frequently used on bold modern fabrics for quick effects. It is important that all embroidery threads, wools, silks or cottons, should be dyed in fast colours, otherwise it is waste of time to work with them.

When any working thread loses its freshness and begins to " fluff " or become untwisted, take a fresh length immediately. A professional worker will twist her wool or silk, with the thumb and finger of the left hand after each stitch, to avoid this untwisting, a movement which soon becomes purely automatic.

Frames. Many amateurs regard the use of a frame as something for professionals only, but it is certain that, once the experiment is made, there will be no desire to work in any other way. It gives greater ease and comfort in working, is a safeguard against puckering, and of great assistance to regularity of stitching.

The mounting of embroidery into a frame is technically known as " dressing " a frame.

The simplest type is the circular or tambour frame, constructed from two rings of wood which fit over each other, the outer provided with a tightening screw. *Fig.* 332 shows the

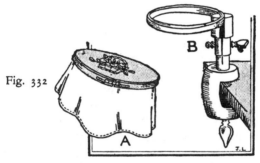

Fig. 332

kind with the material already mounted, and at B a similar frame fixed into a table clamp. This secures it in position and leaves both hands free to manipulate the work. Circular frames are more suitable for working small designs, and for use in larger patterns, care must be taken in △ changing the position of the ring, otherwise the stitching is damaged. This may be partly avoided by inserting a piece of soft material between the two rings. Place the inner ring on a table, and over this the material to be embroidered, and over this a piece of protective muslin, and then the outer ring and tighten the screw. Cut away the protective material to within half-an-inch of the rings. This leaves the under material exposed *f*or embroidery, but protected from the rub and pressure of the rings. Should a fine material tend to sag when working the embroidery, bind the inner ring with a strip of tape to form a better grip.

The slate frame as shown in *Fig.* 333 is the most popular. This consists of two rollers across the top and bottom, and two flat strips of wood or laths provided with little holes down each side. These are slatted into the rollers top and bottom with wooden pegs, inserted in any one of the holes according to the height of the embroidery. Each roller has a strip of tape or webbing nailed along the edge, to which the material of the embroidery is firmly sewn top and bottom. To do this, mark the middle of the roller with a pencil and to this attach the middle of the material and stitch outwards from the centre first left and then to the right, in herringbone stitch or diagonal overcast stitch, taken through a folded hem of the material, on the back of the work. Should the material be longer than the

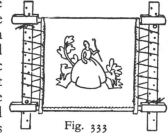

Fig. 333

frame, wind the portion not required round the top or bottom roller as shown on the top roller in *Fig.* 333, and insert a slip of thin soft fabric between to protect and prevent the material creasing. The selvedge sides of the work are then laced over the laths with string as shown in *Fig.* 333. If a firm strong fabric is being used for the embroidery, the sides of the material may be tacked down over a piece of string, like an encased cord, and the lacing done directly into the material. This string method can only be used when the edge of the material is " extra," and can be cut away when the work is finished. If not, sew down each side an odd piece of any material △ of the same strength and with similar " pull " as the one which is being embroidered, and take the string through this. If the frame is not wide enough to take this extra width use the following method. Take a length of tape about $\frac{3}{4}''$ wide, and instead of lacing it *through* the material, pin, with a good ordinary pin, taking care to pick up about $\frac{1}{2}''$ of the material, so that the " pull " does not come on a few threads. This method is often used for fine materials, when string lacing would tear.

To mount odd shapes, such as bags, collars, etc., or small

pictures, get a piece of muslin and lay flat on the table, and to this sew the bag shape. Frame as before, △ and then cut away the muslin from beneath the bag *after* all the framing is completed. All kinds of different materials, light and heavy, can be framed, providing one golden rule is remembered. △ The material used for the embroidery must be mounted at the sides to a fabric of similar weave, so that *both* have an equal " pull " when the frame is tightened up. The old idea of always using tape or webbing at the sides is not suitable to the lighter fabrics now so often used for embroidery, as it can be appreciated that the " pull " would be unequal.

Fig. 334

The table frame as shown in *Fig.* 334 is the same as the slate, but mounted on a stand for use on a table. An even more elaborate frame can be bought mounted on a stand which reaches the floor and therefore requires no table. In working on a " slate " or " table frame " it is a good idea to have a thimble on the middle finger of both hands, as the needle is passed vertically from front to back and back to front.

Materials. The art of choosing the correct material for any embroidery work is determined by the object for which it is intended. For instance, satin on a footstool provokes irritation and the desire to rip it off. That is because it is wrong and irritates accordingly. Almost any material can be embroidered in some form or other and materials suitable to the various kinds of work are given in each chapter, and the correct material is a very important factor in making any work a complete and lasting success. The rich luxury fabrics should only be used for articles that can be cleaned, and linens, etc for those needing constant laundering. Linens with a flattened surface, known as " beetled," should be generally avoided, or used with a transfer, as the threads are difficult to count and the appearance of the work when finished is not so satisfying. Many of the modern furnishing fabrics which suggest bold stitching and gay colours are excellent.

When Buying Linen. Linens purchased from any good embroidery shop are cut dead straight by first removing a thread of the linen across the entire width and cutting along the grain of the material. This avoids that disastrously crooked cut which often leaves the embroideress to choose between making her article smaller or buying another length of linen. See that this is done when buying material.

This method of drawing a single thread as a guide line should always be employed when cutting out a small square or rectangular mats or any straight strips.

To Keep a Hem Straight. A hem can be kept straight on a coarsely-woven fabric by following along a single line of the material, parallel to the edge as a guide. This method would be too trying on fine fabrics, so the needle is slipped under a single thread near the edge and a △ very small loop is drawn up and eased (not withdrawn) across the whole width of the material. This makes quite a pronounced ridge of sufficient visibility to use as a guide for the hemming. Should the hem be finished with decorative stitching, the thread could be cut and withdrawn completely, provided the little gap is afterwards covered.

To Prevent Fraying. In working on a material which easily frays, oversew the cut edges before commencing the work. Should the work be important and likely to take some time to complete, bind each edge with tape, which is removed when the work is finished.

To Correct Puckering. Slight puckering can often be corrected by shrinking the material. Damp on the wrong side and press with a hot iron. Should the puckering be very pronounced, spread several sheets of damp clean blotting-paper over a drawing or pastry board and pin the work to this, using plenty of drawing-pins. The material must be carefully pulled as the pins are being inserted until the normal shape is resumed. (It is advisable to pin through a tape.) The work is then covered with a sheet of paper and placed under a heavy even weight for twenty-four hours.

To correct puckering on canvas work, first draw out the original shape and size of the work on the blotting-paper. Then damp, not soak, the back of the work with cold water, place it face downwards on the blotting-paper and proceed to stretch it to shape on the board as before. The opposite diagonals should be pinned first and then the middle of each side, after which the pins are placed left and right almost touching each other, while the hand smooths and pulls the work to shape in the process. Pin through the canvas margin and not through the embroidery, and if this is too narrow to grip with a turn, pin through a piece of tape. Bad puckering should be left to stretch thus from one to two days.

To avoid puckering on fine materials such as crêpe-de-chine or satin, it is a good plan to tack a piece of organdie, muslin or lawn at the back and take the embroidery stitches through both layers of material. The superfluous backing is cut away afterwards. This idea is only available when the back of the work will be covered, as for a cushion cover, sachet, etc.

POUNCING, TRACING AND TRANSFERRING

There are many ways to offset a design on material for embroidery. The older and more usual is by " pouncing." This method is necessary to offset an original design or drawing. Ready-made designs are offset by the means of printed transfers.

Pouncing a Design. The materials required for pouncing are: (1) a thick pad of felt or ironing blanket, (2) special " pricker " which resembles a thick pin mounted into a handle, (3) tracing paper (unless the drawing itself can be used), (4) emery paper, (5) drawing-pins long and short, (6) drawing-board or old table, (7) pad of soft cloth or felt rolled into a tight bundle and tied round the middle, and (8) powdered charcoal for light materials or powdered chalk for dark materials. Mix charcoal with little chalk, except for very coarse materials, otherwise it is difficult to blow off cleanly. The drawing or tracing is first laid upon the blanket or felt and pinned through to the board. The outline of the design is then pricked all round with the pricker (*see Fig. 335*). (A dressmaker's tracing wheel may be used for very bold outlines.) The little holes must be pricked closely together, particularly where the finer and more intricate parts of the design occur, pricking from 15 to 25 holes per inch as an average number. When this is completed the drawing is removed and the back rubbed over with emery paper, to smooth away the rough

edges of the holes. (It can easily be seen that Pouncing would spoil any good drawing, so if a good picture or an illustration from a book is being copied, then a tracing must be made first

Fig. 335

and the pricking done on this.) The material is laid on the table or drawing-board and secured with drawing-pins, and the pricked design placed over this and also fixed firmly with drawing-pins. (At this point it is necessary to decide if the design

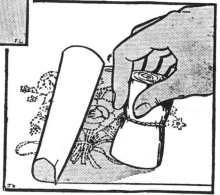

Fig. 336

shall be reversed or used direct, because if the pricked paper is placed right side up, the design will come out the same as the drawing, but placed the *wrong* side up, the design will come out reversed.) Now dip the little pad into charcoal or chalk, according to the colour of the material, and dab, then rub it firmly all over the surface of the paper so that the powder is forced through the little holes on to the material, as shown in *Fig. 336*, where the paper is rolled back to show the impression of the design in little " dots " of powder on the material beneath. When the whole design has been thoroughly rubbed over, remove the paper very carefully and gently blow away any superfluous powder collected on the material.   The design must be fixed on the material with a fine paint brush and thick water-colour paint, as the powder dots would rub away at a touch.   Paint with a suitable colour to show up clearly on the fabric.   Blue is used on most smooth materials, Chinese white on dark, while oil paint mixed with turpentine can be used for rough woollen surfaces.   △ Paint carefully over the dotted outline and, when quite dry, shake off any remaining powder and the material is ready for the embroidery.

Transparent Materials. Transparent materials such as fine silks or lawns can be pinned direct over the drawing and the design traced directly on to the material with water-colour paint and a fine brush or even pencil.

Tracing on Difficult Materials. The best method to offset a design on coarse rough fabric is to trace the pattern out on tissue paper and tack this to the material.   The design is then outlined with running stitches through both paper and material and the paper then torn away, leaving the design roughly outlined in stitches upon the material.

Tracing by Means of Carbon Paper. Carbon paper, as used for typewriting, is sometimes used to offset designs on fine materials.   The carbon is placed face downwards on the material with the drawing over it and the design pencilled over in firm outlines, sufficient to leave an impression on the material.   This method is not recommended as the carbon is apt to smudge and mark the fabric, and it is better to rest the hand on a ruler, slanted off the drawing in making the outline.

Tracing by Means of Transfer Inks. A few successful transfer inks are now on the market and greatly simplify the business of transferring designs, as the outline of the design can be painted over on tracing paper, placed above the drawing and, when dry, be ironed on to the material like a printed transfer. This method, of course, will give the design in the reverse, and in cases where this is not desirable the tracing must be turned over to face the table and another tracing made over this, as it is not advisable to retrace over the back as the front side would be covered with sticky ink and difficult to iron.

A substitute for transfer ink is made in the following way: Dissolve one teaspoonful of Reckitt's washing blue with 3 or 4 teaspoonfuls of sugar in a very little water and pound well together until the grain of the sugar quite disappears. Use as described and, when dry, the design is offset with a warm iron.

The Use of Printed Transfers. For those who are unable to draw or adapt their own designs, a printed transfer is necessary, and providing a careful choice is made, with an eye to good design, some very good results are obtained.

Printed transfers are sold in blue, yellow and black print. Yellow is only satisfactory on black material. Blue is the best colour for all light shades. Black is better for blue, green or brown materials.

Place the transfer with the shiny side downwards and iron over with a hot iron. An indistinct outline is frequently the result of using the iron too cold, and as a test iron off the trade mark (which must always be carefully removed or disaster results) on an odd scrap of similar fabric, or on the back of the work. If the transfer appears to be sticking, a damp cloth should be placed over it and a hot iron run over the surface again.

In offsetting a printed transfer on rough coarse material, first press the fabric with a hot iron through a damp cloth. This temporarily flattens the surface. The transfer should be stamped on quickly before this has time to rise again, and the iron should be held for a second or two in different places until the whole surface has been covered, as the usual ironing movement is not sufficient. If, in spite of these precautions, the outline remains undefined, then it must be strengthened with paint over the faint impression.

Stamping Transfers on Velvet. Four hands are better than two in ironing off a transfer on velvet. Pin the transfer in position and get a second person to hold it taut, and then run the tip of a very hot iron along the transfer lines. In this way but little of the pile will be disturbed and that which is inadvertently pressed down will generally " come up " with steaming. If the work is attempted alone, just iron over a very thick blanket in the same way.

Repeating a Transfer. Any transfer offset correctly should be quite clear and smooth with all the shiny paint transferred to the material. In this case, if the reverse of a design is required for, say, the opposite corner, and it cannot be bought, the outline of the transfer can be painted over with transfer ink as described.

Removing Transfer Marks. The simplest way to remove the marks of printed transfers on linens, etc., is to wash with pure soap flakes and hot water. For an unwashable material, the marks must be carefully and gently rubbed with a clean soft rag dipped into benzine, and placed before a closed window, in the sun.

ENLARGING AND REDUCING A DESIGN

To enlarge or reduce the size of a design is not such a difficult matter as generally supposed. First enclose the original picture, design or floral motif in a square or rectangle as the case may be (*see Fig.* 337, A, B, C, D). Take a large piece of paper and lay the original picture at the corner as in *Fig.* 337, and draw a diagonal line from C, through B to Y. This line can be extended to any length, but to get the required height

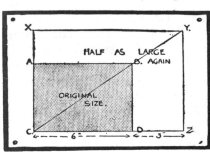

Fig. 337

for a particular enlargement, extend the line CA, and measure off on this the height desired, which we will call X. Supposing the original design be 6″ in height and you desire a design 12″ in height, the line CAX will measure 12″ high. From here the line drawn from X to Y must be parallel to the base of the original design, and cut the diagonal line at the point Y. This gives the correct position for dropping the line YZ.

Any line dropped in this manner to meet the extended base line as shown gives the required new proportion. The next process is to divide the original design into equal squares all over the surface as at *Fig.* 338 A, and then square up the paper on which the enlargement is being made in the same way, making the squares proportionately larger, but *using the same number of divisions* (*Fig.* 338 B). The design is then drawn in freehand upon the enlargement. The cloud appearing in division 2 in the smaller drawing is enlarged proportionately in square 2 of the larger drawing at *Fig.* 338 B. The whole design is drawn out in this way, square by square, and the finished drawing will be a faithful enlargement of the original.

The same principle is applied when reducing a design, only in the reverse order. The diagonal line is made on the large drawing, and the height A represented on the line CX is

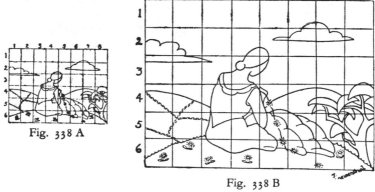

Fig. 338 A

Fig. 338 B

measured off as before, and the parallel lines drawn to meet the diagonal. The large design is divided up into squares as before and the smaller design into an equal number of squares, and the design copied out in freehand.

The number of divisions made in squaring up a design depends on the complexity of the drawing, as intricate designs need a greater number of divisions.

To Evolve a Corner from a Border Design. The problem of forming a suitable corner from a straight border design is overcome by the use of a small mirror which can be purchased from any shop selling artist's materials. The mirror must reflect up to the extreme edge; one with bevelled edges or fitted into a frame of any kind is useless. Place the mirror as shown in

Fig. 339 diagonally across the border at a suitable spot, where the reflection of a right-angles repeat of the pattern with a symmetrical corner will appear. This operation should be repeated until a suitable corner is found as some parts of the design will make a better decoration than others.

Evolving a Square from a Border Design.   By using two mirrors placed at right angles to each other and diagonally across the border as shown in *Fig.* 340 a square motif suitable for a centre

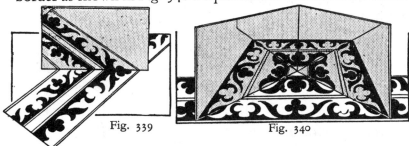

Fig. 339   Fig. 340

decoration can be obtained from the same simple border. A little experiment in moving the mirrors backwards and forwards is required to find the most suitable spot to reflect.

Mounting Finished Work.   An embroidered picture, fire-screen, etc., should be first mounted on cardboard before framing, and a good margin of material left all round the edges of the embroidery for this purpose. Use stiff cardboard and cut to size about a quarter of an inch wider all round than the edge of the embroidery to allow for any overlapping of the wooden frame. The side edges of the material are then folded back over the cardboard and caught together with long stitches taken from side to side. The material top and bottom is folded back and sewn in the same way (*see Fig.* 341.) The stitches must be pulled tightly in

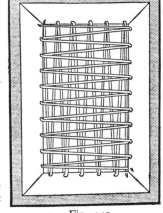

Fig. 341

order to stretch the material firmly over the picture surface, after which it is framed in the usual way.

Canvas-worked chair seats are first mitre-joined at the corners, a space being left for this purpose on the design. Use strong thread for the sewing and afterwards overcast with matching wool to hide any vestige of canvas or thread stitching. Cut away surplus canvas from corners and fit over chair or loose seat. Turn upside-down and tin-tack in position, and then back with hessian or linen slipstitched to the canvas beneath.

Washing and Ironing Embroidery. Most modern embroidery threads will stand washing and some boiling, and provided the material is also of a washable nature, the work can be laundered without any qualms. Dissolve pure soap or good soap flakes in hot water and afterwards dilute with cold until little more than lukewarm. Immerse the embroidery and move gently about, but do not rub. Next rinse in warm and then cold water. Dry quickly. △ Iron on the *wrong* side, placing the work face downwards on to an extra thick blanket so that the embroidery is not flattened out with the iron. (Test to see that it is not too hot.) A damp cloth placed over the work will prevent any possibility of singeing.

To wash delicate embroideries, soak overnight in strong salt and warm water (provided of course the colours are fast). This will remove a great deal of surface dirt, after which carefully immerse in soap and warm water, and move very gently with the hand but never rub. Roll up in a towel and iron as described.

HOW TO MITRE A CORNER

To mitre a corner, first plan the depth of hem to be turned up and allow an extra ¼″ for turning, and crease the lines as shown in *Fig.* 342 A, which also shows how to turn over the corner ABC. Point C is the corner of the cloth and gives the depth of the triangular fold, the line of which is firmly creased

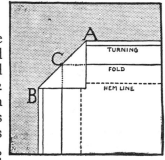

Fig. 342 A

as shown by the dotted line in *Fig.* 342 B. Allow $\frac{1}{4}''$ for turning beyond this creased line and cut off corner as shown, after which the two sides are folded as in *Fig.* 342 C, so that A falls directly over B.   Backstitch the two layers to-

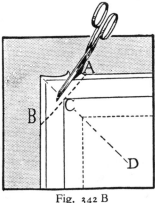

Fig. 342 B

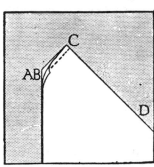

Fig. 342 C

gether along the crease, to within $\frac{1}{4}''$ of the two edges, halting at the creased line of the turnings.   Open out the seam and turn corner to right side when it automatically assumes its correct shape (*Fig.* 342 D).   Tack and hem in the usual way.

Fig. 342 D

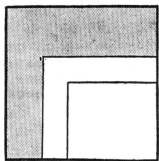

Fig. 342 E

Fig 342 E shows the right side of the corner where no stitching is visible.

How to Mount Lace or Crochet.   A border of crochet squared to fit a tea-cloth, tray-mat, etc., is mounted in the following way, by which method fancy corners present no difficulty at all. The linen used for mounting should be about $1''$ larger all round than the interior measurement of the crochet square. First lay the crochet upon the linen square, making the interior edge of the crochet fall accurately along the thread of the linen. Here pin the crochet in position, and with chalk or pencil, draw along the exact lines of the linen threads where the edges of the crochet fall. Now remove the crochet (*Fig.* 343), and the exact outline of its shape will be left upon the linen as at A. △ Examine the outline and correct any crooked spots as this preparation is so important, and cannot be corrected afterwards. This outline is then button stitched, arranging the

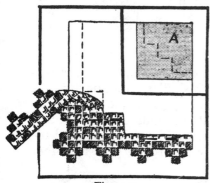
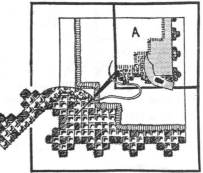

Fig. 343   Fig. 344

looped edge to fall on the outside and along the pencilled outline (*see Fig.* 344). Now lay the crochet back into its original position again so that it fits exactly along the buttonholed outline. Tack, and then whip the edge of the crochet to the looped edge of the buttonhole stitching (*Fig.* 344) without taking the needle through the superfluous material beneath. When the crochet is safely attached to the linen in this way, turn the work over and cut away the superfluous material from the back outside the buttonhole stitching and quite close up to the edge as shown at A, *Fig.* 344.

How to Make a Pad for a Tea-cosy. The secret of making a good firm cosy pad to " sit well " on a tray, is to avoid any seam round the bottom edge (*see Fig.* 345). The average size

Fig. 345

of a cosy pad is 14" by 12" high. Breakfast size 10½" by 7½"
high. The pad is usually made of soft silk or sateen and
filled with cotton wadding. First cut out or procure a paper
pattern of the shape (*Fig.* 346 A). Now take the silk and
fold it in half and place the paper pattern along the folded
edge as in *Fig.* 346 B and cut round the edges. Open out flat

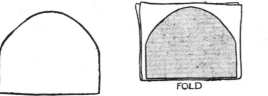

Fig. 346 A   Fig. 346 B   Fig. 346 C

and the resulting shape will be that in *Fig.* 346 C. Use this
oval as a pattern and cut another similar oval in silk and
two similar ovals in cotton wadding. △ Lay one oval of silk
flat on a table and over this an oval of wadding folded in half
as in *Fig.* 346 D. Tack the double wadding and material together (*Fig.* 346 E), and repeat the same process with the other

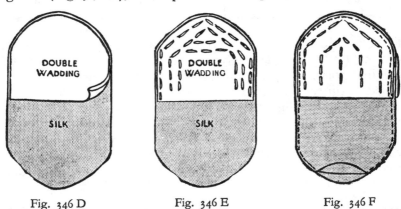

Fig. 346 D   Fig. 346 E   Fig. 346 F

oval of silk and wadding. Both ovals are then placed together
with the silk sides facing in the middle, and the wadded
portions on the outer sides. Tack all firmly together, after
which machine or back stitch together as in *Fig.* 346 F. Leave
an opening at base as shown. △ Be sure that the stitches
pierce all four thicknesses of the wadding. The object of the

opening is shown in *Fig.* 346 G, where the lower half of the silk has been drawn up over the wadding. The opening now comes to the top of the cosy, here the edges are neatly turned in and overcast or slipstitched together (*Fig.* 346 H) and the pad is completed.

Fig. 346 G   Fig. 346 H

EMBROIDERY IN DRESSMAKING

The practical adaptation of embroidery stitches to dressmaking is evidenced in the tailor's buttonhole and the Sprat's Head, Arrow Head and Crow's Foot motifs used to secure the sides of a pocket or the folds of a box pleat.

TAILOR'S BUTTONHOLE

A Tailor's Buttonhole has several distinctive features, quite apart from the actual working of the stitch. The coat front must be prepared with four thicknesses of material: (1) Cloth; (2) A strip of linen to match the cloth, which is laid down from top to bottom of the coat over the positions of the buttonholes; (3) Canvas; (4) Cloth for facing. The first three are made up with the coat, but before the final cloth facings are added the position of the buttonholes is chalked out on the coat front and repeated again on the canvas. △ The canvas only is then cut away round the hole, leaving a space like a letter-box, larger of course than the actual hole. (This prevents the light canvas showing through the stitches and the rough edges from fraying the buttonhole twist.) The facings are then added and the coat finished. The buttonholes are then finally cut. The scissors will, of course, cut through three thicknesses of material only, two of cloth and one of matching linen, as the canvas has been previously cut away as described.

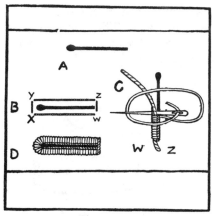

Fig. 347

The diagram in *Fig.* 347 gives the working method. A shows how the buttonhole is cut. The end nearest the coat edge is the "head" and the rounded open part the "eye" of the buttonhole, shaped thus to take the shank of the button. Decorative buttonholes in lapels, etc., are cut without an eye and shaped with a bodkin (or Eversharp pencil) after the hole is worked.

The size of the buttonhole should be a good $\frac{1}{8}''$ longer than the button, and the head placed within the edge about $\frac{3}{4}''$, according to size of button and never less than three-quarters the width of the diameter of the button.

Mark out the buttonholes with tailor's chalk and cut out the eye with fine embroidery scissors (A, *Fig.* 347). Should the material be stretchy or inclined to fray, it is advisable to baste round the hole before cutting.

There are two methods of preparation. The first at B, where the hole is just barred, a method now favoured by the "exclusive" West End tailors as it is softer and more pliable. The second is at C, where the stitches are worked over a gimp which is drawn up when the buttonhole is finished so that it keeps its shape. This latter method is used for overcoats, but a twisted thread is preferable to gimp as it is softer and does not fray the twist. This thread is twisted by placing the double ends between the teeth and bringing it taut over the hand and twisting the threaded needle *towards* you, as any twist made towards the body remains intact while working. Wax the thread when finished. (The thread is prepared in the same way for sewing on the buttons.)

Letter B, *Fig.* 347, shows how a hole is barred. Use a No. 5 needle and tailor's twist and insert between the thicknesses of the material and come up about $\frac{1}{16}''$ from the edge of the hole as at W. Send the needle down again at X and bring it up almost in the same spot at X and take it down again at Y and so on to Z and back to W again. Keep the stitches tight. Send needle up again at W and go round a second time as before. The buttonhole is then worked as at C.

The second method is shown at C.

The buttonhole is not barred but worked with tailor's buttonhole twist over a four-cord thread twisted as described. Leave the needle at the end of the twisted thread as it is then ready to fasten off upon reaching Z. Thread a second with the twist. The twisted thread is then laid along the edge of the buttonhole (leave an end as at CW), and is regulated by the left thumb as the stitching is worked. The ends are afterwards passed through the buttonhole to wrong side of the garment, and drawn up to keep the hole from stretching.

A tailor works his buttonhole *upwards* (this keeps it from gaping), and puts the needle in from right to left, throwing the thread beneath the needle as shown at C. First prepare the twist by drawing it smartly over a cork (not wax as this dulls the surface and soils the twist) to keep it from " snarling," to use a tailor's term. Commence at the lower left side marked W, and secure with a back stitch made on the lining and bring through $\frac{1}{8}''$ away from cut edge of buttonhole. The ends of the twist which come from the eye of the needle are then passed under the point of the needle, in the same direction as the stitch is progressing, and the needle pulled through gently to keep the knotted part of the stitch regulated along the top of the buttonhole and to avoid gaping (*see* C). The working is continued in this way, making each stitch straight and even, and the knots nicely pearled along the edge. The stitches at the " head " must be worked closely together. When the point Z is reached, the ends of the twisted thread are pulled through to the back and drawn up slightly and secured with one or two back stitches. To finish the buttonhole of an overcoat, use the needle threaded with the twist, and work two or three stitches across at the end marked ZW to form a " bar tack." These are then covered with ordinary buttonhole or overcasting stitches made without taking the needle into the material beneath (*see* D). Finish off securely on the wrong side and shape the eye of the buttonhole with a bodkin (or Eversharp pencil). Press.

SPRAT'S HEAD

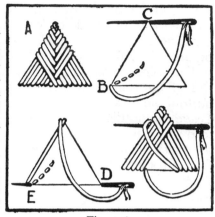

Fig. 348

The method of working a Sprat's Head is shown in *Fig.* 348, with the completed Sprat's Head which forms a triangle at A. The outline of the triangle is first chalked on the material round a shape cut out of thin cardboard (the triangle is equilateral, each side measuring about half an inch). A small running stitch is better worked over the chalked outline for additional clearness, as the chalk line generally disappears. This is afterwards removed.

A fine buttonhole twist to match the material is used for working, and the thread run in from the centre of the triangle emerges at the bottom left-hand corner (B). A small stitch is then made at the apex of the triangle (C) and the needle inserted at D, bottom right-hand corner, to emerge again just inside the first stitch (E). The working continues in this way, taking first a stitch across the top, just below the last, and then across the bottom and just within the previous stitch. In this way each stitch at the top will of necessity get wider and wider as it descends, while each stitch at the bottom will become smaller and smaller as it approaches the middle until the whole triangle is filled in and completed as shown at A.

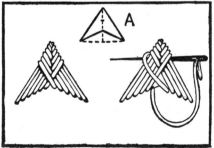

Fig. 349

This triangle is worked over the end of a slit or pleat with the broad end facing the pleat.

ARROW HEAD

A variation of the Sprat's Head known as Arrow Head is shown in *Fig.* 349. The working method is exactly the same except that the stitches taken at the base of the triangle are arranged just above as well as inside each other so that they slant up in triangular formation. The plan of the stitch is shown at A, and the apex of the base line is one third the height of the centre line.

CROW'S FOOT

This is a much more elaborate motif and very interesting to work and not difficult, providing attention is paid to the direction in which the arrows on *Fig.* 350 are pointing, when

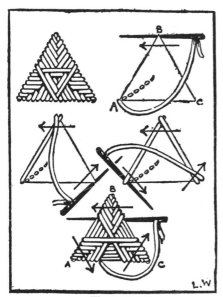

making the stitches at the corners. Both the working method and completed triangle of the Crow's Foot are shown in *Fig.* 350, and it will be seen that the motif is really a more closely interwoven variation of the Sprat's Head. The triangle should be traced in the same way with a cardboard guide, and the buttonhole twist brought out at the bottom left corner (A). A small stitch is then made at the apex (B), another tiny stitch across the bottom right corner (C) in the direction of the arrow, and then a third across the bottom left corner (A), also in the direction of the arrow. △ The working is continued in this way, making a stitch across each corner just within the last and *always* in the direction of the arrow. This is very important in order to achieve the correct interlocking of the threads. As the work progresses, each stitch will approach nearer and nearer towards the middle until the whole triangle is filled.

Fig. 350

ILLUSTRATIONS

ILLUSTRATIONS 299

INDEX

A CATALOG OF SELECTED
DOVER BOOKS
IN ALL FIELDS OF INTEREST

A CATALOG OF SELECTED DOVER
BOOKS IN ALL FIELDS OF INTEREST

DRAWINGS OF REMBRANDT, edited by Seymour Slive. Updated Lippmann, Hofstede de Groot edition, with definitive scholarly apparatus. All portraits, biblical sketches, landscapes, nudes. Oriental figures, classical studies, together with selection of work by followers. 550 illustrations. Total of 630pp. 9⅛ × 12¼.
21485-0, 21486-9 Pa., Two-vol. set $25.00

GHOST AND HORROR STORIES OF AMBROSE BIERCE, Ambrose Bierce. 24 tales vividly imagined, strangely prophetic, and decades ahead of their time in technical skill: "The Damned Thing," "An Inhabitant of Carcosa," "The Eyes of the Panther," "Moxon's Master," and 20 more. 199pp. 5⅜ × 8½. 20767-6 Pa. $3.95

ETHICAL WRITINGS OF MAIMONIDES, Maimonides. Most significant ethical works of great medieval sage, newly translated for utmost precision, readability. Laws Concerning Character Traits, Eight Chapters, more. 192pp. 5⅜ × 8½.
24522-5 Pa. $4.50

THE EXPLORATION OF THE COLORADO RIVER AND ITS CANYONS, J. W. Powell. Full text of Powell's 1,000-mile expedition down the fabled Colorado in 1869. Superb account of terrain, geology, vegetation, Indians, famine, mutiny, treacherous rapids, mighty canyons, during exploration of last unknown part of continental U.S. 400pp. 5⅜ × 8½. 20094-9 Pa. $6.95

HISTORY OF PHILOSOPHY, Julián Marías. Clearest one-volume history on the market. Every major philosopher and dozens of others, to Existentialism and later. 505pp. 5⅜ × 8½. 21739-6 Pa. $8.50

ALL ABOUT LIGHTNING, Martin A. Uman. Highly readable non-technical survey of nature and causes of lightning, thunderstorms, ball lightning, St. Elmo's Fire, much more. Illustrated. 192pp. 5⅜ × 8½. 25237-X Pa. $5.95

SAILING ALONE AROUND THE WORLD, Captain Joshua Slocum. First man to sail around the world, alone, in small boat. One of great feats of seamanship told in delightful manner. 67 illustrations. 294pp. 5⅜ × 8½. 20326-3 Pa. $4.95

LETTERS AND NOTES ON THE MANNERS, CUSTOMS AND CONDITIONS OF THE NORTH AMERICAN INDIANS, George Catlin. Classic account of life among Plains Indians: ceremonies, hunt, warfare, etc. 312 plates. 572pp. of text. 6⅛ × 9¼. 22118-0, 22119-9 Pa. Two-vol. set $15.90

ALASKA: The Harriman Expedition, 1899, John Burroughs, John Muir, et al. Informative, engrossing accounts of two-month, 9,000-mile expedition. Native peoples, wildlife, forests, geography, salmon industry, glaciers, more. Profusely illustrated. 240 black-and-white line drawings. 124 black-and-white photographs. 3 maps. Index. 576pp. 5⅜ × 8½. 25109-8 Pa. $11.95

THE BOOK OF BEASTS: Being a Translation from a Latin Bestiary of the Twelfth Century, T. H. White. Wonderful catalog real and fanciful beasts: manticore, griffin, phoenix, amphivius, jaculus, many more. White's witty erudite commentary on scientific, historical aspects. Fascinating glimpse of medieval mind. Illustrated. 296pp. 5⅜ × 8¼. (Available in U.S. only) 24609-4 Pa. $5.95

FRANK LLOYD WRIGHT: ARCHITECTURE AND NATURE With 160 Illustrations, Donald Hoffmann. Profusely illustrated study of influence of nature—especially prairie—on Wright's designs for Fallingwater, Robie House, Guggenheim Museum, other masterpieces. 96pp. 9¼ × 10¾. 25098-9 Pa. $7.95

FRANK LLOYD WRIGHT'S FALLINGWATER, Donald Hoffmann. Wright's famous waterfall house: planning and construction of organic idea. History of site, owners, Wright's personal involvement. Photographs of various stages of building. Preface by Edgar Kaufmann, Jr. 100 illustrations. 112pp. 9¼ × 10. 23671-4 Pa. $7.95

YEARS WITH FRANK LLOYD WRIGHT: Apprentice to Genius, Edgar Tafel. Insightful memoir by a former apprentice presents a revealing portrait of Wright the man, the inspired teacher, the greatest American architect. 372 black-and-white illustrations. Preface. Index. vi + 228pp. 8¼ × 11. 24801-1 Pa. $9.95

THE STORY OF KING ARTHUR AND HIS KNIGHTS, Howard Pyle. Enchanting version of King Arthur fable has delighted generations with imaginative narratives of exciting adventures and unforgettable illustrations by the author. 41 illustrations. xviii + 313pp. 6⅛ × 9¼. 21445-1 Pa. $6.50

THE GODS OF THE EGYPTIANS, E. A. Wallis Budge. Thorough coverage of numerous gods of ancient Egypt by foremost Egyptologist. Information on evolution of cults, rites and gods; the cult of Osiris; the Book of the Dead and its rites; the sacred animals and birds; Heaven and Hell; and more. 956pp. 6⅛ × 9¼. 22055-9, 22056-7 Pa., Two-vol. set $20.00

A THEOLOGICO-POLITICAL TREATISE, Benedict Spinoza. Also contains unfinished *Political Treatise*. Great classic on religious liberty, theory of government on common consent. R. Elwes translation. Total of 421pp. 5⅜ × 8½. 20249-6 Pa. $6.95

INCIDENTS OF TRAVEL IN CENTRAL AMERICA, CHIAPAS, AND YUCATAN, John L. Stephens. Almost single-handed discovery of Maya culture; exploration of ruined cities, monuments, temples; customs of Indians. 115 drawings. 892pp. 5⅜ × 8½. 22404-X, 22405-8 Pa., Two-vol. set $15.90

LOS CAPRICHOS, Francisco Goya. 80 plates of wild, grotesque monsters and caricatures. Prado manuscript included. 183pp. 6⅝ × 9⅝. 22384-1 Pa. $4.95

AUTOBIOGRAPHY: The Story of My Experiments with Truth, Mohandas K. Gandhi. Not hagiography, but Gandhi in his own words. Boyhood, legal studies, purification, the growth of the Satyagraha (nonviolent protest) movement. Critical, inspiring work of the man who freed India. 480pp. 5⅜ × 8½. (Available in U.S. only) 24593-4 Pa. $6.95

ILLUSTRATED DICTIONARY OF HISTORIC ARCHITECTURE, edited by Cyril M. Harris. Extraordinary compendium of clear, concise definitions for over 5,000 important architectural terms complemented by over 2,000 line drawings. Covers full spectrum of architecture from ancient ruins to 20th-century Modernism. Preface. 592pp. 7½ × 9⅜. 24444-X Pa. $14.95

THE NIGHT BEFORE CHRISTMAS, Clement Moore. Full text, and woodcuts from original 1848 book. Also critical, historical material. 19 illustrations. 40pp. 4⅝ × 6. 22797-9 Pa. $2.25

THE LESSON OF JAPANESE ARCHITECTURE: 165 Photographs, Jiro Harada. Memorable gallery of 165 photographs taken in the 1930's of exquisite Japanese homes of the well-to-do and historic buildings. 13 line diagrams. 192pp. 8⅜ × 11¼. 24778-3 Pa. $8.95

THE AUTOBIOGRAPHY OF CHARLES DARWIN AND SELECTED LETTERS, edited by Francis Darwin. The fascinating life of eccentric genius composed of an intimate memoir by Darwin (intended for his children); commentary by his son, Francis; hundreds of fragments from notebooks, journals, papers; and letters to and from Lyell, Hooker, Huxley, Wallace and Henslow. xi + 365pp. 5⅜ × 8. 20479-0 Pa. $6.95

WONDERS OF THE SKY: Observing Rainbows, Comets, Eclipses, the Stars and Other Phenomena, Fred Schaaf. Charming, easy-to-read poetic guide to all manner of celestial events visible to the naked eye. Mock suns, glories, Belt of Venus, more. Illustrated. 299pp. 5¼ × 8¼. 24402-4 Pa. $7.95

BURNHAM'S CELESTIAL HANDBOOK, Robert Burnham, Jr. Thorough guide to the stars beyond our solar system. Exhaustive treatment. Alphabetical by constellation: Andromeda to Cetus in Vol. 1; Chamaeleon to Orion in Vol. 2; and Pavo to Vulpecula in Vol. 3. Hundreds of illustrations. Index in Vol. 3. 2,000pp. 6⅛ × 9¼. 23567-X, 23568-8, 23673-0 Pa., Three-vol. set $38.85

STAR NAMES: Their Lore and Meaning, Richard Hinckley Allen. Fascinating history of names various cultures have given to constellations and literary and folkloristic uses that have been made of stars. Indexes to subjects. Arabic and Greek names. Biblical references. Bibliography. 563pp. 5⅜ × 8½. 21079-0 Pa. $7.95

THIRTY YEARS THAT SHOOK PHYSICS: The Story of Quantum Theory, George Gamow. Lucid, accessible introduction to influential theory of energy and matter. Careful explanations of Dirac's anti-particles, Bohr's model of the atom, much more. 12 plates. Numerous drawings. 240pp. 5⅜ × 8½. 24895-X Pa. $4.95

CHINESE DOMESTIC FURNITURE IN PHOTOGRAPHS AND MEASURED DRAWINGS, Gustav Ecke. A rare volume, now affordably priced for antique collectors, furniture buffs and art historians. Detailed review of styles ranging from early Shang to late Ming. Unabridged republication. 161 black-and-white drawings, photos. Total of 224pp. 8⅜ × 11¼. (Available in U.S. only) 25171-3 Pa. $12.95

VINCENT VAN GOGH: A Biography, Julius Meier-Graefe. Dynamic, penetrating study of artist's life, relationship with brother, Theo, painting techniques, travels, more. Readable, engrossing. 160pp. 5⅜ × 8½. (Available in U.S. only) 25253-1 Pa. $3.95

HOW TO WRITE, Gertrude Stein. Gertrude Stein claimed anyone could understand her unconventional writing—here are clues to help. Fascinating improvisations, language experiments, explanations illuminate Stein's craft and the art of writing. Total of 414pp. 4⅜ × 6⅜. 23144-5 Pa. $5.95

ADVENTURES AT SEA IN THE GREAT AGE OF SAIL: Five Firsthand Narratives, edited by Elliot Snow. Rare true accounts of exploration, whaling, shipwreck, fierce natives, trade, shipboard life, more. 33 illustrations. Introduction. 353pp. 5⅜ × 8½. 25177-2 Pa. $7.95

THE HERBAL OR GENERAL HISTORY OF PLANTS, John Gerard. Classic descriptions of about 2,850 plants—with over 2,700 illustrations—includes Latin and English names, physical descriptions, varieties, time and place of growth, more. 2,706 illustrations. xlv + 1,678pp. 8½ × 12¼. 23147-X Cloth. $75.00

DOROTHY AND THE WIZARD IN OZ, L. Frank Baum. Dorothy and the Wizard visit the center of the Earth, where people are vegetables, glass houses grow and Oz characters reappear. Classic sequel to *Wizard of Oz.* 256pp. 5⅜ × 8. 24714-7 Pa. $4.95

SONGS OF EXPERIENCE: Facsimile Reproduction with 26 Plates in Full Color, William Blake. This facsimile of Blake's original "Illuminated Book" reproduces 26 full-color plates from a rare 1826 edition. Includes "The Tyger," "London," "Holy Thursday," and other immortal poems. 26 color plates. Printed text of poems. 48pp. 5¼ × 7. 24636-1 Pa. $3.50

SONGS OF INNOCENCE, William Blake. The first and most popular of Blake's famous "Illuminated Books," in a facsimile edition reproducing all 31 brightly colored plates. Additional printed text of each poem. 64pp. 5¼ × 7. 22764-2 Pa. $3.50

PRECIOUS STONES, Max Bauer. Classic, thorough study of diamonds, rubies, emeralds, garnets, etc.: physical character, occurrence, properties, use, similar topics. 20 plates, 8 in color. 94 figures. 659pp. 6⅛ × 9¼. 21910-0, 21911-9 Pa., Two-vol. set $15.90

ENCYCLOPEDIA OF VICTORIAN NEEDLEWORK, S. F. A. Caulfeild and Blanche Saward. Full, precise descriptions of stitches, techniques for dozens of needlecrafts—most exhaustive reference of its kind. Over 800 figures. Total of 679pp. 8⅛ × 11. Two volumes. Vol. 1 22800-2 Pa. $11.95
Vol. 2 22801-0 Pa. $11.95

THE MARVELOUS LAND OF OZ, L. Frank Baum. Second Oz book, the Scarecrow and Tin Woodman are back with hero named Tip, Oz magic. 136 illustrations. 287pp. 5⅜ × 8½. 20692-0 Pa. $5.95

WILD FOWL DECOYS, Joel Barber. Basic book on the subject, by foremost authority and collector. Reveals history of decoy making and rigging, place in American culture, different kinds of decoys, how to make them, and how to use them. 140 plates. 156pp. 7⅞ × 10¾. 20011-6 Pa. $8.95

HISTORY OF LACE, Mrs. Bury Palliser. Definitive, profusely illustrated chronicle of lace from earliest times to late 19th century. Laces of Italy, Greece, England, France, Belgium, etc. Landmark of needlework scholarship. 266 illustrations. 672pp. 6⅛ × 9¼. 24742-2 Pa. $14.95

ILLUSTRATED GUIDE TO SHAKER FURNITURE, Robert Meader. All furniture and appurtenances, with much on unknown local styles. 235 photos. 146pp. 9 × 12. 22819-3 Pa. $7.95

WHALE SHIPS AND WHALING: A Pictorial Survey, George Francis Dow. Over 200 vintage engravings, drawings, photographs of barks, brigs, cutters, other vessels. Also harpoons, lances, whaling guns, many other artifacts. Comprehensive text by foremost authority. 207 black-and-white illustrations. 288pp. 6 × 9. 24808-9 Pa. $8.95

THE BERTRAMS, Anthony Trollope. Powerful portrayal of blind self-will and thwarted ambition includes one of Trollope's most heartrending love stories. 497pp. 5⅜ × 8½. 25119-5 Pa. $8.95

ADVENTURES WITH A HAND LENS, Richard Headstrom. Clearly written guide to observing and studying flowers and grasses, fish scales, moth and insect wings, egg cases, buds, feathers, seeds, leaf scars, moss, molds, ferns, common crystals, etc.—all with an ordinary, inexpensive magnifying glass. 209 exact line drawings aid in your discoveries. 220pp. 5⅜ × 8½. 23330-8 Pa. $3.95

RODIN ON ART AND ARTISTS, Auguste Rodin. Great sculptor's candid, wide-ranging comments on meaning of art; great artists; relation of sculpture to poetry, painting, music; philosophy of life, more. 76 superb black-and-white illustrations of Rodin's sculpture, drawings and prints. 119pp. 8⅜ × 11¼. 24487-3 Pa. $6.95

FIFTY CLASSIC FRENCH FILMS, 1912–1982: A Pictorial Record, Anthony Slide. Memorable stills from Grand Illusion, Beauty and the Beast, Hiroshima, Mon Amour, many more. Credits, plot synopses, reviews, etc. 160pp. 8¼ × 11. 25256-6 Pa. $11.95

THE PRINCIPLES OF PSYCHOLOGY, William James. Famous long course complete, unabridged. Stream of thought, time perception, memory, experimental methods; great work decades ahead of its time. 94 figures. 1,391pp. 5⅜ × 8½. 20381-6, 20382-4 Pa., Two-vol. set $19.90

BODIES IN A BOOKSHOP, R. T. Campbell. Challenging mystery of blackmail and murder with ingenious plot and superbly drawn characters. In the best tradition of British suspense fiction. 192pp. 5⅜ × 8½. 24720-1 Pa. $3.95

CALLAS: PORTRAIT OF A PRIMA DONNA, George Jellinek. Renowned commentator on the musical scene chronicles incredible career and life of the most controversial, fascinating, influential operatic personality of our time. 64 black-and-white photographs. 416pp. 5⅜ × 8¼. 25047-4 Pa. $7.95

GEOMETRY, RELATIVITY AND THE FOURTH DIMENSION, Rudolph Rucker. Exposition of fourth dimension, concepts of relativity as Flatland characters continue adventures. Popular, easily followed yet accurate, profound. 141 illustrations. 133pp. 5⅜ × 8½. 23400-2 Pa. $3.95

HOUSEHOLD STORIES BY THE BROTHERS GRIMM, with pictures by Walter Crane. 53 classic stories—Rumpelstiltskin, Rapunzel, Hansel and Gretel, the Fisherman and his Wife, Snow White, Tom Thumb, Sleeping Beauty, Cinderella, and so much more—lavishly illustrated with original 19th century drawings. 114 illustrations. x + 269pp. 5⅜ × 8½. 21080-4 Pa. $4.50

CATALOG OF DOVER BOOKS

SUNDIALS, Albert Waugh. Far and away the best, most thorough coverage of ideas, mathematics concerned, types, construction, adjusting anywhere. Over 100 illustrations. 230pp. 5⅜ × 8½. 22947-5 Pa. $4.50

PICTURE HISTORY OF THE NORMANDIE: With 190 Illustrations, Frank O. Braynard. Full story of legendary French ocean liner: Art Deco interiors, design innovations, furnishings, celebrities, maiden voyage, tragic fire, much more. Extensive text. 144pp. 8⅞ × 11¾. 25257-4 Pa. $9.95

THE FIRST AMERICAN COOKBOOK: A Facsimile of "American Cookery," 1796, Amelia Simmons. Facsimile of the first American-written cookbook published in the United States contains authentic recipes for colonial favorites—pumpkin pudding, winter squash pudding, spruce beer, Indian slapjacks, and more. Introductory Essay and Glossary of colonial cooking terms. 80pp. 5⅜ × 8½. 24710-4 Pa. $3.50

101 PUZZLES IN THOUGHT AND LOGIC, C. R. Wylie, Jr. Solve murders and robberies, find out which fishermen are liars, how a blind man could possibly identify a color—purely by your own reasoning! 107pp. 5⅜ × 8½. 20367-0 Pa. $2.50

THE BOOK OF WORLD-FAMOUS MUSIC—CLASSICAL, POPULAR AND FOLK, James J. Fuld. Revised and enlarged republication of landmark work in musico-bibliography. Full information about nearly 1,000 songs and compositions including first lines of music and lyrics. New supplement. Index. 800pp. 5⅜ × 8¼. 24857-7 Pa. $14.95

ANTHROPOLOGY AND MODERN LIFE, Franz Boas. Great anthropologist's classic treatise on race and culture. Introduction by Ruth Bunzel. Only inexpensive paperback edition. 255pp. 5⅜ × 8½. 25245-0 Pa. $5.95

THE TALE OF PETER RABBIT, Beatrix Potter. The inimitable Peter's terrifying adventure in Mr. McGregor's garden, with all 27 wonderful, full-color Potter illustrations. 55pp. 4¼ × 5½. (Available in U.S. only) 22827-4 Pa. $1.75

THREE PROPHETIC SCIENCE FICTION NOVELS, H. G. Wells. *When the Sleeper Wakes, A Story of the Days to Come* and *The Time Machine* (full version). 335pp. 5⅜ × 8½. (Available in U.S. only) 20605-X Pa. $5.95

APICIUS COOKERY AND DINING IN IMPERIAL ROME, edited and translated by Joseph Dommers Vehling. Oldest known cookbook in existence offers readers a clear picture of what foods Romans ate, how they prepared them, etc. 49 illustrations. 301pp. 6⅛ × 9¼. 23563-7 Pa. $6.50

SHAKESPEARE LEXICON AND QUOTATION DICTIONARY, Alexander Schmidt. Full definitions, locations, shades of meaning of every word in plays and poems. More than 50,000 exact quotations. 1,485pp. 6½ × 9¼. 22726-X, 22727-8 Pa., Two-vol. set $27.90

THE WORLD'S GREAT SPEECHES, edited by Lewis Copeland and Lawrence W. Lamm. Vast collection of 278 speeches from Greeks to 1970. Powerful and effective models; unique look at history. 842pp. 5⅜ × 8½. 20468-5 Pa. $11.95

THE BLUE FAIRY BOOK, Andrew Lang. The first, most famous collection, with many familiar tales: Little Red Riding Hood, Aladdin and the Wonderful Lamp, Puss in Boots, Sleeping Beauty, Hansel and Gretel, Rumpelstiltskin; 37 in all. 138 illustrations. 390pp. 5⅜ × 8½. 21437-0 Pa. $5.95

THE STORY OF THE CHAMPIONS OF THE ROUND TABLE, Howard Pyle. Sir Launcelot, Sir Tristram and Sir Percival in spirited adventures of love and triumph retold in Pyle's inimitable style. 50 drawings, 31 full-page. xviii + 329pp. 6½ × 9¼. 21883-X Pa. $6.95

AUDUBON AND HIS JOURNALS, Maria Audubon. Unmatched two-volume portrait of the great artist, naturalist and author contains his journals, an excellent biography by his granddaughter, expert annotations by the noted ornithologist, Dr. Elliott Coues, and 37 superb illustrations. Total of 1,200pp. 5⅜ × 8.
Vol. I 25143-8 Pa. $8.95
Vol. II 25144-6 Pa. $8.95

GREAT DINOSAUR HUNTERS AND THEIR DISCOVERIES, Edwin H. Colbert. Fascinating, lavishly illustrated chronicle of dinosaur research, 1820's to 1960. Achievements of Cope, Marsh, Brown, Buckland, Mantell, Huxley, many others. 384pp. 5¼ × 8¼. 24701-5 Pa. $6.95

THE TASTEMAKERS, Russell Lynes. Informal, illustrated social history of American taste 1850's-1950's. First popularized categories Highbrow, Lowbrow, Middlebrow. 129 illustrations. New (1979) afterword. 384pp. 6 × 9. 23993-4 Pa. $6.95

DOUBLE CROSS PURPOSES, Ronald A. Knox. A treasure hunt in the Scottish Highlands, an old map, unidentified corpse, surprise discoveries keep reader guessing in this cleverly intricate tale of financial skullduggery. 2 black-and-white maps. 320pp. 5⅜ × 8½. (Available in U.S. only) 25032-6 Pa. $5.95

AUTHENTIC VICTORIAN DECORATION AND ORNAMENTATION IN FULL COLOR: 46 Plates from "Studies in Design," Christopher Dresser. Superb full-color lithographs reproduced from rare original portfolio of a major Victorian designer. 48pp. 9¼ × 12¼. 25083-0 Pa. $7.95

PRIMITIVE ART, Franz Boas. Remains the best text ever prepared on subject, thoroughly discussing Indian, African, Asian, Australian, and, especially, Northern American primitive art. Over 950 illustrations show ceramics, masks, totem poles, weapons, textiles, paintings, much more. 376pp. 5⅜ × 8. 20025-6 Pa. $6.95

SIDELIGHTS ON RELATIVITY, Albert Einstein. Unabridged republication of two lectures delivered by the great physicist in 1920-21. *Ether and Relativity* and *Geometry and Experience*. Elegant ideas in non-mathematical form, accessible to intelligent layman. vi + 56pp. 5⅜ × 8½. 24511-X Pa. $2.95

THE WIT AND HUMOR OF OSCAR WILDE, edited by Alvin Redman. More than 1,000 ripostes, paradoxes, wisecracks: Work is the curse of the drinking classes, I can resist everything except temptation, etc. 258pp. 5⅜ × 8½. 20602-5 Pa. $4.50

ADVENTURES WITH A MICROSCOPE, Richard Headstrom. 59 adventures with clothing fibers, protozoa, ferns and lichens, roots and leaves, much more. 142 illustrations. 232pp. 5⅜ × 8½. 23471-1 Pa. $3.95

PLANTS OF THE BIBLE, Harold N. Moldenke and Alma L. Moldenke. Standard reference to all 230 plants mentioned in Scriptures. Latin name, biblical reference, uses, modern identity, much more. Unsurpassed encyclopedic resource for scholars, botanists, nature lovers, students of Bible. Bibliography. Indexes. 123 black-and-white illustrations. 384pp. 6 × 9. 25069-5 Pa. $8.95

FAMOUS AMERICAN WOMEN: A Biographical Dictionary from Colonial Times to the Present, Robert McHenry, ed. From Pocahontas to Rosa Parks, 1,035 distinguished American women documented in separate biographical entries. Accurate, up-to-date data, numerous categories, spans 400 years. Indices. 493pp. 6½ × 9¼. 24523-3 Pa. $9.95

THE FABULOUS INTERIORS OF THE GREAT OCEAN LINERS IN HISTORIC PHOTOGRAPHS, William H. Miller, Jr. Some 200 superb photographs capture exquisite interiors of world's great "floating palaces"—1890's to 1980's: *Titanic, Ile de France, Queen Elizabeth, United States, Europa,* more. Approx. 200 black-and-white photographs. Captions. Text. Introduction. 160pp. 8⅞ × 11¾. 24756-2 Pa. $9.95

THE GREAT LUXURY LINERS, 1927–1954: A Photographic Record, William H. Miller, Jr. Nostalgic tribute to heyday of ocean liners. 186 photos of Ile de France, Normandie, Leviathan, Queen Elizabeth, United States, many others. Interior and exterior views. Introduction. Captions. 160pp. 9 × 12. 24056-8 Pa. $9.95

A NATURAL HISTORY OF THE DUCKS, John Charles Phillips. Great landmark of ornithology offers complete detailed coverage of nearly 200 species and subspecies of ducks: gadwall, sheldrake, merganser, pintail, many more. 74 full-color plates, 102 black-and-white. Bibliography. Total of 1,920pp. 8⅝ × 11¼. 25141-1, 25142-X Cloth. Two-vol. set $100.00

THE SEAWEED HANDBOOK: An Illustrated Guide to Seaweeds from North Carolina to Canada, Thomas F. Lee. Concise reference covers 78 species. Scientific and common names, habitat, distribution, more. Finding keys for easy identification. 224pp. 5⅜ × 8½. 25215-9 Pa. $5.95

THE TEN BOOKS OF ARCHITECTURE: The 1755 Leoni Edition, Leon Battista Alberti. Rare classic helped introduce the glories of ancient architecture to the Renaissance. 68 black-and-white plates. 336pp. 8⅜ × 11¼. 25239-6 Pa. $14.95

MISS MACKENZIE, Anthony Trollope. Minor masterpieces by Victorian master unmasks many truths about life in 19th-century England. First inexpensive edition in years. 392pp. 5⅜ × 8½. 25201-9 Pa. $7.95

THE RIME OF THE ANCIENT MARINER, Gustave Doré, Samuel Taylor Coleridge. Dramatic engravings considered by many to be his greatest work. The terrifying space of the open sea, the storms and whirlpools of an unknown ocean, the ice of Antarctica, more—all rendered in a powerful, chilling manner. Full text. 38 plates. 77pp. 9¼ × 12. 22305-1 Pa. $4.95

THE EXPEDITIONS OF ZEBULON MONTGOMERY PIKE, Zebulon Montgomery Pike. Fascinating first-hand accounts (1805–6) of exploration of Mississippi River, Indian wars, capture by Spanish dragoons, much more. 1,088pp. 5⅜ × 8½. 25254-X, 25255-8 Pa. Two-vol. set $23.90

A CONCISE HISTORY OF PHOTOGRAPHY: Third Revised Edition, Helmut Gernsheim. Best one-volume history—camera obscura, photochemistry, daguerreotypes, evolution of cameras, film, more. Also artistic aspects—landscape, portraits, fine art, etc. 281 black-and-white photographs. 26 in color. 176pp. 8⅜ × 11¼. 25128-4 Pa. $12.95

THE DORÉ BIBLE ILLUSTRATIONS, Gustave Doré. 241 detailed plates from the Bible: the Creation scenes, Adam and Eve, Flood, Babylon, battle sequences, life of Jesus, etc. Each plate is accompanied by the verses from the King James version of the Bible. 241pp. 9 × 12. 23004-X Pa. $8.95

HUGGER-MUGGER IN THE LOUVRE, Elliot Paul. Second Homer Evans mystery-comedy. Theft at the Louvre involves sleuth in hilarious, madcap caper. "A knockout."—Books. 336pp. 5⅜ × 8½. 25185-3 Pa. $5.95

FLATLAND, E. A. Abbott. Intriguing and enormously popular science-fiction classic explores the complexities of trying to survive as a two-dimensional being in a three-dimensional world. Amusingly illustrated by the author. 16 illustrations. 103pp. 5⅜ × 8½. 20001-9 Pa. $2.25

THE HISTORY OF THE LEWIS AND CLARK EXPEDITION, Meriwether Lewis and William Clark, edited by Elliott Coues. Classic edition of Lewis and Clark's day-by-day journals that later became the basis for U.S. claims to Oregon and the West. Accurate and invaluable geographical, botanical, biological, meteorological and anthropological material. Total of 1,508pp. 5⅜ × 8½.
21268-8, 21269-6, 21270-X Pa. Three-vol. set $25.50

LANGUAGE, TRUTH AND LOGIC, Alfred J. Ayer. Famous, clear introduction to Vienna, Cambridge schools of Logical Positivism. Role of philosophy, elimination of metaphysics, nature of analysis, etc. 160pp. 5⅜ × 8½. (Available in U.S. and Canada only) 20010-8 Pa. $2.95

MATHEMATICS FOR THE NONMATHEMATICIAN, Morris Kline. Detailed, college-level treatment of mathematics in cultural and historical context, with numerous exercises. For liberal arts students. Preface. Recommended Reading Lists. Tables. Index. Numerous black-and-white figures. xvi + 641pp. 5⅜ × 8½.
24823-2 Pa. $11.95

28 SCIENCE FICTION STORIES, H. G. Wells. Novels, *Star Begotten* and *Men Like Gods,* plus 26 short stories: "Empire of the Ants," "A Story of the Stone Age," "The Stolen Bacillus," "In the Abyss," etc. 915pp. 5⅜ × 8½. (Available in U.S. only)
20265-8 Cloth. $10.95

HANDBOOK OF PICTORIAL SYMBOLS, Rudolph Modley. 3,250 signs and symbols, many systems in full; official or heavy commercial use. Arranged by subject. Most in Pictorial Archive series. 143pp. 8⅛ × 11. 23357-X Pa. $5.95

INCIDENTS OF TRAVEL IN YUCATAN, John L. Stephens. Classic (1843) exploration of jungles of Yucatan, looking for evidences of Maya civilization. Travel adventures, Mexican and Indian culture, etc. Total of 669pp. 5⅜ × 8½.
20926-1, 20927-X Pa., Two-vol. set $9.90

DEGAS: An Intimate Portrait, Ambroise Vollard. Charming, anecdotal memoir by famous art dealer of one of the greatest 19th-century French painters. 14 black-and-white illustrations. Introduction by Harold L. Van Doren. 96pp. 5⅜ × 8½.
25131-4 Pa. $3.95

PERSONAL NARRATIVE OF A PILGRIMAGE TO ALMANDINAH AND MECCAH, Richard Burton. Great travel classic by remarkably colorful personality. Burton, disguised as a Moroccan, visited sacred shrines of Islam, narrowly escaping death. 47 illustrations. 959pp. 5⅜ × 8½. 21217-3, 21218-1 Pa., Two-vol. set $19.90

PHRASE AND WORD ORIGINS, A. H. Holt. Entertaining, reliable, modern study of more than 1,200 colorful words, phrases, origins and histories. Much unexpected information. 254pp. 5⅜ × 8½. 20758-7 Pa. $4.95

THE RED THUMB MARK, R. Austin Freeman. In this first Dr. Thorndyke case, the great scientific detective draws fascinating conclusions from the nature of a single fingerprint. Exciting story, authentic science. 320pp. 5⅜ × 8½. (Available in U.S. only) 25210-8 Pa. $5.95

AN EGYPTIAN HIEROGLYPHIC DICTIONARY, E. A. Wallis Budge. Monumental work containing about 25,000 words or terms that occur in texts ranging from 3000 B.C. to 600 A.D. Each entry consists of a transliteration of the word, the word in hieroglyphs, and the meaning in English. 1,314pp. 6⅜ × 10.
23615-3, 23616-1 Pa., Two-vol. set $27.90

THE COMPLEAT STRATEGYST: Being a Primer on the Theory of Games of Strategy, J. D. Williams. Highly entertaining classic describes, with many illustrated examples, how to select best strategies in conflict situations. Prefaces. Appendices. xvi + 268pp. 5⅜ × 8½. 25101-2 Pa. $5.95

THE ROAD TO OZ, L. Frank Baum. Dorothy meets the Shaggy Man, little Button-Bright and the Rainbow's beautiful daughter in this delightful trip to the magical Land of Oz. 272pp. 5⅜ × 8. 25208-6 Pa. $4.95

POINT AND LINE TO PLANE, Wassily Kandinsky. Seminal exposition of role of point, line, other elements in non-objective painting. Essential to understanding 20th-century art. 127 illustrations. 192pp. 6½ × 9¼. 23808-3 Pa. $4.50

LADY ANNA, Anthony Trollope. Moving chronicle of Countess Lovel's bitter struggle to win for herself and daughter Anna their rightful rank and fortune— perhaps at cost of sanity itself. 384pp. 5⅜ × 8½. 24669-8 Pa. $6.95

EGYPTIAN MAGIC, E. A. Wallis Budge. Sums up all that is known about magic in Ancient Egypt: the role of magic in controlling the gods, powerful amulets that warded off evil spirits, scarabs of immortality, use of wax images, formulas and spells, the secret name, much more. 253pp. 5⅜ × 8½. 22681-6 Pa. $4.00

THE DANCE OF SIVA, Ananda Coomaraswamy. Preeminent authority unfolds the vast metaphysic of India: the revelation of her art, conception of the universe, social organization, etc. 27 reproductions of art masterpieces. 192pp. 5⅜ × 8½.
24817-8 Pa. $5.95

CHRISTMAS CUSTOMS AND TRADITIONS, Clement A. Miles. Origin, evolution, significance of religious, secular practices. Caroling, gifts, yule logs, much more. Full, scholarly yet fascinating; non-sectarian. 400pp. 5⅜ × 8½.
23354-5 Pa. $6.50

THE HUMAN FIGURE IN MOTION, Eadweard Muybridge. More than 4,500 stopped-action photos, in action series, showing undraped men, women, children jumping, lying down, throwing, sitting, wrestling, carrying, etc. 390pp. 7⅞ × 10⅝.
20204-6 Cloth. $21.95

THE MAN WHO WAS THURSDAY, Gilbert Keith Chesterton. Witty, fast-paced novel about a club of anarchists in turn-of-the-century London. Brilliant social, religious, philosophical speculations. 128pp. 5⅜ × 8½. 25121-7 Pa. $3.95

A CEZANNE SKETCHBOOK: Figures, Portraits, Landscapes and Still Lifes, Paul Cezanne. Great artist experiments with tonal effects, light, mass, other qualities in over 100 drawings. A revealing view of developing master painter, precursor of Cubism. 102 black-and-white illustrations. 144pp. 8¾ × 6⅜. 24790-2 Pa. $5.95

AN ENCYCLOPEDIA OF BATTLES: Accounts of Over 1,560 Battles from 1479 B.C. to the Present, David Eggenberger. Presents essential details of every major battle in recorded history, from the first battle of Megiddo in 1479 B.C. to Grenada in 1984. List of Battle Maps. New Appendix covering the years 1967–1984. Index. 99 illustrations. 544pp. 6½ × 9¼. 24913-1 Pa. $14.95

AN ETYMOLOGICAL DICTIONARY OF MODERN ENGLISH, Ernest Weekley. Richest, fullest work, by foremost British lexicographer. Detailed word histories. Inexhaustible. Total of 856pp. 6½ × 9¼.
21873-2, 21874-0 Pa., Two-vol. set $17.00

WEBSTER'S AMERICAN MILITARY BIOGRAPHIES, edited by Robert McHenry. Over 1,000 figures who shaped 3 centuries of American military history. Detailed biographies of Nathan Hale, Douglas MacArthur, Mary Hallaren, others. Chronologies of engagements, more. Introduction. Addenda. 1,033 entries in alphabetical order. xi + 548pp. 6½ × 9¼. (Available in U.S. only)
24758-9 Pa. $11.95

LIFE IN ANCIENT EGYPT, Adolf Erman. Detailed older account, with much not in more recent books: domestic life, religion, magic, medicine, commerce, and whatever else needed for complete picture. Many illustrations. 597pp. 5⅜ × 8½.
22632-8 Pa. $8.50

HISTORIC COSTUME IN PICTURES, Braun & Schneider. Over 1,450 costumed figures shown, covering a wide variety of peoples: kings, emperors, nobles, priests, servants, soldiers, scholars, townsfolk, peasants, merchants, courtiers, cavaliers, and more. 256pp. 8⅜ × 11¼. 23150-X Pa. $7.95

THE NOTEBOOKS OF LEONARDO DA VINCI, edited by J. P. Richter. Extracts from manuscripts reveal great genius; on painting, sculpture, anatomy, sciences, geography, etc. Both Italian and English. 186 ms. pages reproduced, plus 500 additional drawings, including studies for *Last Supper, Sforza* monument, etc. 860pp. 7⅞ × 10¾. (Available in U.S. only) 22572-0, 22573-9 Pa., Two-vol. set $25.90

THE ART NOUVEAU STYLE BOOK OF ALPHONSE MUCHA: All 72 Plates from "Documents Decoratifs" in Original Color, Alphonse Mucha. Rare copyright-free design portfolio by high priest of Art Nouveau. Jewelry, wallpaper, stained glass, furniture, figure studies, plant and animal motifs, etc. Only complete one-volume edition. 80pp. 9⅜ × 12¼. 24044-4 Pa. $8.95

ANIMALS: 1,419 COPYRIGHT-FREE ILLUSTRATIONS OF MAMMALS, BIRDS, FISH, INSECTS, ETC., edited by Jim Harter. Clear wood engravings present, in extremely lifelike poses, over 1,000 species of animals. One of the most extensive pictorial sourcebooks of its kind. Captions. Index. 284pp. 9 × 12. 23766-4 Pa. $9.95

OBELISTS FLY HIGH, C. Daly King. Masterpiece of American detective fiction, long out of print, involves murder on a 1935 transcontinental flight—"a very thrilling story"—NY Times. Unabridged and unaltered republication of the edition published by William Collins Sons & Co. Ltd., London, 1935. 288pp. 5⅜ × 8½. (Available in U.S. only) 25036-9 Pa. $4.95

VICTORIAN AND EDWARDIAN FASHION: A Photographic Survey, Alison Gernsheim. First fashion history completely illustrated by contemporary photographs. Full text plus 235 photos, 1840–1914, in which many celebrities appear. 240pp. 6½ × 9¼. 24205-6 Pa. $6.00

THE ART OF THE FRENCH ILLUSTRATED BOOK, 1700–1914, Gordon N. Ray. Over 630 superb book illustrations by Fragonard, Delacroix, Daumier, Doré, Grandville, Manet, Mucha, Steinlen, Toulouse-Lautrec and many others. Preface. Introduction. 633 halftones. Indices of artists, authors & titles, binders and provenances. Appendices. Bibliography. 608pp. 8⅜ × 11¼. 25086-5 Pa. $24.95

THE WONDERFUL WIZARD OF OZ, L. Frank Baum. Facsimile in full color of America's finest children's classic. 143 illustrations by W. W. Denslow. 267pp. 5⅜ × 8½. 20691-2 Pa. $5.95

FRONTIERS OF MODERN PHYSICS: New Perspectives on Cosmology, Relativity, Black Holes and Extraterrestrial Intelligence, Tony Rothman, et al. For the intelligent layman. Subjects include: cosmological models of the universe; black holes; the neutrino; the search for extraterrestrial intelligence. Introduction. 46 black-and-white illustrations. 192pp. 5⅜ × 8½. 24587-X Pa. $6.95

THE FRIENDLY STARS, Martha Evans Martin & Donald Howard Menzel. Classic text marshalls the stars together in an engaging, non-technical survey, presenting them as sources of beauty in night sky. 23 illustrations. Foreword. 2 star charts. Index. 147pp. 5⅜ × 8½. 21099-5 Pa. $3.50

FADS AND FALLACIES IN THE NAME OF SCIENCE, Martin Gardner. Fair, witty appraisal of cranks, quacks, and quackeries of science and pseudoscience: hollow earth, Velikovsky, orgone energy, Dianetics, flying saucers, Bridey Murphy, food and medical fads, etc. Revised, expanded In the Name of Science. "A very able and even-tempered presentation."—The New Yorker. 363pp. 5⅜ × 8. 20394-8 Pa. $6.50

ANCIENT EGYPT: ITS CULTURE AND HISTORY, J. E Manchip White. From pre-dynastics through Ptolemies: society, history, political structure, religion, daily life, literature, cultural heritage. 48 plates. 217pp. 5⅜ × 8½. 22548-8 Pa. $4.95

SIR HARRY HOTSPUR OF HUMBLETHWAITE, Anthony Trollope. Incisive, unconventional psychological study of a conflict between a wealthy baronet, his idealistic daughter, and their scapegrace cousin. The 1870 novel in its first inexpensive edition in years. 250pp. 5⅜ × 8½.   24953-0 Pa. $5.95

LASERS AND HOLOGRAPHY, Winston E. Kock. Sound introduction to burgeoning field, expanded (1981) for second edition. Wave patterns, coherence, lasers, diffraction, zone plates, properties of holograms, recent advances. 84 illustrations. 160pp. 5⅜ × 8¼. (Except in United Kingdom)   24041-X Pa. $3.50

INTRODUCTION TO ARTIFICIAL INTELLIGENCE: SECOND, EN-LARGED EDITION, Philip C. Jackson, Jr. Comprehensive survey of artificial intelligence—the study of how machines (computers) can be made to act intelligently. Includes introductory and advanced material. Extensive notes updating the main text. 132 black-and-white illustrations. 512pp. 5⅜ × 8½.   24864-X Pa. $8.95

HISTORY OF INDIAN AND INDONESIAN ART, Ananda K. Coomaraswamy. Over 400 illustrations illuminate classic study of Indian art from earliest Harappa finds to early 20th century. Provides philosophical, religious and social insights. 304pp. 6⅜ × 9⅜.   25005-9 Pa. $8.95

THE GOLEM, Gustav Meyrink. Most famous supernatural novel in modern European literature, set in Ghetto of Old Prague around 1890. Compelling story of mystical experiences, strange transformations, profound terror. 13 black-and-white illustrations. 224pp. 5⅜ × 8½. (Available in U.S. only)   25025-3 Pa. $5.95

ARMADALE, Wilkie Collins. Third great mystery novel by the author of *The Woman in White* and *The Moonstone*. Original magazine version with 40 illustrations. 597pp. 5⅜ × 8½.   23429-0 Pa. $9.95

PICTORIAL ENCYCLOPEDIA OF HISTORIC ARCHITECTURAL PLANS, DETAILS AND ELEMENTS: With 1,880 Line Drawings of Arches, Domes, Doorways, Facades, Gables, Windows, etc., John Theodore Haneman. Sourcebook of inspiration for architects, designers, others. Bibliography. Captions. 141pp. 9 × 12.   24605-1 Pa. $6.95

BENCHLEY LOST AND FOUND, Robert Benchley. Finest humor from early 30's, about pet peeves, child psychologists, post office and others. Mostly unavailable elsewhere. 73 illustrations by Peter Arno and others. 183pp. 5⅜ × 8½.
22410-4 Pa. $3.95

ERTÉ GRAPHICS, Erté. Collection of striking color graphics: *Seasons, Alphabet, Numerals, Aces* and *Precious Stones*. 50 plates, including 4 on covers. 48pp. 9⅜ × 12¼.   23580-7 Pa. $6.95

THE JOURNAL OF HENRY D. THOREAU, edited by Bradford Torrey, F. H. Allen. Complete reprinting of 14 volumes, 1837–61, over two million words; the sourcebooks for *Walden*, etc. Definitive. All original sketches, plus 75 photographs. 1,804pp. 8½ × 12¼.   20312-3, 20313-1 Cloth., Two-vol. set $80.00

CASTLES: THEIR CONSTRUCTION AND HISTORY, Sidney Toy. Traces castle development from ancient roots. Nearly 200 photographs and drawings illustrate moats, keeps, baileys, many other features. Caernarvon, Dover Castles, Hadrian's Wall, Tower of London, dozens more. 256pp. 5⅜ × 8¼.
24898-4 Pa. $5.95

AMERICAN CLIPPER SHIPS: 1833–1858, Octavius T. Howe & Frederick C. Matthews. Fully-illustrated, encyclopedic review of 352 clipper ships from the period of America's greatest maritime supremacy. Introduction. 109 halftones. 5 black-and-white line illustrations. Index. Total of 928pp. 5⅜ × 8½.
25115-2, 25116-0 Pa., Two-vol. set $17.90

TOWARDS A NEW ARCHITECTURE, Le Corbusier. Pioneering manifesto by great architect, near legendary founder of "International School." Technical and aesthetic theories, views on industry, economics, relation of form to function, "mass-production spirit," much more. Profusely illustrated. Unabridged translation of 13th French edition. Introduction by Frederick Etchells. 320pp. 6⅛ × 9¼. (Available in U.S. only) 25023-7 Pa. $8.95

THE BOOK OF KELLS, edited by Blanche Cirker. Inexpensive collection of 32 full-color, full-page plates from the greatest illuminated manuscript of the Middle Ages, painstakingly reproduced from rare facsimile edition. Publisher's Note. Captions. 32pp. 9⅜ × 12¼. 24345-1 Pa. $4.95

BEST SCIENCE FICTION STORIES OF H. G. WELLS, H. G. Wells. Full novel *The Invisible Man*, plus 17 short stories: "The Crystal Egg," "Aepyornis Island," "The Strange Orchid," etc. 303pp. 5⅜ × 8½. (Available in U.S. only)
21531-8 Pa. $4.95

AMERICAN SAILING SHIPS: Their Plans and History, Charles G. Davis. Photos, construction details of schooners, frigates, clippers, other sailcraft of 18th to early 20th centuries—plus entertaining discourse on design, rigging, nautical lore, much more. 137 black-and-white illustrations. 240pp. 6⅛ × 9¼.
24658-2 Pa. $5.95

ENTERTAINING MATHEMATICAL PUZZLES, Martin Gardner. Selection of author's favorite conundrums involving arithmetic, money, speed, etc., with lively commentary. Complete solutions. 112pp. 5⅜ × 8½. 25211-6 Pa. $2.95

THE WILL TO BELIEVE, HUMAN IMMORTALITY, William James. Two books bound together. Effect of irrational on logical, and arguments for human immortality. 402pp. 5⅜ × 8½. 20291-7 Pa. $7.50

THE HAUNTED MONASTERY and THE CHINESE MAZE MURDERS, Robert Van Gulik. 2 full novels by Van Gulik continue adventures of Judge Dee and his companions. An evil Taoist monastery, seemingly supernatural events; overgrown topiary maze that hides strange crimes. Set in 7th-century China. 27 illustrations. 328pp. 5⅜ × 8½. 23502-5 Pa. $5.95

CELEBRATED CASES OF JUDGE DEE (DEE GOONG AN), translated by Robert Van Gulik. Authentic 18th-century Chinese detective novel; Dee and associates solve three interlocked cases. Led to Van Gulik's own stories with same characters. Extensive introduction. 9 illustrations. 237pp. 5⅜ × 8½.
23337-5 Pa. $4.95

Prices subject to change without notice.
Available at your book dealer or write for free catalog to Dept. GI, Dover Publications, Inc., 31 East 2nd St., Mineola, N.Y. 11501. Dover publishes more than 175 books each year on science, elementary and advanced mathematics, biology, music, art, literary history, social sciences and other areas.